COMMUNAL SOCIETIES IN AMERICA
AN AMS REPRINT SERIES

FROM

PALMYRA, NEW YORK, 1830,

TO

Independence, Missouri, 1894.

AMS PRESS
NEW YORK

FROM

PALMYRA, NEW YORK, 1830,

TO

Independence, Missouri, 1894.

PART I.
The Book Unsealed, Revised and Enlarged.

PART II.
Eleven Works Against Mormonism, Six United States School Histories, Four Leading Encyclopedias and Reissues Compared with Each Other and Reviewed in the Light of Facts on the Subject Treated.

PART III.
A Compendium of Evidences of Material Value Mainly from Outside Parties and Embracing Three Court Decisions.

By ELDER R. ETZENHOUSER,

OF THE

Reorganized Church of Jesus Christ of Latter Day Saints.

INDEPENDENCE, MO,
ENSIGN PUBLISHING HOUSE.
1894.

The Library of Congress Cataloged the AMS Printing of this Title
as Follows:

Etzenhouser, Rudolph, 1856-
   From Palmyra, New York, 1830, to
Independence, Missouri, 1894.
Independence, Mo., Ensign Pub. House,
1894. [New York, AMS Press, 1971]
   444 p. 22 cm.
   The Book unsealed, rev. and enl.,
which was first published in 1892,
forms part one of this work.

   1. Book of Mormon.   2. Mormons and
Mormonism—Doctrinal and controversial
works. 3. Smith, Joseph, 1805-1844.
I. Title
BX8627   E78   1971
ISBN 0-404-08435-4   73-134393

Reprinted from the edition of 1894, Independence
First AMS edition published in 1971
Manufactured in the United States of America

AMS PRESS INC.
NEW YORK, N.Y. 10003

PREFACE.

The author of this work makes no claim to scholarship in the presentation of its pages, and prefers that it shall be judged by the measure of truth it contains, rather than by its quality as a literary production.

The "Book Unsealed" in a revised and enlarged form constitutes Part I of this work. Extreme care has been used in the preparation of its matter. A very few quotations taken from accepted reliable sources and which have NOT been compared with originals, appear designated as such by a dagger (†). These quotations could have been dispensed with, as on all points upon which they bear a sufficient quantity would still remain. Different editions of a number of authors are quoted from, as for instance, Priest's of 1833 and 1838. As the quotations not compared with originals are DESIGNATED as before mentioned, the different editions of works cited are not given accompanying quotations.

Libraries at St. Louis, Kansas City, St. Joseph, Denver, Salt Lake City, Des Moines, Chicago, Cincinnati, Philadelphia, Brooklyn and New Brunswick have been searched, and for aid in this, the author is indebted to Elders F. G. Pitt, A. H. Parsons and J. B. Roush, also to Miss Etta M. Izatt.

Part II is the only production of the kind, and something of the kind has long been recognized as needed. It embraces the review and exposure of eleven works written against "Mormonism," with other matter of the kind.

Also, a review of six United States School Histories as a sample in general upon the subject from that source. Four of the leading encyclopedias and their later editions are examined and reviewed. Statements of encyclopedias and the press relative to the Reorganized Church of Latter Day Saints, are given.

Part III presents Joseph Smith as the founder of the Latter Day Work, his character, etc., by those not members but directly acquainted with him.

Evidences of the same class relative to the early scenes in New York, Ohio, Missouri and Illinois, the character of the Saints, etc. Three prominent court decisions, that of Kirtland Temple, Ohio, 1880; the Canada Court on the rights of the Reorganized Church of Latter Day Saints, 1893, and the Temple Lot case of 1894.

The title, "From Palmyra, New York, to Independence, Missouri," is not indicative of continuous narative but embracing material facts during that lapse of years.

In Part II appears two articles from the pen of Elder Heman C. Smith and one from Elder C. Scott, taken from the Saints' Herald. Matter furnished by Elder I. M. Smith, as also valuable suggestions are acknowledged with pleasure; also, matter from brethren A. H. Parsons and Albert Carmichael.

A glance through the manuscript with the author led Elders Joseph Luff, I. N. White, F. M. Sheehy and I. M. Smith to say, "The work will be a useful one." With this end in view the work is now submitted to its readers.   R. E.

INDEPENDENCE, Mo., May 12, 1894.

THE

BOOK UNSEALED.

Exposition of Prophecy

AND

AMERICAN ANTIQUITIES.

The Claims of the Book of Mormon Examined and Sustained.

CHAPTER I.

THE BOOK OF MORMON.

The Book of Mormon derives its name from the writer of one of the several books of which it is composed, whose name was Mormon, and who compiled the several books as they appear. The book, by those not acquainted with it, has been supposed to countenance and sanction the institution of polygamy, while just the opposite is true; nothing in the realm of literature being more condemnatory of polygamy.

"Wherefore, my brethren, hear me, and harken to the word of the Lord: For there shall not any man among you have save it be one wife: and concubines he shall have none, for I the Lord God delighteth in the chastity of women."—Book of Mormon, p. 116. (All

citations from Plano edition except where other's works
are quoted).

The time the Book of Mormon covers is divided
into two periods; the first, from the confusion of languages at Babel, from whence the first colony, the Jaredites came to the western continent, to the time they
became extinct, which was wrought through a series of
bloody wars before the Nephite colony came over from
Jerusalem, which migration occurred during the reign
of Zedekiah, king of Judah, about 600 B. C.   This colony having become possessed of the Jaredite record,
and having completed their own, added the record of
the former people in an abridged form.

The second colony, some years after their arrival
here, divided, each party taking the name of its respective leader, and so were known as Nephites and Lamanites.

The Jaredites, like the Nephites and Lamanites,
were of the white race.   The Lamanites, because of
their rebellion against God and his appointments, were
cursed with a dark or copper colored skin, their descendants being the American Indians of today.   Both
of the colonies were a highly civilized, enlightened and
religious people, and attained excellence in art, science,
architecture and agriculture.

The Nephites lost their national existence in war
with the Lamanites about the year 420 of the Christian
era; the remnant of that people were then merged into
the Lamanites.   Their records were hidden in the place
from which they were taken in 1827 by Joseph Smith,
the translator of the book.

From the preface to Delafield's work entitled "An
inquiry into the Origin of the Antiquities of America,"

which was published in 1839, at New York, London and Paris, by the Right Reverand Chas. P. McIlvaine, D. D., bishop of the diocese of Ohio:

"Suppose that in searching the TUMULI that are scattered so widely over this country, the silent, aged, mysterious remembrance of some populous race, once carrying on all the business of life where now are only the wild forests of many centuries, a race of whom we ask so often, who they were, whence they came, whither they went; suppose that under one of those huge structures of earth which remain of their works, a book were discovered, an alphabetic history of that race for a thousand years, containing their written language, and examples of their poetry and other literature, and all undeniably composed many hundreds of years before any of the nations now possessing this continent were here! What a wonder would this be! What intense interest would attach to such a relic! What price would not the learned be willing to give for it!"

The Book of Mormon, published ten years before Mr. McIlvaine wrote, gave the facts he asked and sighed for.

Josiah Priest, in American Antiquities, edition of 1838, p. 361, says:

"But what has finally become of these nations, and where are their descendants, are questions which, could they be answered, would be highly gratifying."

Mr. Wm. Pidgeon, in his Traditions of De-coo-dah and Antiquarian Researches, edition of 1853, p. 11, says: "But it yet remains for America to awake her story from sleep, to string lyre, and nerve the pen, to tell the tale of her antiquities, as seen in the relics of nations, coeval perhaps with the oldest works of man."

These men, with all others who have written on American antiquity, while setting aside the Book of Mormon as a matter of nonsense, pile up the evidences of its divinity as the reader will see as he proceeds.

Rev. John McCalman, of New Bedford, Massachusetts, preached in the Middle Street Christian church in that place, Sunday, March 4th, 1894, in the course of which sermon he said:

"The word of the Lord is divine communication, teaching his children what to do under circumstances in which they find themselves at a given time and place. Sometimes we call it confidence. If today your hearts are open to receive divine communication, the word of the Lord will be present. You ask, how shall I know it is the word of God? Joseph Smith published to the world at large that he had received a divine communication. Now, what right have I to say that that communication was not a divine one?"

"God moves in a mysterious way" in many things. The Book of Mormon he caused to come forth before the Antiquities of America were known, and in their discovery by those who did not accept the book he secures a cloud of witnesses.

The Book of Mormon has been criticised on two lines: First, its literary inelegance, and second, that it is not a true record. Is Peter's part of the New Testament untrue because not so elegant as the writing of the learned Paul?

Here is what some of the writers in the Book of Mormon say of this work:

"And I know that the record which I make is true; and I make it with mine own hand; and I make it according to my knowledge."—B. of M., p. 1, par. 1. The record was made according to Nephi's knowledge, not according to the knowledge of God, but the things recorded are true.

"And it came to pass that I, Jacob, began to be old; and the record of this people being kept on the other plates of Nephi, wherefore I conclude this record, declaring that I have written according to the best of my knowledge."—B. of M., p. 131, par. 8.

"And whoso receiveth this record, and shall not condemn it because of the imperfections which are in it, the same shall know of greater things than these. Behold, I am Moroni; and were it possible, I would make all things known unto you."—B. of M. p. 495, par. 1. The same admission is made by Moroni on page 500, paragraph 8.

The prophets and apostles were inspired of God to write and speak; and yet each one has his distinctive style of expression. This seems to plainly indicate that, as a rule, God gave the sentiment,—the ideas — but these men were left to express these ideas according to their own language, and their own knowledge.

"Horne's Introduction," p. 115:

"When it is said, that Scripture is divinely inspired, we are not to understand that God suggested every word or dictated every expression. From the different styles in which the books are written, and from the different manner in which the same events are related and predicted by different authors, it appears that the sacred penmen were permitted to write as their several tempers, understandings, and habits of life, directed; and that the knowledge communicated to them by inspiration on the subject of their writings, was applied in the same manner as any knowledge acquired by or-

dinary means.   Nor is it to be supposed that they were
even thus inspired in every fact which they related, or
in every precept which they delivered.   They were left
to the common use of their faculties, and did not, upon
every occasion, stand in need of supernatural communi-
cations; but whenever, and as far as divine assistance
was necessary, it was always afforded."

Also, page 521:   "But with respect to the choice
of words in which they wrote, I know not but they
might be left to the free and rational exercise of their
own minds, to express themselves in the manner that
was natural and familiar to them, while at the same
time they were preserved from error, in the ideas they
conveyed.   If this were the case, it would sufficiently
account for the over observable diversity of style and
manner among the inspired writers.   The Spirit guided
them to write nothing but truth concerning religion,
yet they might be left to express that truth in their own
language."   Quoted by Horne from "Parry's Inquiry
into the Nature and Extent of the Inspiration of the
Apotsles."

A few facts are now presented in a miscellaneous
manner in the remainder of this chapter.

"For sure it is the earth that moves and not the
sun."—B. of M., Helaman, 4: 8.

"The scriptures are laid before thee, yea, and all
things denote there is a God; yea, even the earth, and
all things that are upon the face of it, yea, and its motion; yea, and also all the planets which move in their
regular form, doth witness that there is a Supreme Cre-
ator."—B. of M., Alma, 16 : 7.

Now let a voice from the World's Fair confirm this,
for the Book of Mormon has been charged with having

claimed to contain knowledge of the rotary motion of the earth before it had been discovered, and now it is authenticated:

"ANCIENT AMERICANS.

"THEY WERE GREAT ASTRONOMERS.

"WORLD'S FAIR GROUNDS, Chicago, August 29. — What is claimed to be a correct interpretation of the ancient Aztec calendar was made public for the first time today at a meeting of the anthropological congress at the Fair. Scholars pronounce it to be the most important discovery in its line of this century.

"The interpretation was made by a woman, Mrs. Zelia Nuttal, one of the judges of ethnology at the Fair, who explained the wonderful calendar to the anthropological congress. Dr. Daniel G. Drinton, A. B., president of the congress, said it would eventually lead to a translation of the hieroglyphics carved on the ruins of Mexico and Central America and thus reveal the history of the wonderful people who built them.

"The accuracy and perfection of the calendar is convincing evidence of the civilization and mathematical attainments of the ancient inhabitants of America. It was estimated that no less than 4,000 years of astronomical observations would have been necessary to perfect the calendar. A complete cycle of the calendar referring to the revolution of the moon and earth about the sun covers a period of 1,094 years. It shows that the ancient inhabitants of America were familiar with the movements of the planets, Jupiter, Venus, Mercury, and perhaps Mars, as well as those of the Earth and Moon."

The above clipping is from the St. Joseph, Missouri, weekly News, of September 1st, 1893.

Book of Mormon, Nephi, 4th chapter, sets forth in a graphic manner the convulsions that took place on this continent of North America and says: "But behold, there was a more great and terrible destruction in the land northward: for behold, the whole face of the land was changed." (The reader is referred to the entire chapter.)

John T. Short, in his American Antiquties page 233, writing of a race of giants says: A great convulsion of nature which shook the earth, and caused the mountains and volcanoes to swallow up and kill them." On page 125, "In 1857, a portion of a human cranium was found associated with bones of the mastodon at the depth of one hundred and eighty feet below the surface in a mining shaft at Table Mountain, California."

Baldwin, in his Ancient America, page 176, says of Central America: "The land was shaken by frightful earthquakes, and the waves of the sea combined with volcanic fire to overwhelm and engulf it."

Josiah Priest describes three wells near Cincinnati, Ohio, the shallowest being eighty feet deep, in each of which when dug, the stump of a tree was taken out at that depth.   The citations are given in chapter ten of this book.

And in addition to the above a very singular discovery was reported in the Leadville, Colorado, papers in March, 1891.   A man by the name of John Sunger had brought to the city an arrowhead, made of tempered copper, and a number of human bones, which were found in a mine, four hundred and sixty feet below the surface of the earth, imbeded in a vein of silver bearing oar.   Over one hundred dollars worth of ore clung to the bones when they were removed from the mine.

The arrowhead is four inches long, and one and one half inches wide at the widest part. The shank is one and one half inches long and has a hole pierced through the center by which the shaft was fastened to the spike. The oar clung to it when taken from the vein, and was with some difficulty removed."

Any one who has crossed Wyoming on the Union Pacific railroad in day light has seen what is by many believed to have been the bottom of a great inland sea, which it appears clearly to have been.

All who have seen the famous Salt Lake Valley of Utah, could trace what is called the water line. It is far up the Wasatch mountains, and is to be seen all around the valley and marks where the lake waters once stood. "The face of the land was changed."

A number of works on Antiquity relate similar facts. See chapter nine of this work, citation from Pittsburg Leader, telling of brick and a coin found at the depth of one hundred and twenty five feet in a well at Helena, Arkansas.

A remarkable corroboration of the above is found in a paper written by Dr. D. L. Yates, the same having been read by T. H. Hittel before the Historical Society, in a meeting of that body held in San Francisco. The same appeared in the Bulletin in March, 1888, as follows:

"It was said that California possessed some of the oldest known relics on the continent. The first authenticated record of the original occupants was found on the table mountain region in Tuolumne county, and is of an age prior to the great volcanic outburst. Fossil remains of the rhinoceros and an extinct horse are found under the lava layers forming the table

mountains which are 1,400 feet thick, 1,700 feet wide
* * * where the river beds have been washed out,
and have been covered again to the depth of from three
thousand to four thousand feet more since the flow of
the lava.   This lava rests on a bed of detritus, which
is often entered by running tunnels (in mining).   The
human relics and stone implements found in these
formations give evidence of human habitants differing
from any known since.   There have been found spearheads, a pipe of polished stone, two scoop of stalactite
rock (resembling the grocer's scoop), an implement of
aragonite, resembling an unbent bow, but the use of
which is unknown and cannot be conjectured, a stone
needle with notches at the larger end, and the finest
charmstones that have ever been found.

"There have been brought to light the fossils of
nine mastodons, twenty elephants, various pachyderms
in the Table Mountains, numerous evidences of animal
life in the calcareous formations in the Texas flats, obsidian spearheads, fossils of the elephant, horse and
camel about Hornitos, bones and evidences of prehistoric human industry in Tulare, and in Trinity and
Sisklyon many proofs of the contemporaneous existence of man and extinct mammals.

"In the San Jose Valley are deep layers of coniferous trees in such a carbonized state that they crumble
into dust when exposed to the air.   They are of the
pliocene period, and show that the entire topography
of the region has changed, and that where now the
valleys and mountains are destitute of timber, they
were once coniferous and deciduous trees, affording
food and shelter to monster mammals in comparison to
which, man was but an insignificant mite.   In the lay-

ers of the miocene period are found in California the remains of amphibious animals not to be found elsewhere."

Thus it is seen, that east, west, north and south, unmistakable evidences abound to show that "the face of the land was changed," as stated in the Book of Mormon.

On pages 399, 408, 426–428, Book of Mormon, the Gadianton robbers are described and their strongholds in their mountain home in the cliffs. Any one who was at the World's Fair could well appreciate the account, having seen the exhibit of the Cliff Dwellers. The Independent Patriot of September 14th, 1893, contains the following:

"In this exhibit may be seen what is intended to represent the mountain homes of the cliff dwellers; the methods by which they obtained ingress and egress; the rugs, mats, implements of war and peace which they had; some of the corn they raised, with cob, grain and husk quite well preserved. When we reached this point in the exhibit the lecturer was asked how long ago he supposed this race to have lived upon this continent. He answered, 'From two to four thousand years.' 'From what part of the earth, and what branch of the human family do you suppose these people to have come?' 'From the ancient Aryan branch of Asia, which sent out portions of its descendants to Africa, Europe, and I think also to America.'

"The skulls of the cliff dwellers were exhibited in profusion, and presented, as we were told by the lecturer, the appearance of having belonged to a highly intelligent and well developed race of people. Some days previous to our visit, he informed us, a professional phrenologist had visited the room, and to him had been handed an Indian skull along with a cliff dweller's. He at once stated that the latter was a well developed type of a highly civilized and intelligent race; while the former looked more like the skull of an American Indian than anything else. These were handed the professor, as we were told, without his being informed as to what race or races they belonged."

All who saw the hair on skulls, and several bunches besides, will attest it was of fine texture and of various shades of brown and auburn. Very unlike Indian hair; but like that of the white race. Being there, I saw it.

Baldwin, on page 173, says:

"Tradition of the native Mexicans and Central Americans described the first civilizers as "bearded white men," who "came from the east in ships."

This accords with the Book of Mormon, pages 502–505.

Bancroft, volumn 5, page 24, says:

"There are numerous vague traditions of settlements or nations of white men who lived apart from the other people of the country, and were possessed of an advanced civilization."

Josiah Priest, in his edition of 1838, page 390, American Antiquities, gives headlines for a chapter thus: "Traits of white nations in Georgia and Kentucky before Columbus' time and the traditions of the Indians respecting them."

Donnely says of the Peruvians: "The native traditions said this city was built by bearded white men, who came there long before the time of the Incas, and established a settlement." – Atlantis, p. 393.

The Jaredites and Nephites were both white.

AN ACCOUNT OF RELICS AT THE WORLD'S FAIR.

Don McGuire, Chief Dept. Mines and Archæology, of Utah, contributing to Salt Lake City Tribune, in its issue for October 29th, 1893 says:

"In the department of anthropology at Jackson Park, man has an opportunity of becoming acquainted with the remains and relics of many races. * * * In the Wisconsin state collection there is a fine lot of copper implements and arms, consisting of axes, chisels, lance heads, arrow points, needles, combs, cups, crowns, armlets, finger rings, and hundreds of articles, the use of which is wholly a mystery to us. From the same state comes stone axes and stone lance heads. The copper was taken from the present copper mines of Lake Superior; it was hammered into form, and this hammering rendered it quite hard. The tools are very well fashioned and show considerable skill.

"There is a fine exhibit from south, central and northern Illinois, which comes from the mounds of this state. The work is well done and it is varied in its makeup. Flint, steatite, clay, limestone and copper were used as in Wisconsin, and amongst the Illinois collection we are struck with the beauty of the great array of pipes found in the mounds, some of which are exceedingly beautiful.

"But when the collection of the Ohio Valley is reached we are before the greatest find, and at the same time most varied collection that has been made for many years from the mounds of that region, and one that surpasses in many ways all that we found in any of the state exhibits east of the Missouri river.

One Charles Morehead for the two past years has been engaged in excavating in the great mounds of Central Ohio, around Marietta and through the Sceota valley. From a few mounds of that state we see here a collection of copper tools of every description, also of tools of obsidian and also of flint, and beautiful ornaments of abalone shell, and mother of pearl, and thousands of pearls, along with articles of bone, stone and copper, long since perished. There was cloth and feather work, but it is now in dust.

"The fortress in which these were found would conveniently contain forty thousand people, and when we see the articles of agriculture we have little doubt but that this people who occupied this land in remote ages were a great commercial and far travelling race of men"

Writes of Colorado relics: "These relics and discoveries consist of fifteen very well preserved mummies of the ancient cliff-dwellers, and a great variety of their pottery, stone weapons and wooden implements, cotton cloth, feather cloth, cordage, tanned leather, bone and shellwork, haircloth, hair cordage, and husk matting and carpets, corn, cotton seed, squash, pumpkin and gourd seed; in a word, it represents that ingenious and lost people as they were, and the mummies are, as they lie there, about as interesting, repulsive and ill-odored a lot of human junk as ever startled a weak-nerved mortal of this world."

Of a Utah skeleton and relics: "It is the finest specimen of desiccated humanity ever discovered on the American continent, and with him were found the most interesting and valuable lot of relics yet brought forth from a cliff-dweller's tomb. They consist of pottery, corn, beans, cotton cloth, feather cloth, cordage of various kinds, wooden implements, pipes, arrow and lance heads."

Of Central American ruins: "These remains were taken from the desolate and long abandoned cities that are buried deep amid the forests of Central America, where beyond question at one time remote in the bygone years a great city and a proud nation flourished As we look out of the building we behold sections of those old palaces that were built here as fac-similes of the architecture of these races that are found in Yucatan. Old palaces represented here show wonderful architecture, which even in our own day of great buildings compare favorably with the most substantial of man's work. There is a mystery, dark, deep, unfathomable in all these traces of a lost race, those altars rich in sculptured relief work, these raised inscriptions in an unknown and lost tongue, all are as a wild, undistinguishable voice coming back from vanished generations that have crossed the flood."

Of Peruvian relics: "There is here also from Peru a large number of pots, vases, cups, dishes of very fine workmanship by the artisans of the Inca empire. Their cotton, their vicuna wool, their tanned leather, their corn, dried fruit, their weapons, arms and jewels of obsidian, jasper, copper, gold and silver. "No such exhibit was ever made outside of Peru, and as one gazes spellbound upon this rich and ancient lot of skeletons, mummies, pottery, gold and silver from Peru, he regrets that the fair is not to last twelve months longer."

"The uniform and constant report of Peruvian tradition places the beginning of this old civilization in the valley of Cuzco, near lake Titicaca."--Baldwin's Ancient America, page 236.

"Those who criticise Montesinos admit that 'his advantages were great,' that 'no one equaled him in archælogical knowledge of Peru,' and that 'he became acquainted with original instruments which he occasonally transferred to his own pages * * * difficult to meet elsewhere.' "--Ibid 263.

Of Peruvian civilization he says: " 'It was originated,' he says, 'by a people led by four brothers, who settled in the Valley of Cuzco. * * * The youngest of these brothers assumed supreme authority and became the first of a long line of sovereigns.' "--Ibid 264.

The above agrees exactly to the Nephite colony as any one will discover by reading the Book of Mormon.   Laman, Lemuel, Samuel and Nephi were the brothers, and position, no doubt, that of Peru.   Nephi, the youngest of the four was the first of a long line of rulers.

The Marqueis De Nadaillac in his work "Prehistoric People," on pages 268-9 and elsewhere, sets forth that the ancient American's trepanned skulls, tells of the skulls being found showing the operation, he suggests it was done with stone.   His imagination must be strong, trepanning is by no means a common piece of surgery with the instruments of to-day.   The steel instruments of the ancient Americans all having decayed by rust, therefore stone would do for anything is concluded.   The wonderful and extensive buildings of Central America, are passed by many in silence as to what the tools were that were used in their construction.

It is recently admitted that the builders of Egyptian pyramids had some tools, possibly it will be, some day, that the Americans had also.

"TOOLS OF THE PYRAMID BUILDERS.

"A two years' study at Gizeh has convinced Mr. Flinders Petrie that the Egyptian stone workers of four thousand years ago had a surprising acquaintance with what have been considered modern tools. Among the many tools used by the pyramid-builders were both solid and tubular drills and straight and circular saws. The drills, like those of to-day, were set with jewels (probably corundum, as the diamond was very scarce), and even lathe tools had such cutting edges. So remarkable was the quality of the tubular drills and the skill of the workmen, that the cutting-marks in hard granite give no indication of wear of the tool, while a cut of a tenth of an inch was made in the hardest rock at each revolution, and a hole through both the hardest and softest material was bored perfectly smooth and uniform throughout."—American Analyst, New York.

CHAPTER II.
CONTINENTS AND NATIONS.

There being two continents, nothing is more reasonable than that the people of each may have had recognition from, and communication with God.

That this is clearly admissable, is evident from Acts 17: 24–27. "God that made the world, and all things * * hath made of one blood all nations of men for to dwell on all the face of the earth, and hath determined the times before appointed, and the bounds

of their habitation. That they should seek the Lord,
if haply they might feel after him and find him, though
he be not very far from every one of us."

The following points are clear:

1st.—All nations were from one source.

2d.—By God's decree they were to inhabit "All
the face of the earth."

3d.—Their distribution as to "times" and "bounds"
God directs.

4th.—"They should seek the Lord." He would
not command them to seek unless it were possible that
he should be found. Peter said, "Of a truth I perceive
that God is no respecter of persons, but in every nation he that feareth him and worketh righteousness is
accepted with him."—Acts 10: 34.

As the nations of the eastern continent sought and
found God, and had revelation and covenant relation
with him, so could the nations of the western continent, in fulfillment of God's covenant to Abraham:
"And in thy seed shall all the nations of the earth be
blessed, because thou hast obeyed my voice."—Gen.
22: 18. The Prophet Ezekiel, in chapter 37, mentions
two "sticks," (records), one for Judah and the children of Israel his companions, "another stick [record]
for Joseph and for all the house of Israel, his companions."

The stick for Judah being the Bible, a similiar
record or "another stick" should appear for Joseph.
This is realized in the Book of Mormon, which is a
record of the dealings of God with the descendants of
Joseph on the western continent. It is therefore of
equal authority with other sacred writings, and throws
light upon doctrine, promise and prophecy. For as

Paul says, "All scripture is given by inspiration of God and is profitable for doctrine, for reproof, for correction, for instruction in righteousness, that the man of God may be thoroughly furnished in all good works." —2 Tim. 3: 19. It does not in any sense supplant the Bible or take its place, but is a companion volume thereto.

We quote Bishop McIlvaine again from preface to Delafield's work. He is right, that American Antiquity is to confirm the Scriptures. The gospel of Christ had been taught here as the PRIESTS SUPPOSED. The universal and uniform traditions of the nations of both continents are strong evidence of a common origin as set forth in this chapter from the Bible:

"Traditions have been distinctly traced, in opposite regions of the globe, and in the most unconnected nations of the creation; of the production of all living creatures out of water by the power of the Supreme mind; the formation of man, last, in the image of God, his being invested with dominion over all other animals; the primitive state of innocence and happiness; Paradise; the Sabbath; the division of time into weeks; the fall of man; (the mother of mankind is represented in American tradition as fallen and accompanied by a serpent); the promise of a deliverer; Cain and Abel; the general degeneracy of mankind; the longevity of the Patriarchs; the general deluge; the escape of only a single family in an ark; the dove sent out by Noah; the rainbow as a sign; the number of persons in the ark; the Tower of Babel; the destruction of Sodom and Gomorrah—these with divers circumstances and details illustrating the main particulars. So remarkable were the traditions of several of these facts, among the inhabitants of America, at the time of the Spanish conquest, that the priests, who accompanied the army, were induced to suppose that Christianity, or at least Judiasm, had been inculcated among them at some very distant period.   Humboldt, however, sees no need of such explanation 'since similiar traditions, (he says) of high and venerable antiquity, are found among the followers of Brama, and among the Shamans of the eastern stepps of Tartary.'

"The traditions of the deluge are particularly numerous.   They are derived from the oldest nations of antiquity—the Chaldeans, Egyptians, Greeks (and mentioned by Berosus, Hesiod, Plato, Plutarch, Lucian, &c), as well as from people the most recently discovered; as the natives of North and South America and of the islands of the South Sea.   The antipodes of the earth unite in testimony to the deluge.   Chinese and Sanscrit literature concurs with Chilian and Peruvian and Mexican tradition in bearing witness to that catastrophe.   Among the natives of America it is commemorated by a fable similar to that of Pyrrha and Deucalion.   'These ancient traditions of the human race (says Humboldt) which we find dispersed over the surface of the globe, like the fragments of a vast shipwreck, are of the greatest interest in the philosophical study of our species. * * *

"The Antiquities of America are an immense field for inquiry, hardly entered; abounding in promise of reward for the most devoted investigations.   Let it be thoroughly explored for the truth's sake.   The Scriptures have yet to gather a richer cabinet of illustrative and corroborating collections from the long buried and unknown depositories of American antiquity.

"In reference to the question, whether all the races of men have descended from one common stock, the antiquities of this continent are especially interesting, and may prove of very great value. It is a question, indeed, forever settled by the researches of Bryant, Faber and Sir William Jones: 'The dark Negro, the white European, and the swarthy Asiatic, being plainly traced to their respective ancestors in the family of Noah.' But much confirmatory testimony may yet be obtained. The contingent of America to the host of evidence already in array is yet to take its entire place in the line. If the present volume shall only increase the ardor of investigation and the number of minds turning their energies upon the disinterment of the buried antiquarian treasures of this continent, it will do a good work and deserve the thanks of all lovers of truth.—Kenyon College, Ohio, January, 1839."

CHAPTER III.

THE JAREDITES FROM BABEL.

On pages 501–2, (new edition 445–6), of the Book of Mormon is an account of the Jaredites who were led from the tower of Babel to a "choice land," "beyond the sea." In answer to prayer they were permitted to retain their language, which was the Adamic, and so were not given a new language in the confusion of tongues. The statement found in Gen. 9 : 18, 19, confirms such position: "And of them [sons of Noah] was the whole earth overspread." The foregoing declaration was evidently intended to include in its fulfillment events connected with the confusion of tongues

at Babel.   It is written: "So the Lord scattered
them abroad from thence upon the face of all ·the
earth.   Therefore is the name of it called Babel; because the Lord did there confound the language of all
the earth, and from thence did the Lord scatter them
abroad upon the face of all the earth."—-Gen. 11: 8, 9.

Opinions of many old Spanish writers were expressed in substance by Father Duran in 1585 in his
history, "New Spain."   "Adair the expert, and Eman-
uel De Moraes, agree that the Quichees by tradition
affirm that they made a long journey by land and
crossed the sea from the east.   The tradition of their
origin states that they came from the far east across
immense tracts of land and water."

It is scarcely presumable that from the year 1492
A. D. to the year 1585 A. D., only ninety-three years
having elapsed, that the Indians could have had such
a tradition created and received among them as coming down through their sages, by their limited contact
with the treacherous Spaniards, who had from the very
beginning betrayed all confidence reposed in them.

"In Yucatan the traditions all point to an EASTERN
AND FOREIGN origin for the race.   The early writers
report that the natives believe their ancestors to have
crossed the sea by a passage which was opened for
them."—Landa's Relacion, p. 28.   Atlantis 167.

Dr. Le Plongeon, in a newspaper article states:
"Of the Nahan predecessors of the Toltecs in Mexico
the Olmecs and Xicalancans were the most important.
They were the forerunners of the great race that followed.   According to Ixtlilxochitl, these people—
which are conceded to be one—occupied the world in

the third age; they came from the East in ships or barks to the land of Potonchan, which they commenced to populate." Atlantis, p. 167.

From Josiah Priest: "If so, then it is clear that the inhabitants of America who had the knowledge of this kind of fabrication, did indeed belong to an era as ancient as the first people of Asia itself, and even before the settlement of Europe; this is not a small witness in favor of our opinion of the extreme antiquity of those ancient works of the west."—Priest's American Antiquities, p. 258.

Pidgeon says: "That the present Indians and the ancient Mound Builders were of distinct national origin, is equally evident."—Traditions of Dee-Coo-Dah, p. 101.

Equally as positive upon the distinct race, is Mac-Lean: "An ancient race, entirely distinct from the Indian, possessing A CERTAIN DEGREE OF CIVILIZATION, once inhabited the central portion of the United States."†—Mound Builders, p. 13.

Bancroft says: "Most and the best authorities deem it impossible that the Mound Builders were even the remote ancestors of the Indian tribes; and while inclined to be less positive than most who have written on the subject respecting the possible changes that have been effected by a long course of centuries, I think that the evidence of a race locally extinct, is much stronger here than in any other part of the continent."—Nat. Races of Pacific States, Vol. 4, p. 787.

Stephens, writing of the antiquity of Palenque, says: "Here were the remains of a CULTIVATED, POLISHED AND PECULIAR PEOPLE who had passed through ALL THE STAGES incident to the rise and fall of nations,

reached their golden age and PERISHED ENTIRELY UN-
KNOWN."—Incidents of Travel in Yucatan, Vol. 2, p.
356.

"The most ancient civilization on this continent,
judging from the combined testimony of tradition,
records, and architectural remains, was that which
grew up under the favorable climate and geographical
surroundings which the Central American region southward of the Isthmus of Tehuantepec afforded.   The
great Maya family with its numerous branches, each in
time developing its own dialect, if not its own peculiar
language, at an early date fixed itself in the fertile valley of the river Usumasinta, and produced a civilization which was old and ripe when the Toltecs came in
contact with it.   Here in this picturesque valley region in Tabasco and Chiapas, we may look for the
cradle of American civilization.   Under the shadow
of the magnificent and mysterious ruins of Palenque a
people grew to power, who spread into Guatemala and
Honduras, northward toward Anahuac and southward
into Yucatan, and for a period of, probably twenty-five
centuries, exercised a sway, which at one time, excited
the envy and fear of its neighbors.

"We are fully aware of the uncertainty which at-
taches itself to tradition in general, and of the caution
with which it should be accepted in treating of the
foundation of history; but still, with reference to the
origin and growth of old world nations, nothing better
offers itself in many instances than suspicious legends.
The histories of the Egyptians, the Trogens, the Greeks,
and even of ancient Rome rest on no surer footing.
Clavigero says, the Chiapanese have been the first peo-
plers of the new world, if we give credit to their tradi-

tions.   They say that Votan, the grandson of that respectable old man that built the great ark to save
himself and family from the deluge, and one of those
who undertook the building of that lofty edifice, which
was to reach up to heaven, went by express command
of the Lord to people that land.

"The tradition of Votan, the founder of Maya culture, though somewhat warped, probably by having
passed through priestly hands, is nevertheless one of
the most valuable pieces of information which we have
concerning the Ancient Americans.   Without it our
knowledge of the Mayas would be a hopeless blank and
the ruins of Palenque would be more a mystery than
ever.

"According to this tradition, Votan came from the
East, from Valum Chivim, by the way of Valum Votan,
from across the sea, by divine command, to apportion
the land of the new continent to seven families which
he brought with him."—North Americans of Antiquity,
John T. Short, pages 203–4.

Short says, of Francisco Nunes de la Vega, Bishop
of Chiapas, who had read a book or document discovered by him and which is mentioned as a Votanic document, "He fails to give any definite information from
the document except the most general statements with
reference to Votan's place in the calendar, and his having seen the tower of Babel, at which each people was
given a new language."—Ibid 206.   "While some of
the details of Votanic tradition are not worthy of a
moment's consideration, it is quite certain that in the
general facts we have a key to the origin of what all
Americanists agree in pronouncing the oldest civilization on this continent, one which was already gray and

declining when the Toltecs entered Mexico. There is not the slightest evidence that it originated in any other place than in Chiapas where it is found, and extended itself into Guatemala, Yucatan, and probably branched northward in a colony as remote as Culhuacan "—Ibid 210.

"It is found in the history of the Toltecs that this age and first world, as they call it, lasted 1716 years, that men were destroyed by tremendous rains and lightnings from the sky, and even all the land, without the exception of anything, and the highest mountains were covered up and submerged in water * * fifteen cubits * * and how, after men multiplied, they erected a very high * * tower * * in order to take refuge in it, should the second world [age] be destroyed. Presently the language was confused, and not able to understand each other, they went to different parts of the earth. The Toltecs, consisting of seven friends and their wives, who understood the same language, came to these parts, * * 520 years after the flood."—Ibid 238.

In the introduction to his History General, (Sahagun) in speaking of the origin of this people, expresses the opinion that it is impossible to definitely determine more than that they report, "That all the natives came from seven caves, and that these seven caves are the seven ships or galleys in which the first populators of the land came. This people came in quest of the terrestrial paradise, and were known by the name of Tamoanchan, by which they mean, "We seek our home"—Ibid 242.

Delafield says: "A tradition exists among the native Mexicans bearing close analogy to the Semitic account of the flood, the building of the tower of Babel and its destruction."—Antiquities, p. 33.

And still more important from the same author: "Still farther and more important evidence, however, renders the point conclusive that southern Asia was the birth-place of this people, as we detect among them actual traditions of the flood, the building of Babel and the death of Abel; and from their cosmogony we think we trace farther traditions of the famine and the destruction of the cities of the plain. These historical facts stamp their origin conclusively, as they are peculiar to those who have been once residents of the country where the transactions occurred."—Ibid, p. 41.

Bancroft says: "They believed the rainbow was not only a passive sign that the earth would not be destroyed by a second deluge, but an active instrument to prevent the recurrence of such a catastrophe."—National Races, Vol. 5, p. 17.

Again he says: "Many of these flood myths are supplemented with an account of an attempt to provide against a second deluge, by building a tower of refuge, resembling more or less closely the Biblical legend of the tower of Babel."—Ibid, p. 17.

He extends his remarks as follows: "These myths have lead many writers to believe that the Americans had a knowledge of the tower of Babel, while some think that they are the direct descendants of the builders of that tower, who, after the confusion of tongues, wandered over the earth until they reached America."—Ibid, p. 18.

Speaking of Votan, Bancroft says: "Votan, another mysterious personage, closely resembling Quetzalcoatl in many points, was the supposed founder of

the Maya civilization. He is said to have been a descendant of Noah, and to have assisted at the building of the tower of Babel. After the confusion of tongues, he lead a portion of the dispersed people to America."
--Nat. Rac. Pac. States, Vol. 5, p. 27.

"The polished nations of the new world, and particularly those of Mexico; preserve in their traditions and in their paintings the memory of the creation of the world and of the building of the tower of Babel. the confusion of language and the dispersion of the people."--Short's American Antiquities, p. 140.

All of the above citations are very confirmatory of the account cited in the Book of Mormon, respecting the migration of the Jaredites to the western continent. As to the peculiar construction of the vessels of the Jaredite colony, (which are eight in number, seven of which were used for the people, the remaining one specially for their cargo), the following is very interesting: "The little steamer Norton, which is to sail from Long Island Sound for Southern France to-morrow, is, it is claimed by her builder and captain, a craft that cannot sink. She is only fifty-eight feet in length, but the most conspicuous feature about her is that she has a double bottom and six ballast compartments   Water is admitted through holes in the outer bottom. When the boat careens, the body of water between the bottoms presses the air in the compartments and acts as a ballast, the air serving as a cushion. This prevents the boat from capsizing or from diverging far from its center, even in the roughest seas. It is claimed that the double bottom and air tight compartments make it impossible to sink should the boat be cut in two. If the builder's theory be correct, its application will rev-

olutionize naval architecture. The result of the Norton s first voyage will be awaited with great interest."
—Philadelphia Record, December 13, 1891.

"If Victor Hugo were now alive he would have a new field, or new light on one of his old fields of work. Navigating the sea has always been supposed to mean plowing the surface, whatever the motor might be. But we can now travel under the sea as well as on the surface. Recent experiments have been made at Toulon with a submarine boat, that proves to be a great success. It runs from nine to ten knots, while the light is good and respiration easy. The boat can be moved in any direction, either vertically or horizontally. It will carry five persons. Of course its purport is warfare, but there is no reason why such a boat may not be applied to purposes more peaceful, especially to aid scientific research."—Globe-Democrat, February 3d, 1889.

CHAPTER IV.

TWO DISTINCT AND HIGHLY CIVILIZED PEOPLES.

"The Neolithic and Bronze ages preceded the Palæolithic, at least in the Mississippi basin, not that the last inhabitants deteriorated and lost the high arts which are well known to have been cultivated upon the same soil by them, but that they were preceded by a race possessed of no inferior civilization, who were not their ancestors, but a distinct people with a capacity for progress, for the exercise of government, for the erection of magnificent architectural monuments, and possessed of a respectable knowledge of geometrical principles."—North Americans of Antiquity, (Short), p. 27.

Pidgeon says: "From these facts in connection with the traditions of De Coo Dah, respecting the ancient inhabitants of these regions, as of various languages, customs and color, we are led to the conclusion that at least TWO DISTINCT RACES of men have occupied this territory at different eras, and that both became nationally extinct anterior to the occupation of the present Indian race."—Traditions of De Coo Dah, pp. 176-7.

Bancroft says: "The resemblance in the different groups of ruins in Chiapas, Yucatan and Honduras, are more than sufficient to prove intimate connection between the builders and artists. The differences pointed out prove just as conclusively that the edifices were not all erected and dedicated by the same people, under the same laws and religious control, at the same epoch."—Native Races, Pacific States, Vol. 4, p. 359.

"It is a point of no little interest that these old constructions belong to different periods in the past, and represent somewhat different phases of civilization." * * "The attention of investigators has lingered in speculation. They find in them a significance which is stated as follows by Brasseur de Bourbourg: 'Among the edifices forgotten by time in the forests of Mexico and Central America, we find architectural characteristics so DIFFERENT from each other, that it is impossible to attribute them to the SAME PEOPLE as to believe they were all built at th same epoch.' "—Baldwin's Ancient America, pp. 155, 156.

We have now presented Short, Pidgeon, Bancroft and Baldwin, four eminent authorities on there having been two distinct peoples, and who preceded the abo rigines of America, in the possession of this land, which supports the claim of the Book of Mormon for the Jaredite and Nephite colonizations. These four authorities agreeing as to the "two distinct" peoples, and Mr. Short classing them as having "capacity" for the "exercise of government," "erection of magnificent architectural monuments," and possessed of a "respectable knowledge of geometrical principles," we shall now present evidences of high civilation without classification.

Pidgeon says: "It cannot any longer be denied that there has been a day when this continent swarmed with millions of inhabitants, when the arts and sciences flourished."—Antiquarian Researches, p. 5.

Of ancient America's knowledge of astronomy, Donnelly says: "It will be conceded, that a considerable degree of astronomical knowledge must have been necessary to reach conclusively that the true year consisted of 365 days and six hours; (modern science has demonstrated that it consists of 365 days, five hours, less ten seconds), and a higher degree of civilization was requisite to insist that the year must be brought around by the intercalation of a certain number of days in a certain period of time, to its true relation to the season. Both were the outgrowth of a vast ancient civilization of the highest order."—Atlantis, p. 368.

That Abraham was an astronomer, appears from a statement made by Josephus: "Berosus," says he, "mentions our father Abraham, not by name, but after this manner: 'In the tenth generation after the flood there were among the Chaldeans a righteous man, who was also skilled in the knowledge of the heavens.' "—Josephus, Book 1, Chapter 7.

Abraham's posterity in Egypt first, then in America were versed in astronomy: "The Egyptians were the first land surveyors, mathematicians and astronomers of the old world. They calculated the eclipses and periods of the planets and constellations from a remote antiquity."— Beginnings of Civilization, p. 05, and Atlantis, p. 364.

The proficiency of the Aztecs in astronomy is thus spoken of by Prescott: "That they should be capable of accurately adjusting their festivals by the movements of the heavenly bodies, and should fix the true length of the tropical year with a precision unknown to the great philosophers of antiquity, could be the result only of a long series of nice and patient observations, evincing no slight progress in civilization." —Atlantis, p. 352.

Delafield says: "The investigations of Mons Bailey in the astronomy of the ancients generally, of Mons. Jomard in that of Egypt, and of Baron Humboldt in that of Mexico and South America, present most striking incidents of coincidence, not only their division of time, but also in the Zodiacal signs."—Delafield, p. 48.

Mr. Jomard says: "I have also recognized in your memoir on the division of time among the Mexican nations, compared with those of Asia, some very striking analogies between the Toltec character, and institutions observed on the banks of the Nile. Among these analogies is one worthy of attention. It is the use of the vague year of three hundred and sixty-five days, composed of equal months and of five complementary days equally employed at Thebes and Mexico, a distance of three thousand leagues."—Ibid, p. 52.

Mr. Schoolcraft gives this account of a discovery made in West Virginia: "Antique tube; telescopic device. In the course of excavations made in 1842 in the easternmost of three mounds of the Elizabethtown group, several tubes of stone were disclosed, the precise object of which have been the subject of various opinions. The longest measured twelve inches, the shortest eight. Three of them were carved out of steatite, being skillfully cut and polished. The diameter of the tube, externally, was one inch and four-tenths. The bore eight-tenths of an inch. The caliber was continued until within three-eighths of an inch of the sight end, when it diminishes to two-tenths of an inch. By placing the eye at the diminished end, the extraneous light is shut from the pupil and distant objects are more clearly discerned." * * "An ancient Peruvian relic found a few years since, shows the figure of a man wrought in silver, in the act of studying the heavens through such a tube."—Baldwin's Ancient America, p. 42.

"It has been already stated that finely wrought telescopic tubes have been found among remains of the Mound Builders. They were used, it seems, by the ancient people of Mexico and Central America, and they were known also in ancient Peru, where a silver figure of a man in the act of using such a tube has been discovered in one of the old tombs."—Baldwin's Ancient America, p. 123.

"Montesinos gives a list of sixty-four sovereigns who reigned (in Peru) in the first period * * The twenty-first Manco-Capac-Amauta, being adicted to astronomy, convened a scientific counsel. * * Amauta, the thirty-eighth of the line, Yahuar-Huquiz, the fifty-first were 'celebrated for astronomical knowledge,' and the latter 'intercalated a year at the end of four centuries.' "—Ibid, pp. 264-6.

"From the earliest ages, we find skill and knowledge in astronomy, and the more we examine, the more we are surprised at the extent of astronomical science in the earliest history of the world."—Delafield's American Antiquity, p. 48.

"This is no slight analogy, to find the system of intercalation and the number of complementary days identical between Mexico and Egypt."—Ibid, p. 50.

In the sanctuaries of Palenque are found sculptured representations of idols which resemble the most ancient gods, both of Egypt and Syria; planispheres and godiacs exist, which exhibit a superior astronomical and chronological system to that which was possessed by the Egyptians."—Ibid, p. 50.

Priest, quoting Atwater: " 'On the whole,' says Atwater, 'I am convinced from an attention to many hundreds of these works in every part of the west which I have visited, that their authors had a knowledge of astronomy.' "—American Antiquity, p. 273.

Le Plongeon, says: "The Troano, (Maya Book) is a very ancient treatise on geology.' —Sacred Mysteries, p. 70.   So it will certainly appear that at that day the science of geology was not without its devotees and propagators in Ancient America.   Of "Chimu," a city of South America, built by the ancients, Donnelly says: "Tombs, temples and palaces arise on every hand, ruined but still traceable, immense pyramidal structures, some of them a half mile in circuit; vast

areas shut in by massive walls, each containing its water tank, its shops, municipal edifices, and the dwellings of its inhabitants, and each a branch of a larger
organization; prisons, furnaces for smelting metals, and
almost every concomitant of civilization existed in the.
ancient Chimu capital."—Atlantis, p. 393.

Baldwin says: "To find the chief seats and most
abundant remains of the most remarkable civilization
of this old American race, we * * go * * into Central
America and * * Mexico. * * Many ancient cities
have been discovered. * * The chief peculiarity of
these ruins, * * is the evidence they furnish that their
builders had remarkable skill in architecture and * *
ornamenation. * * The rooms and corridors in these
edifices were finely and often elaborately finished; plas-
ter, stucco, and sculpture being used. * * "Throughout," he again says, (quoting Stephens), "the laying
and polishing of the stones are as perfect as under the
rules of the best modern masonry. * * The ornamentation is no less remarkable than the masonry and architectural finish."—Ancient America, pp. 93, 99.

The Marquis de Nadaillac, author of Prehistoric
America, says of the old civilization of Peru: "Nowhere in the world, perhaps, has man displayed greater
energy. It was in these desolate regions that arose the
most powerful and most highly civilized empire of the
two Americas, * * imposing ruins, * * fortresses defending it, * * roads intersecting it, * * canals con-
ducting the water for fertilizing the fields, * * houses
of refuge in the mountains for the use of travelers, * *
potteries, linen and cotton cloth, ornaments of gold and
silver, which are sought for by the Tapadas, with in-
satiable zeal." †—Prehistoric America, p. 388.

Priest says: "The Americans were equal in antiquity, civilization and sciences, to the nations of Europe and Africa; like them the children of the Asiatic nations."   Antiquities, p. 305.

Speaking of a portion of the ruins of Labna, Stephens says: "Above the cornice of the building rises a gigantic perpendicular wall to the height of thirty feet, once ornamented from top to bottom and from one side to the other with colossal figures and other designs in stucco, now broken into fragments, but still presenting a curious and extraordinary appearance, such as the art of no other people ever produced."—Incidents of Travel in Yucatan, Vol. 2, p. 51.

Baldwin says: "At Palenque are remains of a well built aqueduct; and near the ruins, especially in Yucatan, are frequently found the remains of many finely constructed aguadas or artificial lakes. * * These antiquities show that this section of the continent was anciently occupied by a people admirably skilled in the arts of masonry, building, and architectural decoration.   Some of their works can not be excelled by the best of our constructors and decorators."—Ancient America, p. 101.

Short says of Mexico: "Here the silver-smith, the sculptor, the artist and the architect, we are led to believe, from the testimony of both tradition and remains, flourished."—American Antiquities, p. 270.

Baldwin, of Central American ruins, says: "As to the ornamentation, the walls, piers, and cornices are covered with it.   Everywhere the masterly workmanship and artistic skill of the old constructors compel admiration, Mr. Stephens going so far as to say of sculptured human figures found in fragments, 'In justness of proportion and symmetry, they must have approached the Greek Models. * * Dupaix says: 'It is impossible to describe adequately the interior decorations of this sumptuous temple.'

"Stephens states, in the Preface to his work on Yucatan, that he visited forty-four cities or places."— Ancient America, pp. 108–9, 125.

Baldwin says: "Here, (Copan) as at Palenque, the ornamentation was 'rich and abundant.' The ruins, greatly worn by decay, still show that 'architecture, sculpture, painting and all the arts that embellish life, had flourished in this overgrown forest.'"— Ancient America, p. 113.

Of ruins at Mitla, "Their beauty," says M. Charney, "can be matched only by the monuments of Greece and Rome in their best days."—Ibid., p. 121.

Of the ruin called "Kabbah," the author says: "The cornice running over the doorways, tried by the severest rules of art recognized among us, would embellish the architecture of any known era."—Ibid., p. 137.

"Many ages must have been required to develop such admirable skill in masonry and ornamentation."—Ibid., p. 153.

In the late work of John T. Short, published in 1882, he tells the following concerning the city of Palenque: "The accompanying cut shows Waldeck's drawing (employed by Mr. Bancroft). Four hundred yards south of the palace stands the ruins of a pyramid and temple, which at the time of Dupaix's and Waldeck's visits were in a good state of preservation, but quite dilapidated when seen by Charney. The temple faces the east, and on the western wall of its inner apartment itself facing the eastern light, is found, (or rather was, for it has now entirely disappeared), the most beautiful specimens of stucco relief in America. M. Waldeck with the critical insight of an experienced artist declares it worthy to be compared to the most beautiful works of the age of Augustus. He therefore named the temple Beau Relief. The above cut is a reduction from Waldeck's drawing used in Mr. Bancroft's work, and is very accurate. However, the peculiar beauty of Waldeck's drawing is such that it must be seen in order to be fully appreciated. It is scarcely necessary for us to call the reader's attention to the details of this picture, in which correctness of designs and graceful outlines predominate to such an extent, that we may safely pronounce the beautiful youth who sits enthroned on his elaborate and artistic throne, the American Apollo. In the original drawing the grace of the arms and wrists is truly matchless, and the chest muscles are displayed in the most perfect manner."— North Americans of Antiquity, p. 387.

The same author further writes of Palenque: "The stuccoed roofs and piers of both the temples—Cross and Sun—may be truly pronounced works of art of a high order. On the former, Stephens observed busts and heads approaching Greek models in symmetry of contour and perfectness of proportion. Mr. Waldeck has preserved in his magnificent drawings some of these figures, which are certainly sufficient to prove beyond controversy that the Ancient Palenqueans were a cultivated and artistic people In passing to Uxmal the transition is from delineations of the human figure, to the elegant and exterior superabundant ornamentation of edifices, and from stucco to stone as the material

em loyed. The human figure, however, when it is represented, is in statuary of a high order. The elegant
square panels of grecques and frets which compose the
cornice of the Casa del Gobernador, delineated in the
works of Stephens, Baldwin and Bancroft, are a marvel
of beauty which must excite the admiration of the most
indifferent student of the subject."—Ibid., p. 392.

Bancroft says in regard to the Peruvian antiquities: "The Peruvians seem to have had a more abundant supply of metals than the civilized nations of North
America, and to have been at least equally skillful in
working them. The cuts show specimens of copper
cutting implements, of which a great variety are found.
Besides copper, they had gold and silver in much
greater abundance than the northern artisans, and the
arts of melting, casting, soldering, beating, inlaying
and carving these metals, were carried to a high degree
of perfection."—Native Races, Vol. 4, p. 792.

Bancroft says: "Closely enveloped in the dense
forests of Chiapas, Guatemala, Yucatan and Honduras,
the ruins of several ancient cities have been discovered, which are far superior in extent and magnificence
to any seen in Aztec territory, and of which a detailed description may be found in the fourth volume
of this work. They bear hieroglyphic descriptions apparently identical in character; in other respects they
resemble each other more than they resemble the Aztec
ruins, or even other and apparently later works in Guatemala and Honduras. All these remains bear evident
remarks of great antiquity. Their existence and similarity, in the absence of any evidence to the contrary,
would indicate the occupation of the whole country, at
some remote period, by nations far advanced in civili-

zation, and closely allied in manners and customs, if not in blood and language. Furthermore, the traditions of several of the most advanced nations point to a wide-spread civilization, introduced among a numerous and powerful people by Votan and Zamna, who, or their successors, built the cities referred to, and founded great allied empires in Chiapas, Yucatan and Guatemala. And moreover, the tradition is confirmed by the universality of one family of languages or dialects spoken among the civilized nations, and among their descendants to this day. I deem the grounds sufficient, therefore, for accepting this Central American civilization of the past as a fact."--Native Races of Pacific States, Vol. 2, p. 116.

In regard to the ruins of Palenque, Stephens says: "The intermediate country is now occupied by races of Indians speaking many different languages, and entirely unintelligible to each other; but there is room for belief that the whole of this country was once occupied by the same race, speaking the same language, or at least having the same written characters."--Travels in Central America, Chiapas and Yucatan, Vol. 2, p. 343.

William Hosea Bullou, in Scientific American for January 26th, 1889, quoting Le Plongeon, says: "Here (at Chichen) were many beautiful mineral paintings, probably the only vestiges now existing of ancient American art."

With regard to the calendar stone of Mexico, Bancroft says: "The calendar stone was a rectangular parallelopipedon of porphyry, 13 feet, 1½ inches square, 3 feet, 3½ inches thick, and weighing in its present mutilated state, 24 tons."--Native Races, Vol. 4, p. 506.

The concentric circles, the divisions, and the sub-
divisions, without numbers are traced with mathematical
exactitude."—Ibid., p. 508.

Of this stone Short says: "Thus it is that the
stone speaks and testifies to the astronomical knowledge
of the Aztecs, the accuracy of which casts into the
shade the imperfect Julian Calendar in use by Europeans at the time of the conquest."—American Antiquities, p. 455.

Thus it will be seen that these various authors
clearly and distinctly affirm that the ancient denizens
of America possessed high culture, polish and civilization. And so do they add their testimony in support
of the Book of Mormon, for that is in line with its
statements touching these things.

CHAPTER V.
BOOKS, WEAVING AND DYEING,

Elder Wm. Woodhead, in writing for Herald, says:
"The following description of the 'Troano' will probably be a fair one, as to the merit of the 'many ancient
Maya books said to have been destroyed by the vandalism of Landa and other early fathers.' 'The Troano,'
says Dr. Le Plongeon, 'is a very encient treatise on
geology.' "—Sacred Mysteries, p. 70.

Of writing in Central America, Baldwin says: "The
ruins show that they had the art of writing, and that at
the south this art was more developed, more like a
phonetic system of writing than that found in use among
the Aztecs. * * It is known that books or manuscript writings were abundant among them in the ages
previous to the Aztec period."—Ancient America, p.
187.

It is evident then that these books were not the fruits of association with the Spaniards, for the Aztec period antedated the Spaniards by some centuries.

Baldwin says: "These chroniclers had likewise to calculate the days, months and years, and though they had no writings like ours, they had their symbols and characters through which they understood everything, and they had great books, which were composed with such ingenuity and art, that our characters were really of no great assistance to them. Our priests have seen those books, and I myself, * * many were burned at the instigation of the monks. * * Books, such as those here described by Las Cassas must have contained important historical information."—Ancient America, p. 188. Again: "We learn from Spanish writers that a still greater destruction of the old books was effected by the more ignorant and fanatical of the Spanish priests who were established in the country as missionaries after the conquest. This is said by Las Cassas, himself, one of the missionaries"—Ibid., 188-9

"There are existing monuments of an American ancient history which invites study, and most of which might, doubtless, have been studied more successfully in the first part of the sixteenth century, before nearly all the old books of Central America had been destroyed by Spanish fanaticism, than at present."—Baldwin's Ancient America, p. 14.

"They were highly skilled, also, in the appliances of civilized life, and they had the art of writing, a fact placed beyond dispute by their many inscriptions."—Ibid., 101.

"Sahagun wrote such a history, which shows that he had studied the traditions and some of the old books; this work is printed in the great collection of Lord Kingsborough."—Ibid., 191.

Delafield says: "Their buildings, particularly the sacred houses, were covered with hieroglyphics. Each race, Egyptian, Mexican and Peruvian recorded the deeds of their gods upon the walls of their temples."—American Antiquities, p. 60.

Speaking of a sculptured figure at Uxmal, Stephens says: "Around the head of the principal figure are rows of characters. We now discovered that these characters were hieroglyphics."—Incidents of Travel in Yucatan, Vol. 1, p. 167.

"In Peru a paper was made of plantain leaves, and books were common in the earlier ages. Humboldt mentions books of hieroglyphical writings among the Panoes, which were 'bundles of their paper resembling our volumes of quarto.' "—Atlantis, p. 451.

Of the Aztec writing, Baldwin says: "Their skill in architecture and architectural ornamentation did not enable them to build such cities as Mitla and Palenque, and their 'picture writing' was a much ruder form of the graphic art than the phonetic system of the Mayas and the Quiches."—Ancient America, p. 221.

From the above we are led to believe that a wide contrast existed in the writings of the Ancient Americans. Some were elegant in their artistic appearance, while some were rude.

Bancroft describes one of them (the Troano) in these words: "The original is written on a strip of maguey paper about fourteen feet long and nine inches wide, the surface of which is covered with a white varnish, on which the figures are painted in black, red, blue, and brown. It is folded fan-like in thirty-five

folds; presenting, when shut, much the appearance of a
modern large octavo volume. The hieroglyphics cover
both sides of the paper, and the writing is consequently divided into seventy columns, each about five by
nine inches, apparently having been executed after the
paper was folded, so that the folding does not interfere with the written matter. * * The regular lines
of written characters are uniformly black, while the
pictorial portions of what may perhaps be considered
representative signs are in red and blue, chiefly the
former, and the blue appears for the most part as a
background in some of the pages."--J. T Short, p. 422

This description of the Troano will probably be a
fair description of the "many" ancient Maya books
said to have been "destroyed by the vandalism of
Landa and other early Fathers."

Desire Charney says: "Documents were not wanting; and had the religious zeal of the men of that time
been less ill-judged, they would have found in the various multiform manuscripts, in the charts or maps, in
the idols, in the pottery and living traditions, ample
and reliable materials from which to write an exhaust-
ive history of the Maya civilization."--Ancient Cities,
p. 270.

Some of the Peruvian tongues had names for paper, and according to Montesino's writing, books
were common in the older times, that is to say, in ages
long previous to the Incas."--Baldwin's Ancient America, p. 255.

"Humboldt mentions books of hieroglyphical
writings found among the Panoes, on the river Ucayli.

* * A Franciscan missionary found an old man * * reading one of these books to several young persons." —Ibid., 255-6.

Boudinot says: "There is a tradition related by an aged Indian of the Stockbridge Tribe, that their fathers were once in possession of a SACRED BOOK, which was handed down from generation to generation, and at last HID IN THE EARTH, since which time they have been under the feet of their enemies."†—Star of the West."

Baldwin says of Mound Builders: "They manufactured cloth, but their intelligence, skill and civilized ways are shown not only by their constructions and manufactures, but also by their mining works."—Ancient America, p. 61.

McLean says: "The Mound Builders * * for their principal raiment used cloth regularly spun with a uniform thread, and woven with a warp and woof. Fragments of clothing have been taken from a low mound near Charleston, Jackson county, Ohio. In constructing the Cincinnati, Hamilton and Dayton R. R., a mound was cut through near Middleton, Ohio, and in it * * was found cloth connected with tassals and ornaments.—Mound Builders," p. 73.

Donnelly says: "Their works in cotton and wool exceed in fineness anything known in Egypt at that time " (Time of conquest).—Atlantis, p. 395.

Of cloth made from the wool of Peruvian sheep, Prescott says: "The cloth was finished on both sides alike; the delicacy of the texture was such as to give to it the lustre of silk; and the brilliancy of the dyes excited the admiration and envy of the European artizan." —Prescott's Conquest of Peru, Vol. 1, p. 149.

Desire Charney says: "Toltecs * * had sculptors, Mosaists, painters, and smelters of gold and silver; and by means of molds, knew how to give metals every variety of shape; their jewelers and lapidaries could imitate all manner of animals, plants, flowers, birds, etc. Cotton was spun by the women, and given a brilliant coloring, both from animal and mineral substances; it was manufactured of every degree of fineness so that some looked like muslin, some like cloth and some like velvet. They had also the art of interweaving with these the delicate hair of animals and birds' feathers, which made a cloth of great beauty."— Ancient Cities, p. 88.

Fragments of such cloth were to be seen at the World's Fair. There are also some on exhibition at the Chamber of Commerce Library, Denver, Colorado.

Baldwin in speaking of the Peruvians says: "They had great proficiency in the arts of spinning, weaving and dyeing. For their cloth they used cotton and wool of four varieties of the llama; that of the vicuna being the finest. Some of their cloth had interwoven designs and ornaments very skillfully executed. * * They possessed the secret of fixing the dye of all colors, flesh-color, yellow, gray, blue, green, black, etc., so firmly in the thread, or in the cloth already woven, that they never faded during the lapse of ages, even when exposed to the air, or buried (in tombs) under the ground. Only the cotton became slightly discolored, while the woolen fabrics preserved their primitive lustre. It is a circumstance worth remarking that chemical analysis made of pieces of cloth of all the different dyes prove that the Peruvians extracted all their colors from the vegetable and none of the mineral

kingdom.   In fact, the natives of the Peruvian mountains now use plants unknown to Europeans, producing
from them bright and lasting colors."--Ancient America, pp. 247-8.

"The American nations manufactured woolen and
cotton goods, they made pottery as beautiful as the
wares of Egypt.   They manufactured glass, they engraved gems and precious stones."--Atlantis, p. 142.

"In both continents we find brick, glassware and
even porcelain."--Ibid., p. 350.

Priest mentioning a Mr. Brown says: "He discovered in one mound an article of glass, in form
resembling the bottom of a tumbler, weighing five
ounces; it was concave on both of its sides.   It is true
that although glass is said not to have been found out
till 644 of the Christian era, yet it was known to the
ancient Romans, * * Pompeii and Herculaneum buried
by the volcanic eruption of Mount Vesuvius.   Among
the vast discoveries * * has been found one bow win-
dow, lighted with glass of a green tinge, or color."--
American Antiquities, p. 280.

Chambers says: "The invention of glass dates from
the earliest antiquity, and the honor of its discovery
has been contested by several nations.   As the oldest
known specimens are Egyptian, its invention may with
great probability be attributed to that people." (1445
B. C.)--Chambers' Encyclopedia, Article, Glass.

I give one citation of many in the Book of Mormon which are amply sustainsd by the above mentioned
authorities on weaving: "Behold their women did toil
and spin and did make all manner of cloth of fine
twined linen, and cloth of every kind."--Plano Edition, Book of Mormon, p. 394.

CHAPTER VI.
ISRAEL IN AMERICA.

That Israel was to be scattered far wider than the eastern continent, is evident from Isaiah 11: 11, 12: "And it shall come to pass that the Lord shall set his hand again the second time to recover the remnant of his people which shall be left, from Assyria, and from Egypt, and from Pathros, and from Cush, and from Elam, and from Shinar, and from Hammath, and from the islands of the sea. And he shall set up an ensign for the nations and assemble the outcasts of Israel, and gather the dispersed of Judah from the four corners of the earth."

The liberal mention of lands, supplemented by "and from the islands of the sea," covers all lands in its scope. The "ensign for the nations," and to "assemble the outcasts of Israel, and gather together the dispersed of Judah, from the four corners of the earth," contemplates the entire earth. The effort to "recover' outcast Israel and dispersed Judah must occur after the year 70 A. D., when Judah was dispersed and Jerulalem destroyed.

The first desolation and scattering of Israel occurred about 590 B. C., when the power of Babylon wrought the complete overthrow of the Jews, and destroyed Jerusalem and burned the magnificent temple erected by Solomon.

The first restoration occurred about 520 B. C., when their beloved Jerusalem was restored, and the temple rebuilt, under the splendid patronage and aid of Cyrus, king of Persia, the great ruler of the east.

The second desolation and scattering came in the year 70 of the Christian era, when the famed city, "beautiful for situation," and "the joy of the whole earth," was laid in ruins, and the second temple razed to the ground, when the Jews perished by pestilence, famine and war; and only a remnant escaped, to endure exile and captivity under the yoke of the Roman Empire.

The second restoration, which is so plainly predicted by the prophet, can only occur after the second scattering and exile of that people; and therefore, must have its fulfillment subsequent to the year 70 of the Christian era.

The prophet Amos said: "And I will plant them upon their own land, and they shall no more be pulled up out of their land, which I have given them, saith the Lord thy God "—Amos 9: 15.

"My sheep wandered through all the mountains, and upon every high hill; yea, my flock was scattered upon all the face of the earth, and none did search or seek after them. For thus saith the Lord God: Behold, I, even I, will both search my sheep and seek them out. As a shepherd seeketh out his flock, * * so will I seek out my sheep * * out of all places * * I will bring them out from the people, and gather them from the countries, and will bring them into their own land."— Ezek. 6: 11, 13.

The above, presents vividly, the extensive scattering of the past, and the complete gathering yet to be,

and Israel being planted in "their own land" from
which they were "outcast" and "dispersed." Israel
here called "sheep" are so mentioned by Christ; "Go
not into the way of the Gentiles, and into any city of
the Samaritans enter ye not: But go rather to the lost
sheep of the house of Israel"—Matt. 10: 5, 6.   God,
who "hath determined the times before appointed"
and the "bounds" of "habitation," gave the "sure
word of prophecy" portraying the history of his chosen
people, ere it came to pass; and so we are enabled to
trace Israel, by ancient promise and prophecy to the
land of America.

Genesis 48: 11–20, relates the blessing of Joseph's
sons, Manasseh and Ephriam, by Jacob; Ephriam, the
younger receives the special, or "right hand" blessing,
while the custom was in favor of the first born.   Of the
two, Jacob said, "He [Manasseh] also shall be great,
but truly his younger brother shall be greater than he,
and his seed shall become a multitude of nations * *
and he set Ephriam before Manasseh.   Genesis 49: 22–
26, presents the blessings of God to Joseph's posterity.
"Joseph is a fruitful bough, even a fruitful bough by a
well, whose branches run over the wall, [or that surrounding that continent, the sea].   The God of thy
fathers * * shall help thee, * * the Almighty * *
shall bless thee with blessings of heaven above [reve-
lation]; blessings of the deep that lieth under: blessings
of the breast and of the womb.   The blessings of thy
father have prevailed above the blessings of my progenitors unto the utmost bound [afar off] of the everlasting hills: they shall be on the head of Joseph and on
the crown of the head of him that was separated from
his brethren."

The geographical extent of the lands of the progenitors of Jacob, (Abraham and Isaac) is described
minutely, and nations mentioned who were occupying
it. "And the Lord appeared unto Abraham and said,
Unto thy seed will I give this land: and there he builded
an altar unto the Lord, who appeared unto him."—
Gen. 13: 15. "For all the land which thou seest, to
thee will I give it, and to thy seed forever."—Gen. 12:
7. "In that same day the Lord made a covenant with
Abraham, saying, Unto thy seed have I given this land,
from the river of Egypt unto the great river, the river
Euphrates: The Kennites, Kenizzites, * * Kadmon-
ites, * * Hittites, Perizzites, * * Rephaim, * * Am-
orites, * * Canaanites, Girgashites, * * and the Jebu-
sites."—Gen. 15: 18–21.

"And I will give unto thee, and to thy seed after
thee, the land wherein thou art a stranger, all the land
of Canaan, for an everlasting possession, and I will be
their God."—Gen. 17: 18.

While the above described and limited country was
given to Abraham and his seed, to Joseph and his seed,
God added that "over the wall, [sea] unto the utmost
bounds of the everlasting hills," or those farthest away.

Deut. 33: 13–17, gives a description of Joseph's
land. "And of Joseph he said, Blessed of the Lord be
his land, for the precious things of heaven, for the dew
and the deep that coucheth beneath, * * precious
fruits brought forth by the sun, * * the moon, * *
chief things of ancient mountains, * * precious things
of the lasting hills, and for the precious things of the
earth and the fullness thereof, and for the good will of
him that dwelt in the bush, let the blessings come upon

the head of Joseph, and upon the top of the head of
him that was separated from his brethren."

The description thus given through Moses of
Joseph's land must certainly apply to that land "afar
off" "the utmost bounds of the everlasting hills,"
and cannot describe that little strip of tribal inheritance
upon the coast of the Mediterranean sea.   There was
nothing of special significance in the blessing of the
land upon the Mediterranean, that such a glowing and
enlarged statement of its luxuriance and richness should
have been given.   "Blessed be his [Joseph's] land for
the precious things of heaven above."   This we understand to be revelation from God.

Now we ask, What special blessing of God did
Joseph receive in his first or tribal inheritance?   We
know of none.   But after going over and beyond the
sea, or "wall" as the prophet describes it, their record,
the Book of Mormon, tells us that God in his loving
kindness and eternal wisdom, gave to them the revelation of his will concerning them from time to time.
The land of America will certainly do justice to the
splendid description of Joseph's land given by the
prophet.   For this is a choice land above all other
lands of the earth; varied in its richness of climate, of
soil, of mineral resources, abounding in all things the
heart could desire, from the ice-bound regions to those
of the tropics, affording almost all the fruits of the
earth.   All of these things point to the Western continent as Joseph's land.   This theory is supported by the
following texts: "O vine of Sibmah, I will weep for
thee with the weeping of Jazer; thy plants are gone
over the sea."—Jer. 48:32.   "For the fields of Hesh-
bon languish, and the vine of Sibmah; the lords of the

heathen have broken down the principal plants thereof
* * they have gone over the sea."—Isaiah 16: 18.

As identifying the "vine of Sibmah," "whose plants
are gone over the sea," "for of old time have I broken
thy yoke, and burst thy bands."—Jer. 2: 20. This
clearly describes the freeing of Israel from Egyptian
bondage, as does also: "Thou hast brought a vine out
of Egypt, thou hast cast out the heathen and planted
it."—Ps. 80: 8. Joseph's posterity, the "branches of
the fruitful bough," which were to "run over the wall;"
the plants of the "vine of Sibmah," are, without doubt,
of Israel.

Now if they went over the sea, or "wall," as the
prophet termed it, where did they go? What other
land save the Western Continent can fulfill the terms of
prophetic description, as given by Moses? We know
of none. Surely it is not found in Europe, or among
the nations of Asia. Here was the land, "choice above
all other lands."

Besides this evidence of a portion of Israel emi-
grating from the eastern to the western continent is the
warning of the Prophet Jeremiah, disclosing King Nebuchadnezzar's "purpose," and the warning of God, commanding them to flee. "Flee, get you far off; dwell
deep, [go secretly, unobserved], O ye inhabitants of
Hazor, saith the Lord, for Nebuchadnezzar hath taken
counsel against you, and hath conceived a purpose
against you. Arise, get you up unto the wealthy nation, that dwelleth without care saith the Lord, which
have neither gates nor bars, which dwell alone. And
their camels shall be a booty, and the multitude of their
cattle a spoil, and I will scatter into all winds them

that are in the utmost corners, and I will bring their calamity from all sides thereof, saith the Lord."—Jer. 49: 30–32.

The following points are prominent: First, They were to "flee;" "get you far off;" "dwell deep;" (go unobserved). Second, They were to go to a "wealthy nation that dwelleth without care," one occupying a land "alone," and, therefore, had neither "gates nor bars" to keep away others, as was the case upon the eastern continent. Third, The camels of the "wealthy nation" were to be a "booty;" "the multitude of their cattle a spoil." Fourth, Those by whom the "booty" and the "spoil" should be left, were to be "scattered to all winds," carried away, obliterated, become extinct; "them that are in the utmost corners" their "calamity" was to "come from all sides;" such was the case with the Jaredite nation in every point. They were "afar off," "wealthy," "dwelt alone," without gates or bars; having grown wicked, were in a continual war, for the last battle of which the armies were four years in gathering, and in which their extinction was accomplished. (See close of Book of Esther, Book of Mormon.)

The Nephites wrote: "And we did find upon the land of promise as we journeyed in the wilderness, that there were beasts in the forests of every kind, both the cow, and the ox, and the ass, and the horse, and the goat, and the wild goat, and all manner of wild animals, which were for the use of men, and we did find all manner of ore, both of gold, silver and of copper." —Book of Mormon, p. 43.

When the Book of Mormon was published, the horse in particular, as also other of the domestic animals, was supposed not to have been on the Western

Continent until brought by the Spaniards "In North America * * in the Champlain period there were great elephants, and mastodons, oxen, horses, stags, beaver, and some edentates in quarternary North America, unsurpassed by any in the world."—Text Book of Geology, J. D. Dana, L. L. D., p. 325.

The Marquis de Naidaillac says: "It is the same in America, animals of the equine race that were so numerous in early geologic times, had long since disappeared on the arrival of the Spaniards."--Prehistoric Peoples, p. 158.

Prof. F. V. Hayden, U. S. Surveyor, Report 1873: "The skeleton, which I excavated with my own hands from the side of a bluff, adds considerably to our knowledge of this genus of horses."—Page 524.

Speaking of the Aceratherium, Megalodus says: "This large species and the A. Crassus Leidy, were very abundant during the Pliocene period in Western North America. Their remains are everywhere mingled with those of horses and camels."—Page 520.

The American Encyclopedia says: "Its fossil remains, chiefly molar teeth, have been so frequently found, especially in the southern and western states and in South America, and have been so carefully examined by competent palæontologists, that no doubt can remain of the former existence of the horse in the western world. * * Prof. Leidy says there is no room to doubt the former existence of the horse on the American continent, at the same time with the mastodon, and that 'man probably was his companion.'"--See article Horse.

Prof. Alexander Winchell says: "I have myself observed the bones of the mastodon and elephant im-

bedded in peat at depths so shallow that I could readily believe the animals to have occupied the country
during its possession by the Indians, and gave publication to this conviction in 1862.   More recently, Prof.
Holmes, of Charleston, has informed the Academy of
Natural Science of Philadelphia, that he finds upon the
banks of the Ashley river a remarkable conglomeration
of fossil remains in deposit of post-tertiary age.   Remains of the hog, horse and other animals of recent
date, together with human bones, stone arrow-heads,
hatchets and fragments of pottery, are there lying mingled with the bones of the mastodon and extinct
gigantic lizards.   Cotemporary with these American
animals, but not yet found associated in their remains
with the relics of the human species, lived in North
America horses much larger than the existing species,
grazing in company with wild oxen and herds of bison
and shrub-loving tapirs.   The streams were dammed
by the labors of gigantic beavers, while the forests afforded a range for a species of hog, and a grateful dwelling place for numerous edentate quadrupeds related to
the sloth, but of gigantic proportions."—Sketches of
Creation, pp. 356–7.

"It is a curious fact that so many genera, now extinct from the continent, but living in other quarters of
the globe, were once abundant on the plains of North
America.   Various species of the horse have dwelt
here for ages, and the question reasonably arises
whether the wild horses of the Pampas may not have
been indigenous.   Here, too, the camel found a suitable home."—Ibid., p. 210.

"Recent discoveries in the fossil beds of the Bad
Lands of Nebraska prove that the norse originated in

America. Professor Marsh, of Yale College, has identified the several preceding forms from which it was developed, rising, in the course of ages, from a creature
not larger than a fox until, by successive steps, it developed in the true horse. * * The fossil remains
of the camel are found in India, Africa, South America and in Kansas. The existing alpacas and llamas
of South America are but varieties of the camel family."—Atlantis, p 54-5.

Desire Charney believes that he has found in the
ruins of Tula the bones of "swine and sheep" "in a fossil state, indicating an immense antiquity."--Ibid., p.
330.

Of four varieties of the Peruvian sheep, the llama,
the one most familiarly known, is the least valuable on
account of its wool."—Prescott's Conquest of Peru,
Vol. 1, p. 147.

In The Youth's Companion of March 30th, 1882,
is the following article: "The Mastodon a Recent
Animal.—It has been common with a class of scientists
to class the mastodon among animals which became
extinct many ages ago. And as the bones of men and
extinct species of animals have been found mingled
together, it was inferred that man may have had a remote antiquity, reaching back a hundred thousand
years or more. But the following facts from Prof.
Collett's Geological Report of Indiana, go to show
that the mastodon disappeared at a quite recent period.
A skeleton was discovered in excavating the bed of the
canal a few miles north of Covington, in wet peat.
The teeth are in good preservation, and when the
larger bones were cut open, the marrow, still preserved,
was utilized by the bog cutters to "grease" their boots.

Pieces of sperm-like substance, two and a half or three inches in diameter, occupied the place of the kidney-fat of the monster.   During the summer of 1880, an almost complete skeleton of a mastodon was found in Illinois which must have survived until the vegetation of to-day prevailed.   The tusks formed each a full quarter of a circle; were nine feet long, twenty-two inches in circumference at the base, and weighed one hundred and seventy pounds.   The lower jaw was well preserved with a full set of magnificent teeth, and is nearly three feet long.   On inspecting the remains closely, a mass of fibrous, bark-like material, was found between the ribs, filling the place of the animal's stomach.   When carefully separated, it proved to be a crushed mass of herbs and grasses, similar to those which still grow in the vicinity.   In the same bed of miry clay a multitude of small fresh-water and land shells were observed.   These mollusks prevail all over the State of Illinois, Indiana, and parts of Michigan, and show conclusively that the animal and vegetable life, and consequently climate, are the same now as when this mastodon sank in his grave of mire and clay."

From Independent Patriot, November 20, 1890: The skeleton of a mastodon found at Higate, forty miles west of St. Thomas, Canada, is on exhibition in that town.   The area of the graves where the monster's bones were found is thirty-five by twenty-one feet. bones were scattered over it, one joint fitting into the other in a bed of gray merl about six feet below the ace.   Over the merl is a thick layer of black, loamy soil.   The length of the animal, gauged by the measurements of the bones already found, and allowing for those that have not yet been discovered, is, from the point of the nostril to the root of the tail, about twenty-one feet. This is greater than that of the celebrated "Mastodon giganteus" discovered near Newburg, N. Y., in the summer of 1845, and the skeleton, as a whole, is larger and more complete than any that have been found in Kentucky, Ohio, Missouri, California or Oregon.—Scientific American.

Prof. Wm. Larrabee, A. M., in "Lectures on the Scientific Evidence of Natural and Revealed Religion," says: "The Mastodon was a native of North America. He resembled the elephant, but was much larger."—p. 312.

In the Chicago Times for April 26, 1882, was the following concerning the elephants of Ancient America: "Jumbo wasn't a circumstance to the elephants that used to stamp around this country."

Priest in his American Antiquities says of skeleton of Mastodon in Philadelphia Museum: The ribs are six inches in width, and in thickness three. The whole skeleton as it is, with the exception of a few bones, weighs one thousand pounds."—p. 151.

Of another skeleton discovered in Louisiana, on the Mississippi: "The largest bone, which was thought to be the shoulder-blade, or jaw bone, is twenty feet long, three broad, and weighed one thousand two hundred pounds."—Ibid., p. 155.

In the Chamber of Commerce Library at Denver, Colorado, may be seen and labeled thus: "Tooth of Prehistoric Elephant, unearthed in 1871, Corner Larimee and Sixteenth streets; weight twenty-one pounds."

Another relic labeled: "Portion of tusk of Mammoth, found in Douglas county; the total length of tusk when found, eleven feet."

"We know that the equine type of quadrupeds existed in America from the period of the Eocene. We are in fact, acquainted with twenty one species of horse-like animals, and the genus of true horses has been traced down to the times preceding the present."— Prof. A. Winchell, Chancellor, Syracuse University, Evolution, p. 82.

Prof. Cooper, in a lecture 1875, in San Francisco, said that during the "Pliocene epoch" in California, "through the luxuriant forests roamed a llama as large as a bactrian camel; herds of huge buffalo disported in the meadows along with wild horses of a giant race." †

"In the later fauna were the remains of a number of species of extinct camels, one of which was of the size of the Arabian camel, and a second about two-thirds as large; also a smaller one. * * Although no horses were known to exist on this continent prior to its discovery by Europeans, yet Dr. Leidy has shown that before the age of man, this was emphatically the country of horses. Dr. Leidy has reported twenty-seven species of the horse family which are known to have lived on this continent prior to the advent of man."— U. S. Surveyor, F. V. Hayden's Great West, p. 44.

The Book of Mormon mentions two large, very large animals, classing them with the elephant. The statement as found in Chambers' Encyclopedia, Vol. 6, Article Mastodon, is therefore full of significance: "Eleven or twelve species have been described from the Miocene, Pliocene and Pleistocene strata in Europe, Asia and America."

Of the third and smaller number of people who migrated to the western continent, it is recorded on page 137, Book of Mormon, that they came from Jerusalem when Zedekiah, who was afterward carried captive into Babylon, was king of Judah. Of this people the prophet Ezekiel says: "Thus saith the Lord God, I will also take the highest branch of the high cedar, and will set it; I will crop off from the top of his young twigs a tender one, and will plant it upon a high mountain and eminent. In the mountain of the height of Israel will I plant it; and it shall bring forth boughs, and bear fruit, and be a goodly cedar; and under it shall dwell all fowl of every wing; in the shadow of the branches thereof shall they dwell" Ezek. 17: 22, 23.

First, King Zedekiah was of Israel. Second, Those taken from his household were to be planted in the "mountain of the height of Israel," where a government would arise in which could "dwell" all "fowl of every wing," or men from all the races, as is the case in America.

The Prophet Isaiah, describes in a graphic manner the Western Continent: "Woe to the land shadowing with wings, which is beyond the rivers of Ethiopia."— Isaiah 18: 1.

First, The American continent is in the form of a pair of wings. Second, It lies west, or beyond the rivers of Ethiopia, from where the prophet had his abode, át Jerusalem.

Zephaniah 3: 10, "From beyond the rivers of Ethiopia my suppliants, even the daughters of my dispersed, shall bring mine offering." This text presents the people of the western land, or that land "beyond the rivers of Ethiopia," bringing offering, which supports all that is claimed in the foregoing chapter in regard to the location of Israel.

For Joseph, whose posterity was to come to the Western Continent, as hitherto shown, there was to be a record. "The word of the Lord came again unto me, saying, Moreover, thou son of man, take thee one stick, and write upon it, for Judah, and for the children of Israel his companions; then take another stick, and write upon it, for Joseph, the stick of Ephraim, and for all the house of Israel his companions: And join them one to another into one stick; and they shall become one in thine hand. And when the children of thy people shall speak unto thee, saying, Wilt thou not show us what thou meanest by these? Say unto them, Thus saith the Lord God; Behold, I will take the stick of Joseph, which is in the hands of Ephraim, and the tribes of Israel his fellows, and will put them with him, even with the stick of Judah, and make them one stick, and they shall be one in mine hand."--Ezek. 37: 15-19.

First, there is to be a stick (record) for "Judah" and "Israel his companions." Second, "Another stick" (record) for "Joseph in the hand of Ephraim, and Israel his companions." Third, They are to be joined "one to another," and thus made companion volumes. Fourth, God was to put the stick (record) in the hand of Ephraim with that of Judah, which, in the preservation of the records of the Book of Mormon and their translation was fulfilled. Fifth, Ephraim's pre-eminence, as shown in his blessing, is clearly brought to light, in his possession of the "stick of Joseph," and "Joseph's land." The Western Continent is therefore provided with its record, as was the eastern, with the record of God's dealings with his people upon that land.

The prophet says: "I have written to him the great things of my law, but they were accounted as a strange thing."—Hosea 8: 12.

CHAPTER VII.
HEBREW RELICS, CUSTOMS AND LANGUAGE IN AMERICA.

Bancroft says: "The theory that the Americans are of Jewish descent has been discussed more minutely and at greater length than any other. Its advocates, or at least those of them who have made original researches, are comparatively few, but the extent of their investigations and the multitude of parallelisms they adduce in support of their hypothesis exceed by far anything that we have yet encountered."—Native Races, Vol. 5, pp. 77–8.

Mr. George Catline says: "I believe with many others that the North American Indians are a mixed people; that they have Jewish blood in their veins, though I would not assert, as some have undertaken to prove, that they are Jews, or that they are the "ten lost tribes" of Israel. From the character and composition of their heads, I am compelled to look upon them as an amalgam race, but still savages, and from many of their customs, which seem to me peculiarly Jewish, as well as from the character of their heads, I am forced to believe that some part of those ancient tribes who have been dispersed by Christians in so many ways, and in so many different eras, have found their way to this country where they have entered among the native

stock.   I am led to believe this from the very many
customs which I have witnessed among them, that appear to be decidedly Jewish, and many of them so
peculiarly so, that it would seem almost impossible, or,
at all events, exceedingly improbable, that two peoples
in a state of nature should have hit upon them and
practiced them exactly alike.   The first and most
striking fact among the North American Indians that
refers us to the Jews, is that of their worshiping in all
parts, the "Great Spirit," or Jehovah, as the Jews were
ordered to do by divine precept, instead of a plurality
of gods, as ancient pagans and heathens did, and the
idols of their own formation."— Catlin's North American, Indians, p. 232.

Mr. Catlin then offers "twelve reasons" why he accepted the idea that the American Indians are descendants from the Israelites in some way, and as his investigations contain many facts which enter into this
discussion, I offer them for consideration: First, "The
Jews had their sanctum sanctorum, and so it may be
said the Indians have, in their council or medicine
houses, which are always held as sacred places."   Second, "As the Jews had, they have their high priests
and their prophets."   Third, "Among the Indians, as
among the ancient Hebrews, the women are not allowed
to worship with the men, and in all cases also they eat
separately."   Fourth, "The Indians everywhere believe
that they are certainly like those ancient people, persecuted, as every man's hand seems to be raised against
them."   Fifth, "In their marriages, the Indians, as did
the ancient Jews, uniformly buy their wives by giving
presents, and in many tribes, very closely resemble
them in other forms and ceremonies of their marriages."

Sixth, "In their preparation for war, and in peace-
making, they are strikingly similar." Seventh, "In their
treatment of the sick, burial of the dead, and mourn-
ing, they are also similar." Eighth, "In their bathing
and ablutions, at all seasons of the year, as a part of
their religious observances—having separate places for
men and women to perform these immersions—they resemble again." Ninth, "The customs among women of
absenting themselves during the lunar influences, is exactly consonant to the Mosaic law." Tenth, "After this
season of separation, purification in running water and
annointing, precisely in accordance with the Jewish
command, is required before she can enter the family
lodge." Eleventh, "Many of them have a feast closely resembling the annual feast of the Jewish Passover,
and amongst others, an occasion much like the Israelitish feast of the Tabernacle, which lasted eight days
(when history tells us they carried bundles of wil-
low bows and fasted several days and nights) making
sacrifices of the first fruits and best of everything,
closely resembling the sin offering of the Hebrews.
(See the history in Vol. 1, pp. 159–170 of Religious
Ceremonies of the Mandarins)." Twelfth, "Amongst
the list of their customs, however, we meet a number
which had their origin, it would seem, in the Jewish
ceremonial code, and which are so very peculiar in their
forms that it would seem quite improbable, and almost
impossible, that two different peoples should have hit
upon them alike, without some knowledge of each other.
These, I consider, go farther than anything else, as evidence, and carry, in my mind, conclusive proof that
these people are tinctured with Jewish blood."—Ibid.,
Vol. 2, pp 232–235.

Joseph Merrick gave the following account, that in 1815 he was leveling some ground * * situated on Indian Hill * * discovered * * a black strap, * * threw it into an old tool box, * * later found it, * * was formed of two pieces of thick raw hide, sewed and made water-tight, with sinews of some animal, and gummed over * * in the fold was contained four pieces of parchment. They were of a dark yellow hue and contained some kind of writing. The neighbors * * tore one of the pieces to atoms, * * the other three pieces Mr. Merrick saved and sent them to Cambridge where they were examined and discovered to have been written by a pen in Hebrew, plain and legible. The writing on the remaining pieces of parchment was quotations from the Old Testament."—Ibid., p. 93.

Mr. A. A. Bancroft thus describes a relic: "A slab of stone of hard and fine quality, an inch and a half thick, eight inches long, four and a half inches wide at one end, and tapering to three at the other. Upon the face of the slab was the figure of a man, apparently a priest, with a flowing beard and a robe reaching to his feet. Over his head was a curved line of characters, and upon the edge and back of the stone were closely and neatly carved letters. The slab, which I saw myself, was shown to the Episcopalian clergyman of Newark, and he pronounced the writing to be the Ten Commandments in ancient Hebrew."—Antiquities of Licking Co., Ohio., or Bancroft, Vol. 5, p. 95.

The following is a representation of the supposed "key stone," found 29th of June, 1860, (near Newark, Ohio, by D. Wyrick): "This stone is in the shape and size represented by the cuts, and has upon each of the four sides a Hebrew inscription in the Hebrew charac-

ter, which when translated reads: 'The King of the
earth;' 'The word of the Lord;' 'The laws of Jehovah;'
'The Holy of Holies ' Another stone, 'encased in a stone
box buried some twenty feet in the earth * * was found
on the first of November, 1851,' has 'four cuts on its four
sides,' * * with the characters on each side, the English of which appears to be an abridgement of the Ten
Commandments. The translation was given by J. W.
McCarty. The word 'Moses' and the statement 'Who
brought them out of the land of Egypt,' * * appears
above an image on the stone."—Pamphlet entitled "A
representation of the two stones with the characters inscribed upon them, one found by D. Wyrick during
the summer of 1860, near Newark, Ohio."

Of four stones and Rev. Miller's lecture on relics
found in Ohio, Elder Josiah Ellis, of Pittsburgh, Pa.,
wrote to the Herald in 1866, the following: "Rev. R.
M. Miller, lecturing in the First Presbyterian church,
Alleghany, Pa., on relics found near Newark, Ohio,
containing Hebrew inscriptions, exhibited a photograph
of a stone head, on the forehead of which was written
in Hebrew, 'May the Lord have mercy on an untimely
birth.' The original was owned by Mr. Tenant, of
Newark, Ohio. Another relic owned by Mr. Strock,
of Newark, contained in Hebrew: 'It is good to love
the aged;' and, 'The heart is deceitful.' A third relic,
in the shape of a wedge, had on its respective four sides
in Hebrew: 'The Lord is king of all the earth;' 'The
sword of the Lord is the law;' 'The Holy of Holies;'
'The jew of life is the Lord awakening souls.' A fourth,
called a Teraphim or household god by Mr. Miller,
(he quoted Judges, 17th chapter, to prove it), was eight
inches long, three wide and two thick, having a depres-

sion on one side half an inch deep, in which was carved a figure of a man dressed in priestly robes, over the head the word Moses, on the back and edges was the Ten Commandments. This Teraphim was found by digging into a very large mound, two and a half miles from Newark, Ohio, at some depth, and in a stone box, in 1860, and was owned by David Johnson, of Coshocton, Ohio.

"The Rev. Miller seemed a good Hebrew scholar as he read and criticised the language in the presence of several of the theological professors of the Presbyterian college of Alleghany City. He stated that he had shown them to several learned Rabbis, and they were agreed that the Hebrew characters were of a date beyond Ezra.

"Mr. Miller described on a black-board, the difference of formation of the letters before and after that period. His conclusions were: First, That some of the tribes or parts of tribes of Israel had once inhabited this land; Second, That they were Mound Builders."

Of these stones or similar ones, "The Prophetic Watchman" of September 14th, 1866, said: "We are all more or less acquainted with the so-called 'Indian Mounds,' found in various parts of our country.   *   * For centuries it has been a most interesting subject of inquiry as to who built these mounds and whence came their builders. Within the last few years some relics have been discovered which are thought to throw light upon the subject. The first is a little coarse sand stone, not quite an inch and a half high by two inches long. It was found in the 'Wilson Mound' and bears the face of a human being. On the forehead are five distinct Hebrew characters, which are interpreted to mean

'May the Lord have mercy on him (or me) an untimely birth,' evidently an expression of humiliation. The second relic from the same mound is a stone closely resembling lime stone. It is rather triangular than square in its form, and yet differs widely from both. It represents an animal, and contains four human faces and three inscriptions in Hebrew, signifying devotion, reverence and natural depravity. The third stone was found in 1860, about three miles from Newark. It is shaped like a wedge and is about six inches long, tapering at the end. On one end is a handle and at the top are four Hebrew inscriptions. The last relic is an object of much interest; it was found in 1860, and has engraved upon it, Moses and the Ten Commandments. One side is depressed and the reverse protrudes. Over the figure is a Hebrew word signifying Moses. The other inscriptions are almost literally the words found in some parts of the Bible, and the Ten Commandments are given in part and entirely, the longest being abbreviated. The alphabet used, it is thought, is the original Hebrew one, as there are letters not known in the Hebrew alphabet now in use, but bearing a resemblance to them. All things on this stone point to the time BEFORE Ezra.''

G. R. Lederer, editor "Israelite Indeed," wrote in May, 1861: "We suppose that many if not most of our readers have seen in religious, as well as in secular papers, the accounts of some relics which were found a few months ago in a mound near Newark, Ohio. These relics consist of stones of strange shapes, bearing Hebrew inscriptions, which makes the case particularly interesting to me as a Hebrew. * * In calling a few days ago on my friend, Mr. Theodore Dwight, (the Recording Secretary of the American Ethnological Society and my associate in the editorship of this magazine), my eyes met with the very object of my desire. That I examined these antiquities carefully none of our readers will, I think, entertain any doubt. I recognized all the letters except one, (the ayin) though the forms of many of them are different from those now in use."

According to the statement of the Book of Mormon, that portion of Israel known as the Nephites and Lamanites came over to the Western Continent about 600 B. C. Usher's chronology locates Ezra's prophecy, ending 556 B. C. It would be of the current Hebrew in its letters and forms of the TIMES OF EZRA, that the Nephites would have brought with them. The fact that the Hebrew discovered upon the relics already described, is clearly of that period, is a strong proof in support of the claim made in the Book of Mormon. This is the stronger, when it is known that since A. D. 1829, the searcher and seeker after the curious of antiquity have been at work, constantly increasing the volume and variety of evidence, all in confirmation of the testimony of this book.

Of the Indians, Priest says: "Their Jewish customs are too many to be enumerated in this work. Hebrew words are found among the American Indians in considerable variety."--American Antiquities, pp. 59, 65.

Palacio relates that at Azori in Honduras, the natives circumcised boys before an idol called Icelca."†
—Carta, p. 84

"Both Malvenda and Acosta affirm that the natives observed a jubilee year according to Israel's usage."—A Star in the West, p. 250.

Acosta says: "That the South American Indians dress like the ancient Jews, that they wear a square little poke over a little coat."—Ibid., 249.

Mr. Edwards, in his history of the West Indies says: "The striking conformity of prejudices and customs of the Charivee Indians to the practice of the Jews has not escaped the notice of historians, as Gamella and Du Terte and others."—Ibid., 250.

"The Indians to the eastward say that in Central and eastern America, previous to the white people coming into the country, their ancestors were used to the custom of circumcision, but latterly, not being able to assign any reason for so strange a practice, their young people insisted upon it being absolved."—Ibid., 113.

"Dr. Beattie in Beattie's Journal says, of a visit he paid the Indians on the Ohio about the year 1770, that an old Christian Indian informed him that an old uncle who had died about 1728, related to him several customs and traditions of former times; and among others, that circumcision was practiced among the Indians long ago, but their young, making mock of it, brought it into disrepute, and so it came to be disused."—Ibid., 113.

"Souard, in his Melenges De Literature, or literary miscellanies, speaking of the Indians of Guiana, says, on the authority of a learned Jew, Isaac Nasci, residing at Surinan, * * that the language of the Indians, which he calls the Galibe dialect, * * is soft and agreeable to the ear, abounding in vowels and synonyms, and possessing a syntax as regular as it would have been had it been established by an academy. This Jew asserts that all the substantives are Hebrew. The word expressive of soul in each language, means breath. They have the same word in Hebrew to denominate

God, which means, Master or Lord."—Ibid., 107.

Lact, in his description of South America, says, that he had often heard the Indians repeat the word "Hallelujah;" others attest that "Jehovah" or "Yehovo" is found in frequent use.—Ibid., 249.

H. A. Stebbins reported for the Herald: "A learned Indian, lecturing in Wisconsin in 1868, said that five hundred Indian words within his knowledge were Hebrew."

A table of words and phrases is furnished by Dr. Boudinot, Adair and others, to show the similarity, in some of the Indian languages, to the Hebrew, and that the former must have been derived from the latter. The following is an example afforded from the sources quoted:

WORDS.

ENGLISH.	INDIAN.	HEBRAIC, OR CHALDAIC.
Jehovah,	Yohewah,	Jahoveh.
God,	Ale,	Ale, Aleim.
Jah,	Yah or Wah,	Jah.
Shiloah,	Shilu,	Shiloh.
Heavens,	Chemim,	Shemim.
Father,	Abba,	Abba.
Man,	Ish, Ishie,	Ish.
Woman,	Ishto,	Ishto.
Wife,	Awah,	Ewah, Eve.
Thou,	Keah,	Ka.
His wife,	Liani,	Lihene.
This man,	Uwoh,	Huah.
Nose,	Nichiri,	Neheri.
Roof of a house,	Taubana-ora,	Debonaou.
Winter,	Kora,	Korah.
Canaan,	Canaai,	Canaan.

ENGLISH.	INDIAN.	HEBRAIC, OR CHALDAIC.
To pay,	Phale,	Phalace.
Now,	Na,	Na.
Hind part,	Kesh,	Kish.
Do,	Jennais,	Jannon.
To blow,	Phaubac,	Phauhe.
Rushing wind,	Rowah,	Ruach.
Ararat, or high Mt.,	Ararat,	Ararat.
Assembly,	Kurbet,	Grabit.
My skin,	Nora,	Ourni.
Man of God,	Ashto Allo,	Ishda Alloa.
Waiter of the high priest,	Sagan,	Sagan.

PARTS OF SENTENCES.

ENGLISH.	INDIAN.	HEBREW.
Very Hot,	Heru hara or hala,	Hara hara.
Praise to the first cause,	Hallehuwah,	Hallelujah.
Give me food,	Natoni boman,	Natoni bamen.
Go thy way,	Bayon boorkaa,	Bona bonak.
Good be with you,	Halea tibon,	Ye hali etonboa.
My necklace,	Yene Kali,	Vongali.
I am sick,	Nane guale,	Nance heti.

—Star of the West, pp. 100–107.

Rev. Ethen Smith says: "Their languages in their roots, idioms and particular construction, appear to have the whole genius of the Hebrew; and what is very remarkable, have most of the peculiarities of that language, especially those in which it differs from most other languages."† — The American Indians, pp. 98–101.

In regard to the ruins of Palenque, Stephens says: "The intermediate country is now occupied by races of

Indians speaking many different languages and entirely unintelligible to each other; but there is room for the belief that the whole of this country was once occupied by the same race, speaking the same language, or at least having the same written characters."—Travels in Central America, Chiapas and Yucatan, Vol. 2, p. 343.

CHAPTER VIII.
EGYPTIAN RESEMBLANCE AND LANGUAGE IN AMERICA.

Of Moses it is said: " 'And Moses was learned in all the wisdom of the Egyptians and was mighty in words and deeds.' Acts 7:22. He was also supposed to have entered the Egyptian priesthood, as was the custom for kings' sons, except those who were enthroned."†—Fragmental History, Vol. 2, p. 580.

It will be remembered that during Joseph's sojourn in Egypt, he became distinguished in learning, as no doubt others did during those times. The contact of the children of Israel with the Egyptians for hundreds of years, during which time flourished a Joseph and a Moses, skilled in all the learning of that renowned land, and the services of Moses as their instructor for forty years, would certainly be sufficient to establish Egyptian customs and language with that people. And if Israel came to America, we may reasonably look for and expect Egyptian traces and resemblances in America.

Delafield says: "On a review then of the architectural evidence, we trace identity between the Mexicans and Peruvians and the Egyptians, in (First) the coincidence in the pyramidal sarcophagi and temples, and their peculiar structure. (Second.) The possession of the same architectural and mechanical genius which enabled them to remove masses, which our mechanical skill has not attained to. (Third.) The peculiarity of hieroglyphic inscription of the zodiac and planispheric sculpture in their sacred buildings. (Fourth.) An identity of architectural and sepulchral decorations. (Fifth.) An analogous construction of bridges. (Sixth.) A singular analogy in the specimen given of their sculpture."—Delafield, p. 61.

Bancroft says: "Resemblances have been found between the calendar systems of Egypt and America, based chiefly upon the length and division of the year, and the number of intercalary and complementary days."—Native Races, Vol. 5, p. 62.

Pidgeon says: "Ancient Egypt, first in science and famous in art, has also left her impress here. In 1775 some of the first settlers in Kentucky, whose curiosity was excited by something remarkable in the arrangement of stones that filled the entrance to a cave, removed them, and on entering, discovered a number of mummies, preserved by the art of embalming in as great a state of perfection as was known by the ancient Egyptians 1800 years before Christ, which was about the time the Israelites were in bondage in Egypt. This custom would seem as purely Egyptian, and was practiced in the earliest age of their national existence. A trait of national practice so strong and palpable as is this peculiar art, should lead the mind without hesitation to the belief that wherever it was practiced, its authors or pupils existed."--Traditions of De Coo Dah, p. 19. Also Priest's American Antiquities, pp. 114–117.

"But at Lexington, Kentucky, the traits are too notorious to allow them to be other than pure Egyptian, in full possession of the strongest complexion of their national character, that of embalming, which was connected with their religion."— Priest's American Antiquities, p. 119.

"One of the most interesting sources of comparison between Mexico, Peru, and Egypt, is to be found in an investigation of their hieroglyphic system. Each of these countries had a peculiar method of recording events by means of hieroglyphic signs, sculpturing them on monuments and buildings, and portraying them on papyrus and maguey."—Delafield's American Antiquities, p. 42.

"It is the opinion of the author that further investigations and discoveries in deciphering Mexican hieroglyphic paintings will exhibit a close analogy to the Egyptian in the use of two scriptural systems; the one for monumental inscription, the other for ordinary purposes of record and transmission of information. We find the three species of hieroglyphics common to Mexico and Egypt."—Ibid., p. 46.

Le Plongeon says: "The ancient Maya hieratic alphabet, discovered by me, is as near alike to the ancient hieratic alphabet of the Egyptians, as two alphabets can possibly be, forcing upon us the conclusion that the Mayas and the Egyptians either learned the art of writing from the same masters, or that the Egyptians learned it from the Mayas."—Sacred Mysteries, p. 113.

"In tracing, then, the ancestry of the Mexicans and Peruvians, by analogy in their hieroglyphic system, where shall we take them but to Egypt and southern Asia.?"—Delafield's American Antiquities, p. 47.

Of a comparison of quotations given on page 51, Delafield says: "These quotations we consider very positive evidence of an early identity between the aboriginal race of America and the southern Asiatic and Egyptian family."—American Antiquities, p. 51.

"Let us now take a brief review of the analogical evidence of an identity of the family of Mexico and Peru with that of Hindostan or Egypt to simplify which we name the several coincidences, which have been specified in their proper order."—Ibid., p. 65. On the same page then follows twenty-six coincidences under seven headings.

"As to the Mexicans it would be superfluous to examine how they obtained their knowledge. Such a problem would not soon be solved; but the fact that the intercalation of thirteen days in every cycle, that is, the use of a solar year of three hundred and sixty-five and one fourth days, is proof that it is either borrowed from the Egyptians, or that they had a common origin " —Delafield's American Antiquities, p. 53.

Elder R. M. Elvin in writing for Herald, says: "Wm. Hosea Ballou in the Scientific American of January 6th, 1889, gives the following statement from Dr. Le Plongeon, 'Here (Uxmal) were many beautiful mineral paintings, probably the only vestiges now existing by ancient American Art. * * They were on the walls, which were smoothly and beautifully plastered. The paintings were in vegetable colors the same as upon the tombs of Egypt. They represent the history of the life of the individual buried beneath the mausoleum.' "

Bancroft says: "The columns of Copan stand detached and solitary, so do the obelisks of Egypt do the same, both are square or four sided and covered with the art of the sculptor."—Native Races, Vol. 5, p. 60.

"Strange indeed that even the obelisks of Egypt have their counterpart in America.   Molina, in his history of Chili says: 'Between the hills of Mendoza and La Punta is a pillar of stone one hundred and fifty feet high and twelve feet in diameter.' "† – History of Chili, tom. 1, p. 169.

The report of the Davenport Academy of Science for 1882, in the description of the stone tablet says: "This tablet, * * represents a planetary configuration, the twelve signs of the Zodiac known to all nations of old, and seven planets conjoined with six different signs. * * The figures of the signs are the same which we find depicted on Egyptian, Greek, Roman and other monuments."—Presidency and Priesthood, p. 286.

"There is a very distinct resemblance in some of these hieroglyphics (of Central America) to those of Egypt."—Prehistoric America, p. 328 or Presidency and Priesthood, p. 269.

"Above the door and simulating windows (in the valley of Youcay, one of the tributaries of the Amazon), we meet again with the Egyptian 'tau' that we have already seen at Palenque."—Ibid., p. 417.

"The ornamentations of the buildings resemble that upon Egyptian monuments."—Ibid., p. 324.

"Statues resemble those of Egypt and head dress a little like that of the Assyrians."—Ibid., p. 327.

"They wore a head dress that has been pronounced Egyptian."—Ibid., p. 392.

As to the hieroglyphical writing, Delafield says: "Their buildings, particularly the sacred houses, were covered with hieroglyphics.   Each race, Egyptian,

Mexican and Peruvian recorded the deeds of their gods
upon the walls of their temples."—Inq. Origin American Antiquities, p. 60.

Wm. Woodhead contributing to Herald writes:
"The shape of the temples (in Yucatan and Central
America) was that of the Egyptian letter **M**, called
ma ⬜, a word that also means 'place,' 'country'
and, by extension, 'the Universe.' The Egyptians
adopted it, therefore, not because they believed, as Dr.
Fanton suggests, that the earth was square or oblong;
for they knew full well it was spherical, but becuase the
sign of the word 'ma' conveyed to their mind the idea
of the earth, as the word 'earth' represents it to ours.
But ma is also the radical of Mayax; and likewise, in
the Maya language, it means 'the country.' 'the earth.' "
—Sacred Mysteries, p. 33.

Again he says, concerning prehistoric man in Central America: "In all the buildings, whatever their
size, the ground plan was in the shape of an oblong
square, ⬜ that is of their letter **M**, pronounced ma.
Ma is the contraction of Mam, the ancestor, as they de-
nominated the Earth, and by extension, the Universe.
Ma is also the radical of Mayax, the name of the Yu-
catecan peninsula, in ancient times. * * .in Egypt,
and in Mayax the figure ⬜ in the hieroglyphics,
stands for Earth and Universe."—Ibid., p. 62.

⬜ "It is the letter **M**, pronounced Ma, of the
Maya and Egyptian ancient alphabets.   It is the radical of Mayax, name of the empire.   But Ma in Egypt
as in Mayax, is a word that signifies country, and by
extension, Universe; and in Mayax as in Egypt ⬜ is
one of the signs for land."—Ibid., p. 104.

Now this is curious enough, isn't it, that a people

that sixty years ago were said to have been nearly savages with "no mental culture or intellectual development," should be now found to represent the earth by
the same hieroglyphic that the enlightened Egyptians
did.　Both nations represented the earth by the same
sign, and it is remarkable, too, that the same sign
should not only be the same in form, but also the same
in meaning in both countries, in their hieroglyphics and
alphabets!　The sign ☐ "conveyed to their minds
the idea of the earth, as the word 'earth' represents it
to ours," and did not mean to them an earth with four
corners; "they knew full well it was spherical."　The
fact is, "they knew the rotundity of the earth, which
it was supposed Columbus had discovered."　See Atlantis, p. 364.

We will now proceed a step further, and see what
is said concerning the Yucatan or Landa alphabet.

"It is astonishing to notice that while Landa's **B**
is, according to Valentine, represented by a footprint,
and that path and footprint are pronounced Be in the
Maya dictionary, the Egyptian sign for **B** was the
human leg.　Still more surprising is it that the **H** of
Landa's alphabet is a tie of cord, while the Egyptian
H is a twisted cord. * * But the most striking coincidence of all occurs in the coiled or curled line representing Landa's **U**, for it is absolutely identical with
the Egyptian curled U.　The Mayan word for to wind
or bend is Uuc; but why should the Egyptians, confined as they were to the valley of the Nile, and abhor-
ing, as they did, the sea and sailors, write their **U** precisely like Landa's alphabet **U** in Central America?
There is one other remarkable coincidence between
Landa's and the Egyptian alphabets; and, by the way,

the English and other Teutonic dialects have a curious
share in it. Landa's **D** (**T**) is a disk with lines inside
the four quarters, the allowed Mexican symbol for a
day or sun. So far as sound is concerned, the English
day represents it; so far as form is concerned, the
Egyptian 'cake,' ideograph for (1) country and (2) the
sun's orbit, is essentially the same."—"Proceedings of
the American Philosophical Society," December, 1880,
p. 154, as quoted in Atlantis, p. 231.

Donnelly commenting on the Landa Alphabet says:
"It would appear as if both the Phœnicians and Egyptians drew their alphabets from a common source, of
which the Maya is a survival, but did not borrow from
one another. They followed out different characteristics in the same original hieroglyph, as, for instance,
in the letter b. And yet I have shown that the closest
resemblances exist between the Maya alphabet and the
Egyptian signs [of this system] in the c, h, t, i, k, l,
m, n, o, q, and s eleven letters in all; in some cases,
as in the n and k, the signs are identical; the k, in both
alphabets, is not only a serpent, but a serpent with a
protuberance or convolution in the middle! If we add
to the above the b and u, referred to in the 'Proceedings of the American Philosophical Society,' we have
thirteen letters out of sixteen in the Maya and Egyptian
related to each other. Can any theory of accidental
coincidences account for all this? And it must be remembered that these resemblances are found between
the only two phonetic systems of alphabets in the
world."—Atlantis, p. 232.

The Phœnicians here referred to were the people
that occupied Tyre and Sidon in Bible history, and
were neighbors to the Jews, with whom they appear to

have been related. It was "Hiram," king of Tyre, that furnished skilled workmen to Solomon. (See 1 Kings 7: 13, etc.)

From the above we learn that these three ancient nations, viz:. Egyptians, Phœnicians and Central Americans, seem to have had originally the same alphabet; and either one people learned and derived their alphabet from the other, or each drew from a common source; but each afterward separately followed out different characteristics in the changes they made, and did not borrow from one another. That is precisely what the Book of Mormon teaches about ancient American writing. Lehi and his colony brought with them from Jerusalem to America a knowledge of Egyptian writing as the Jews at Jerusalem taught it. And Moroni says the Egyptian writing known to them had been changed by the Nephites "according to our manner of speech." Now the characters on the plates were not exactly the same as any one of the systems of Egyptian writing; but were one of those systems "reformed."

But to the alphabet again.

Let us suppose that two men agree that each shall construct apart from the other a phonetic alphabet of sixteen letters; that they shall employ only simple forms (combinations of straight or curved lines), and that their signs shall not in any wise resemble the letters now in use. They go to work apart; they have a multitudinous array of forms to draw from—the thousand possible combinations of lines, angles, circles, and curves; when they have finished, they bring their alphabets together for comparison. Under such circumstances it is possible that out of sixteen signs one sign might appear in both alphabets; there is one chance in a hundred that such might be the case; but there is not one chance in five hundred that this sign should in both cases represent the same sound. It is barely possible that two men working thus apart should hit upon two or three identical forms, but altogether impossible that these forms should have same significance; and by no stretch of the imagination can it be supposed that in these alphabets so created, without correspondence, thirteen out of sixteen signs should be the same in form and the same in meaning."—Atlantis, pp. 232, 233.

This Landa alphabet was discovered in Central America, where the Nephite nation was located accorning to the author of the Book of Mormon, which nation appears to have settled there about four hundred and seventy years after Lehi's colony left Jerusalem. If the Nephite system of writing and their language were undergoing changes from time to time, "according to our manner of speech," do we not see that they had in their isolated condition ample time to have made several changes in their style of letters before they reached and settled Central America. And some of these slight changes in the form of these letters may have been made with the Jews, even before they left the "land of Jerusalem." The "learning of the Jew" may be responsible for some of the slight changes found in the Landa alphabet.

On page 219 of Atlantis which is a plate of characters of various alphabets, column one and two are distinct forms of the Maya alphabet, while the third is a column of what are termed intermediate forms so there were three or more kinds of Maya alphabet characters.

Delafield says: "We find three species of hieroglyphics common to Mexico and Egypt."--American Antiquities, p. 46.

"Egyptian writing is of three distinct kinds, which are known respectively by the names of Hyeroglyphic, Hieratic and Demotic or Enchorial."

"The hieroglyphic is that of almost all monuments, and is also occasionally found in manuscripts. The hieratic and demotic occur with extreme rarity upon monuments, but are employed far more commonly than the hieroglyphics in the papyrus rolls or books of the Egyptians."--Rawlinson's Egypt, Vol. 1, p. 120.

Le Plongeon says: "The ancient Maya hieratic alphabet, discovered by me, is as near alike to the ancient hieratic alphabet of the Egyptians, as two alphabets can possibly be, forcing upon us the conclusion that the Mayas and the Egyptians either learned the art of writing from the same masters, or that the Egyptians learned it from the Mayas."--Sacred Mysteries 113.

The Nephite use of language was universal in North, Central, and South America, as clearly set forth in the Book of Mormon. The subjugation of the Nephites by the Lamanites wrought out the decline and overthrow of the common language and its division in to a "multiplicity of tongues."

Bancroft says: "The researches of the few philologists who have given American languages their study have brought to light the following facts: First, that a relationship exists among all the tongues of the Northern and Southern continents; and that while certain characteristics are found in common throughout all the languages of America, these languages are as a whole sufficiently peculiar to be distinguishable from the speech of all the other races of the world. Although some of these characteristics, as a matter of course, are found in some of the languages of the old world, more of them in the Turanian family than any other, yet nowhere on the globe are uniformities of speech carried over vast areas and through innumerable and diversified races with such persistency, as in America; nowhere are tongues so dissimilar and yet so alike as here."— National Races, vol. 3, p. 553.

He says again: "The multiplicity of tongues, even within comparatively narrow areas, rendered the adoption of some sort of universal language absolutely necessary. This international language in America is for the most part confined to gestures, and nowhere has gesture language attained a higher degree of perfection than here; and what is most remarkable, the same representatives are employed from Alaska to Mexico, and even in South America."—Ibid., p. 556.

Professor Benjamin Smith Barton, was the first to collect and classify American words. After him followed Vater, who in his Mithridates, published in Leipsic in 1810, carried out the subject in an extended form. The result of their labors is thus stated: "In eighty-three American languages, one hundred and seventy words have been found, the roots of which have been the same in both continents; and it is easy to perceive that this analogy is not accidental, since it does not rest merely on imitative harmony, or on that conformity of organs which produces almost an identity in the first sounds articulated by children. Of these, three fifths resemble the Mantchou, Tongouse, Mongul, and Samoide languages; and two-fifths the Celtic, Tchoud, Biscayan, Coptic and Congo languages."—Delafield's American Antiquities, p. 23.

"In America there are at least five hundred languages."—Ibid., p. 23.

Priest quoting Prof. Rafinesque says: " 'A multitude of languages exists in America, which may perhaps be reduced to twenty-five radical languages, and two thousand dialects. But they are often unlike the Hebrew, in roots, words and grammar; they have by far, says the author, more analogies with the sanscrit,' (the ancient Chinese), 'Celtic, Bask, Pelasgian, Berber,' (in Europe) 'Lybian, Egyptian,' (in Africa) 'Persian, Turan,' etc., (also in Europe) or in fact, all the primitive languages of mankind."—American Antiquities, p. 78.

"The actual number of American languages and dialects is as yet unascertained, but estimated at nearly thirteen hundred, six hundred of which Mr. Bancroft has classified in his third volume."—Native Races of Pacific States.

"Language in aboriginal America may be pronounced a mystery of mysteries and a babel of babels. Mr. Bancroft has catalogued nearly six hundred distinct languages, existing between northern Alaska and the Isthmus of Panama."—Short's American Antiquities, pp. 190, 469.

The Nephites engraving their plates in reformed Egyptian, is not a strange claim, in the light of their association with Egyptian learning in the times past.

CHAPTER IX.
PLATES—RECORDS.

Elder J. R. Lambert in the Independent Patriot says: "In the days of Job, writing on imperishable material was understood. Job 19: 23, 24: 'Oh that my words were now written! oh that they were printed in a book! That they were graven with an iron pen and lead in the rock forever.' "

It was understood and practiced in the days of Moses. Exodus 39: 30: "And they made the plate of the holy crown of pure gold, and wrote upon it a writing like to the engravings of a signet, Holiness to the Lord."

In the Apocrypha, 1 Macc. 14: 48, 49, we have the following plain statements: "And they commanded that this writing should be put in tables of brass, and that they should be set up within the compass of the sanctuary, in a conspicuous place, and that a copy thereof should be put in the treasury, that Simon and his sons may have it."—Douay Translation.

"After the destruction of Jerusalem, about A. D. 70, Titus, the Roman general, called at Antioch, and the people presented to him a petition against the Jews. Of this translation, Josephus says: 'Whereupon the people of Antioch, when they had failed of success in this their first request, made him a second, for they desired that he would order those tables of brass to be re-

moved, on which the Jews' privileges were engraven,'
etc."—Josephus, vol. 6, p. 132.

The American nations writing on metal plates and
other imperishable materials, is not strange in the light
of this, and it is highly probable in the case of the Nephites, as they were Israelites.

The claim of the Book of Mormon that the ancient
American nations had written on metallic plates, was
thought to be its sure defeat; but plates and various
materials containing hieroglyphical writing have since
been found in such abundance, that the claim is now
fully sustained.

In the Quincy (Ill.) Whig appeared an article describing plates found April 23d, 1843:

"A Mr. J. Roberts from Pike county, called upon
us last Monday with a written description of a discovery which was recently made near Kinderhook in that
county. * * It appeared that a young man by the name
of Wiley, a resident of Kinderhook, commenced digging into a mound, finding it quite laborious, he invited others to assist him; finally a company of ten or
twelve repaired to the mound and assisted. * * After
penetrating the mound about eleven feet they came to a
bed of limestone that had been apparently subjected to
the fire. They removed the stones * * to the depth of
two feet, * * when they found six brass plates secured
or fastened together by two iron wires, but which were
so decayed that they readily crumbled to dust upon being handled. The plates were so completely covered
with dust as almost to obliterate the characters inscribed upon them, but after undergoing a chemical
process, the inscriptions were brought out plain and
distinct. There were six plates four inches in length,

1 ¾ inches wide at the top, and 2 ¾ wide at the bottom, flaring at the points. There are four lines of characters or hieroglyphics on each. * * In the place where the plates were deposited, were also found human bones, in the last stage of decomposition; * * it is believed that it was but the burial place of a small number, perhaps a person or a family · of distinction, in ages long gone by, * * of a people that existed far, far beyond the memory or the present race. * * The plates, above alluded to were exhibited in this city last week."

Wiley and eight bthers testify, in the "Times and Seasons," to the finding of these plates, as follows: "We, the citizens of Kinderhook, whose names are an-nexed, do certify and declare that on the 23d of April, 1843, while excavating a large mound in this vicinity, Mr. Wiley took from said mound six brass plates of a bell shape, covered with ancient characters. Said plates were very much oxidated. The bands and rings on said plates mouldered into dust on a slight pressure. R. Wiley, George Deckenson, W. Longnecker, G. W. F. Ward, J. R. Sharp, Ira S. Curtis, Fayette Grubb, W. P. Harris, W. Fugate."

Of articles discovered opposite Marietta, Ohio, on the Muskingum, Priest says: "Sixth, Under a heap of dust and tennons, shreds of feathered cloth and hair, a parcel of brass rings, cut out of a solid piece of metal, and in such a manner that the rings were suspended from each other, without the aid of solder or any other visible agency whatever. Each ring was three inches in diameter, and the bar of the rings a half inch thick, and were square; a variety of characters were deeply engraved on the sides of the rings resembling the Chinese characters."—American Antiquities, p. 93.

G. W. West of Manchester, Adams county, Ohio,
wrote an· article dated January 19th, 1880, which appeared in Herald, in which it is set forth that, Near
Manchester, Adams county, Ohio, on the old Smith
farm on the Portsmouth pike, in 1880, in a cave where
twenty-five bodies had been entombed as in Egypt,
was found a square package at the head of a tomb,
wrapped in varnished cloth, containing A BOOK of one
hundred leaves of thin COPPER, fastened loosely at the
top and crowded with finely engraved characters. Mr.
Samuel Groom, who owned the farm at the time, is reported as having forwarded these to the Smithsonian
Institute.

The Newport, Vermont, Express and Standard of
August 15th, 1882, quoting from the New Orleans Democrat .says: "The pyramids and mounds which so
often occur in the western states * * have been leveled
* * by zealous searchers for relics of antiquity.   Nor
have their efforts been in vain, copper hatchets, chisels
and various other kinds of tools have been unearthed
with copper plates covered with inscriptions."

"Chillicothe, Ohio, December 15, 1891.—Hundreds came today to see the mound builder relics uncovered by Warren K. Moorehead, Monday.   Of the
five skeletons lying side by side, two were covered with
a sheet of copper six by eight feet.   A large, thick copper ax weighed forty-one pounds and in point of size
and value exceeds any single specimen ever found in
the United States.   There are traces of gold in it.   The
cutting edge is seven inches broad and very sharp.
How it could have been fastened in a handle and used
is a mystery.   All the smaller copper axes are such as
have been found before.

"Thirty copper plates with mound builders' cloth on them overlapped the axes. The average size of the plates was ten by six inches. A great copper eagle, twenty inches in diameter, wings outspread, beak open, tail and wing feathers neatly stamped upon the copper surface, covered the knees of one of the skeletons. This is one of the most artistic designs ever found in copper.

"Remains of a copper stool about a foot in length and several inches in heighth lay near the head of one of the skeletons. The stool had been made out of wood and had been covered with sheet copper. Flint implements, bear tusks, sea-shells and other trinkets were also found."—Chicago Daily News.

In the St. Louis Chronicle in February, 1889, appeared the following: "Rev. S. D. Peet, the well known antiquarian, is reported as having found in Illinois, two cross plates which have all the appearance of being rude musical instruments. These plates are about fifteen inches square and there are places for strings and a bridge. Along the lower edge is a row of hieroglyphics SIMILAR to those on the famous Palmyra plates, said to have been discovered by Joseph Smith and from which he interpreted the Book of Mormon."

John T. Short on pages 38–9 of North Americans of Antiquity, describes two tablets and presents a cut of one, found near Davenport, Iowa, of which he says: "The most remarkable discovery of all, however, (relics of eastern Iowa), was made January 10th, 1877, by Rev. Mr. Gass, * * two tablets of coal slate covered with a variety of figures and hieroglyphics were found."

The Cincinnati tablet is described thus: "The material is a fine grained compact sandstone, of light

brown color.   It measures five inches in length, by
three in breadth at the ends, two and six tenths at the
middle, and is about half an inch in thickness.   The
sculptured face varies very slightly from a perfect plane.
The figures are cut in low relief, (the lines being not
more than one twentieth of an inch in depth), and occupy a rectangular space of four inches and two tenths
long, by two and one tenth wide."—Short's American
Antiquities, pp. 46, 47.   This tablet was found November, 1841, corner Fifth and Mound streets, Cincinnati,
Ohio.

"In 1870 there was found a tablet in a mound near
Lafayette Bayou, * * Miss., which has the same re-
duplication of figures in the carved work as exists in
the Cincinnati Tablet."—Maclean's Mound Builders,
p. 110.

Another, known as the Berlin tablet, found near
Berlin, Ohio, by Dr. J. E. Sylvester, June 14th, 1876,
described on the last page cited, is similar to the last
two treated upon.

Statements concerning other plates and tablets
could have been given, but the foregoing abundantly
establish the claim of the Book of Mormon, as to ancient Americans having written on plates of imperishable material.

The Book of Mormon plates were found in a STONE
BOX in the earth.   The SAME is true of HEBREW TAB-
LETS mentioned in chapter seven of this work.

The Davenport tablet and another plate found are
described in a foot note, on page 38, of J. T. Short's
work, American Antiquities, thus: "The two plates
were closely encircled by a single row of weathered
limestones.   These stones are irregular in shape but al-

most of the same size, their dimensions being about 3x7 or 8 inches, and the diameter of the circle two feet."

Weekly Inter-Ocean, December 23, 1890: "Two inscribed tablets were found near Davenport, Iowa, covered with peculiar figures, and among the figures some strange hieroglyphic letters. Prof. Seyffarth of St. Louis says, that the tablets were descriptive of the flood, and that the people who deposited them had migrated from Asia."

" 'Dr. West of Stockbridge, relates that an old Indian informed him that his fathers in this country had, not long since, been in the possession of a book, which they had for a long time carried with them, but having lost the knowledge of reading it, they buried it with an Indian chief.' View of the Hebrews, p. 223".—Priest's Antiquities, p. 69.

Ellen Russell Emerson says: "The Ujibway Indians, relates 'Mr. Copway,' had three depositories for sacred records near the waters of Lake Superior. Ten of the wisest and most venerable men of the nation dwelt near these, and were appointed guardians of them."†—Indian Myths, pp. 225–6.

Boudinot says: "It is said among their principle, or beloved men, that they have it handed down from their ancestors, that the book which the white people have was once theirs. That while they had it they prospered exceeding, but that the white people bought it of them, and learned many things from it, while the Indians lost their credit, offended the Great Spirit and suffered exceedingly from the neighboring nations. * * They also say that their forefathers were possessed of an extraordinary divine Spirit, by which they foretold

future events, and controlled the common course of
nature, and this they transmitted to their offspring on
condition of their obeying the sacred laws.   That they
did by these means bring down showers of plenty on
the beloved people.   But that this power, for a long
time past, had entirely ceased."—A Star in the West,
pp. 110, 111.

"Dr. West of Stockbridge, (Massachusetts), relates that an old Indian informed him that his fathers
in this country had been in possession of a book,
which, for a long time, they carried with them, but,
having lost the knowledge of reading it, they buried
it with a chief."—Priest's American Antiquities, edition
1833, p. 69, or View of the Hebrews by Dr. West,
p. 223.

The Book of Mormon mentions coins of different
value, used as money.   In the light of this, the following is interesting as well as confirmatory of its statement.   Correspondence to the press, from Helena, Arkansas, bearing date of October 19th, 1891, says: "A
most remarkable find is reported from the little town of
Laconia, about twenty-five miles south of this city.   A
well was being drilled; at the depth of one hundred and
twenty-five feet the drillings showed they were passing
through a layer of brick. * * As there were no brick
houses in the town and never had been it could not be
believed.   While quite a crowd was around the well-
hole, the men brought up to the surface a lot of mud
and examined it, as they had done from the time they
found the brick residue.   In the mass of mud there was
a small piece of metal, which when cleaned off, was
found to be a PIECE OF MONEY.   It was octagonal in
shape and had hieroglyphics on it, which could not be

deciphered, but which were evidently meant to represent the value of the piece. * * It is claimed by antiquarians here that the bricks and COIN are the relics of
a prehistoric race which lived here many years before
the Indians, and built the pavements and roads which
were discovered at Memphis, on the other side of the
river above here."—Pittsburg, Pennsylvania, Leader,
November 6, 1891.

Among relics found at Circleville, Ohio, a coin is
mentioned by Priest.

"Near the same place was dug up from beneath
the roots of a hickory tree, seven feet eight inches, in
circumference, a copper coin, bearing no comparison
with any coin known."—American Antiquities, p. 175.
Another coin is described on page 260.

"At the meeting of the Tennessee Historical Society at Nashville, Tuesday night, there was a letter
read from W. E. McElwee, of Rockwood, Tennessee,
describing a coin found in an Indian mound in that
country. It bears an urn burning incense on one side,
with the inscription in Hebrew, 'shekel of Israel.' On
the other is a fig or olive branch, and the words in Hebrew, 'Jerusalem, the holy land.' A similar coin was
exhibited, but how the coin got into the mound is a
matter of mystery."—Stephenson (Alabama) Chronicle,
of February 20th, 1894.

"A round copper COIN with a serpent stamped on
it was found at Palenque, and T shaped copper coins
are very abundant in the ruins of Central America."—
Atlantis, p. 245.

CHAPTER X.

METALS, IMPLEMENTS AND INSTRUMENTS.

The Book of Mormon on pages 43, 64, 394, and 520, as also elsewhere, mentions gold, silver, brass, copper, steel and iron. The ancient Americans were supposed to have used stone for tools, but not the several precious metals; and for years the Book of Mormon was alone in this claim, for the use of metals on the western continent.

"The Peruvians had such immense numbers of vessels, and ornaments of gold that the Inca paid with them a ransom for himself to Pizzaro of the value of fifteen million dollars."—Atlantis, p. 142.

"The Peruvians called gold, 'The tears wept by the sun.' * * The great temple of the sun at Cuzco was called the 'Place of Gold.' It was as I have shown literally a mine of gold. Walls, cornices, statuary, plate, ornaments, all were of gold; the very sewer-pipes and aqueducts, even the agricultural implements used in the garden of the temple were of gold and sil·ver. The value of the jewels which adorned the temple was equal to one hundred and eighty millions of dollars."—Atlantis, pp. 345.

In speaking of Costa Rica, Mr. Bancroft says: "Mr. Boyle makes the general statement that gold ornaments and idols are constantly found, and that the ancient mines which supplied the precious metal are often seen by modern prospectors."—Native Races, Pacific States, Vol. 4, p. 23.

"Montezuma, in his diplomacy, presents to Cortez, on his arrival to Mexico, gold and native fabrics of the most delicate character; shields, helmets, cuirasses, collars, bracelets, sandals, fans, pearls, precious stones, loads of cotton cloth, extraordinary manufactures of feathers, circular plates of gold and silver, as large as carriage wheels."—History of Mexico, New Mexico and California, Vol. 1, p. 26.

"Calendars made of gold and silver were common in Mexico. Before Cortez reached the capitol, Montezuma sent him two 'as large as cart wheels,' one representing the sun, the other the moon, both 'richly carved.' It was with articles of this gold work that the Inca Alahullpa filled a room in his vain endeavor to purchase release from captivity. One of the old chroniclers mentions 'statuary, jars, vases and every species of vessels, all of fine gold. * * An artificial garden * * of fine gold, * * more than twenty sheep (llamas) with their lambs, attended by shepherds, all made of gold.' * * In the course of twenty-five years after the conquest, the Spandiards sent from Peru to Spain more than four hundred million ducats ($800,-000,000) worth of gold."—Baldwin's Ancient America, pp. 215, 249, 250. Donnely gives substantially the same account on page 395 of Atlantis.

"Gold ornaments are said to have been found in several tumuli. Silver, very well plated on copper, has been found in several mounds, besides those of Circleville and Marietta. An ornament of copper was found in a stone mound near Chillicothe; it was a bracelet for the ankle or wrist."—Priest's Amer. Ant., p. 221.

"Silver was accessible in such quantities that Pizarro found in it a substitute for iron to shoe the horses of his cavalry.   Copper and tin, in like manner, abounded in the mountains, and the Peruvians had learned to alloy the copper, both with tin and silver. * * Discovery of well adjusted silver balances in some of the tombs of the Incas, shows that they made use of weights in determining the value of their commodities." —Prehistoric Man, Geo. Wilson, Vol. 1, page 440.

Mr. Squire says: "These articles have been critically examined and it is beyond doubt that the copper bosses were absolutely plated, not simply overlaid with silver.   Between the copper and the silver exists a connection such as it seems to me could only be produced by heat, and if it is admitted that these are genuine relics of the Mound Builders, it must at the same time be admitted they possessed the difficult art of plating one metal upon another."—Atlantis, p. 378.

Priest says: "In many instances articles made of copper and sometimes plated with silver have been met with on opening their (Mound Builders) works, circular pieces of copper intended either as medals or breast plates, have been found several inches in diameter, very much injured by time."—Inquiry Origin American Antiquities, p. 263.

"In South America * * many interesting specimens have been exhumed. * * 'Among these,' says Dr. Reese, 'are mirrors of various dimensions of hard shining stones, highly polished, * * hatchets and other instruments, * * some were of flint, some of copper, hardened by an unknown process to such a degree as to supply the place of iron."†—Mayer's Mexico, p. 227.

Bryant describes copper instruments found in Wis-

consin: "An adz with wings for fitting. An arrow
head with wings for fitting to arrow. A knife with
socket for handle. A chisel apparently cast, the rough-
ness showing sand-mould, and white spots of melted
silver. An awl. A spear head, eleven inches in
length with socket for handle."—History U. S., Vol. 1,
p. 31.

Of discoveries at Circleville, Ohio, Priest says:
"On this mirror was a plate of IRON which had become
an oxide; but before it was disturbed by the spade, resembled a plate of CAST IRON."—Priest's American Antiquities, pp. 178–9. The size of mirror mentioned is
given as one and a half by three feet.

" 'But besides this, there have been found very well
manufactured swords and knives of IRON and possibly
STEEL,' says Mr. Atwater."—Ibid., p. 265.

Priest gives the following account: "In 1826 near
Cincinnati, Ohio, a gentlemen dug a well. At the
depth of eighty feet there appeared the stump of a tree
three feet in diameter and two feet high, which had
been cut down with an axe. The blows were yet visible." Mr. Priest's fourth reflection is: "Ancient
Americans were acquainted with the use and properties
of iron. The rust of the axe was on top of the stump
when discovered."—Priest's American Antiquities, p.
129.

Mr. Priest mentions two more wells; one ninety, and
another ninty-four feet deep, each containing a stump
of a tree. Of the second he says: "Another stump
was found at ninety-four feet below the surface which
had evident marks of an axe; and on its top there appeared as if some iron tool had been consumed by
rust."—Page 139.

"A piece of a cast iron vessel was taken out of the circular embankment at Circleville, Ohio."—Priest's American Antiquities, p. 175.

Another find is recorded on page 260. In caves on the Gasconade river, a tributary of the Missouri river, were found "axes and hammers made of iron." —Ibid., 239.

"In December, 1827, a planter of South America discovered in a tomb of masonry, two extremely ancient swords, a helmet and shield, which had suffered much from rust."—Ibid., p. 47.

Priest mentions articles found in digging the Louisville canal. "Medals of copper and silver swords, and other implements of iron." "Mr. Flint assures us that he has seen these strange ancient swords. He also examined a small iron shoe, like a horse shoe, encrusted with the rust of ages, and found far beneath the soil, and the copper axe weighing about two pounds, singularly tempered, and of peculiar construction."— American Antiquities, p. 378.

" 'It is remarkable,' says Molina, 'that iron which has been thought unknown to the Ancient Americnas, had particular names in some of their tongues. In official Peruvian it was called, quillary; and in Chilian, panillic. The Mound Builders fashioned implements out of meteoric iron.' "—Atlantis, p. 451.

Again he says: "We find the remains of an iron sword and meteoric weapons in the mounds of the Mississippi Valley, while the name of the metal is found in the ancient languages of Peru and Chili, and the Incas worked in IRON on the shores of Lake Titicaca."—Ibid., p. 462.

"Near the falls of Ohio, six brass ornaments such

as soldiers usually wear in front of their belts, was dug up, attached to six skeletons."—Priest's American Antiquities, p. 232.

Of discoveries in New York: "In Scipio on Salmon Creek, a Mr. Halstead has from time to time, during ten years past, ploughed up * * seven or eight hundred pounds of brass, which appeared to have once been formed into various implements, both of husbandry and war; helmets and working utensils mingled together."—Ibid., p. 261.

Of relics found in mound at Marietta, Ohio: "Three large circular ornaments which had adorned a sword belt or buckler, and were composed of copper, overlaid with a plate of silver."—Ibid., p. 268.

Priest, writing of the town of Pompey, Onondago county, New York, says: "In Pompey, on lot fourteen, is the site of an ancient burying ground, upon which, when the country was first settled, was found timber, growing apparently, of the second growth, judging from the old timber, reduced to mold, lying around which was one hundred years old, ascertained by counting the concentric grains. In one of those graves was found a glass bottle. * * In the same grave with the bottle was found an iron hatchet edged with steel. * * In the same town, on lot number seventeen, was found the remains of a blacksmith's forge; at this spot have been ploughed up crucibles, such as mineralogists use in refining metals."—Priest's American Antiquities, p. 260.

Priest says: "In Virginia, near Blacksburg, eighty miles from Marietta, there was found the half of a STEEL BOW, which when entire would have measured five or six feet."—Priest's American Antiquities, p. 176. (Edition of 1833.)

"In Liberty township, Washington county, Ohio, are yet to be seen twenty or thirty rude furnaces, perhaps used in smelting ore. Large trees are still growing on them and attest their age. They stand in the midst of a rich body of iron ore, and in a wild, hilly, rough part of the country, better adapted to manufacture than to agriculture."—Delafield's American Antiquities, p. 55.

Large earthen vessel. "It was twelve feet across the top and of consequence thirty-six feet in circumference, and otherwise of proportioned depth and form."—Priest's American Antiquities, p. 112.

Jones says: "In 1834, Colonels Meriwether and Lumsden, while engaged in digging a canal in Dukes Creek Valley, Georgia, * * unearthed a subterraneous village * * of thirty-four small cabins. * * They were made of logs hewn at the ends and notched down. * * This hewing and notching had evidently been done with sharp metallic tools, the marks being such as would have been caused by a chopping axe. * * Eleven old shafts have been found varying in depth from ninety to one hundred feet. * * In 1854 one * * was cleaned out, * * at ninety feet was found a windlass of post-oak well hewn, with an inch auger hole bored through each end. Distinct traces appeared where it had been banded with iron. * * The presence of iron and the marks of sharp metallic tools prove that these ancient mining operations cannot be referred to the labor of the Indians."—Antiquity of Southern Indians, pp. 48-9.

GREAT WORKS.

"The most astonishing remains are found still farther south, in Chiapa, Tabasco, Oxaca, Yucatan,

Honduras, Tehauntepec, Guatemala and other parts of Central America, * * of great cities and temples."—Baldwin's Ancient America, p. 77.

"The pyramid of Cholulu covers an area of forty-five acres. It was terraced and built with four stages. When measured by Humboldt it was fourteen hundred feet square at the base, and one hundred and sixty feet high. * * Thousands of other monuments, unrecorded * * invest every sierra and valley of Mexico with profound interest."—Ibid., pp. 90–1.

"Another class of these antiquities consists of enclosures formed by heavy embankments of earth and stone. There is nothing to explain these constructions so clearly as to leave no room for conjecture and speculation It has been suggested that some of them may have been intended for defense, others for religious purposes. A portion of them, it may be, encircled villages and towns. In some cases, the ditches or fosses were on the inside, in others, on the outside. * * Lines of embankment, varying from five to thirty feet in height, and enclosing from one to fifty acres, are very common, while inclosures containing from one hundred to two hundred acres are not infrequent, and occasionally, works are found, inclosing as many as four hundred acres. * * About one hundred inclosures and five hundred mounds have been examined in Ross county, Ohio. The number of mounds in the whole state is estimated at over ten thousand, and the number of inclosures at more than fifteen hundred. * * They were constructed with a geometrical precision which implies a kind of knowledge in the builders that may be called scientific."—Baldwin's Ancient America, pp. 19, 20, 23, 24, 39.

"The number and frequency of tumuli through the country, have led the writer to believe that they have not only been used as the last home of the warrior and his family, but that they served as scopuloi, or beacons, and points of observation, connecting the large and extensive castra."—Delafield's American Antiquities, p. 54.

Compare with the above the Book of Mormon, pp. 337, 341, 344, 346.

See Prescott's Peru, as cited by Donnelly on Public Works: "The American nations built public works as great as, or greater than any known in Europe. The Peruvians had public roads, one thousand five hundred to two thousand miles long, made so thoroughly as to elicit the astonishment of the Spaniards. At every few miles taverns or hotels were established for the accommodation of travelers. Humboldt pronounced these Peruvian roads 'among the most useful and stupendous works ever executed by man.' They built aqueducts for purposes of irrigation, some of which were five hundred miles long. They constructed magnificent bridges of stone, and had even invented suspension bridges thousands of years before they were introduced into Europe. They had, both in Peru and Mexico, a system of posts, by means of which news was transmitted hundreds of miles in a day, precisely like those known among the Persians in the time of Herodotus, and subsequently among the Romans. Stones similar to milestones were placed along the roads in Peru."—Atlantis, pp. 141–2.

Baldwin says in relation to mining: "Remains of their mining works were first discovered in 1848 by Mr. S. O. Knapp, agent of the Minnesota mining company, and in 1849 they were described by Dr. Charles T. Jackson, in his geographical report to the national government."—Ancient America, p. 43.

"Mr. Knapp discovered a detatched mass of copper weighing nearly six tons."—Ibid., p. 43.

"All who have examined these works agree with Colonel Whittlesy that they (Mound Builders) worked the Lake Superior copper mines for a great length of time."—Ibid., 53.

"We find one feature common to the architectural genius of these races, which is to be discovered nowhere else. We allude to the surprising mechanical power they must have employed in constructing their works of massive masonry, such as the present race of man has attempted in vain to move. Travelers in Egypt invariably are filled with amazement at the stupendous blocks of stone with which the pyramids, temples and tombs are constructed, and the size of the obelisks and monuments yet remaining. In Peru the same is observed."—Delafield's American Antiquities, p. 59.

"It surprised me to see these enormous gateways made of great masses of stone, some of which were thirty feet long, fifteen feet high and six feet thick. * * In one case, large masses of sculptured stone, ten yards in length and six in width, were used to make grinding stones for a chocolate mill."—Baldwin's Ancient America, p. 233.

"Ruins of towns, castles, fortresses and other structures are found all about the country. * * It is noticed everywhere that the ancient Peruvians made large use of aqueducts, which they built with notable skill, using hewn stones and cement, and making them very substantial. Some of them are still in use. They were used to carry water to the cities and to irrigate the cultivated lands. A few of them were very long. There is mention of one which was one hundred and fifty miles long, and of another which was extended four hundred and fifty miles across sierras and over rivers, from south to north."--Ibid , 243.

"The American nations built public works as great or greater than any known in Europe. * * Humbolt pronounces these Peruvian roads, 'among the most useful and stupendous works ever executed by man. They built aqueducts for purposes of irrigation, some of which were five hundred miles long. They constructed magnificent bridges of stone, and had even invented suspension bridges thousands of years before they were introduced into Europe. They had, both in Peru and Mexico, a system of posts, by means of which news was transmitted hundreds of miles a day."—Atlantis, p. 141–2.

THE GREAT PERUVIAN ROADS.

"Nothing in ancient Peru was more remarkable than the public roads. No ancient people has left traces of works more astonishing than these, so vast was their extent, and so great the skill and labor required to construct them. One of these roads ran along the mountains through the whole length of the empire, from Quito to Chili. Another, starting from Cuzco, went down to the coast and extended northward to the equator. These roads were built on beds or deep understructures of masonry. The width of the roadways varied from twenty to twenty-five feet, and they were made level and smooth by paving, and in some places by a sort of macadamizing with pulverized stone mixed with lime and bituminous cement. This cement was used in all the masonry. On each side of the roadway was a very strong wall more than a fathom in thickness. This road went over marshes, rivers, and great chasms of the sierras, and through rocky precipices and mountain-sides. The great road passing along the mountains was a marvelous work. In many places its way was cut through rock for leagues. Great ravines were filled up with solid masonry Rivers were crossed by means of a curious kind of suspension bridges, and no obstruction was encountered which the builders did not overcome. The builders of our Pacific Railroad, with their superior engineering skill and mechanical appliances, might reasonably shrink from the cost and the difficulties of such a work as this. Extending from one degree north of Quito to Cuzco, and from Cuzco to Chili, it was quite as long as the two Pacific railroads, and its wild route among the mountains was far more difficult. * * Along these roads at equal distances were edifices, a kind of caravanseras, built of hewn stone, for the accommodation of travelers."--Baldwin's Ancient America, pp. 243, 244-5. Also Atlantis, 392-5.

The class of works found in chapter four, setting forth clearly the civilizations of ancient America, together with the stupendous works named in this chapter, especially the great Peruvian roads, will convince reasonable minds that the metals, and especially STEEL, was in common use. To grant that such tasks were performed without it, would be to admit for those ancient workmen far more skill than if they possessed it.

Since the confusion of Babel was followed by the scattering of man from "Thence upon the face of all the earth," (Gen. 11:8) and as a knowledge of metals must then have been obtained in order to the building of the ark, there is no reason why the knowledge of the metals may not have been brought to the western continent by its first inhabitants.

Wilkinson says: "Iron and copper mines are found in the Egyptian desert which were worked in old times, and the monuments of Thebes and even their tombs about Memphis, dating more than four thousand years ago, represent butchers sharpening their knives on a round bar of metal, attached to their aprons, which from its blue color can only be STEEL; and the distinction between the bronzed and iron weapons in the tomb of Ramases III, one painted red and the other blue, leaves no doubt of both having been used (as in Rome) at the same period."--American Encyclopedia, Vol. 9, p. 585.

The Nephites used a compass or instrument similar to it, as recorded in the Book of Mormon. Of the compass, Donelly says: "In A. D. 868 it was employed by the Northmen." (The Landnamabok, Vol. 1, chap. 2.)

An Italian poem of A. D. 1190, referred to it as in use among the Italian sailors at that date. In the ancient language of the Hindoos, the Sanscrit, which has been a dead language for a period of twenty-two hundred years, the magnet was called "The precious stone beloved of Iron." The Talmud speaks of it as "The stone of attraction," and it is alluded to in the early Hebrew prayers as "kalamitah," the name given it by the Greeks, from the reed upon which the compass floated.

In the year 2700 B. C. the Emperor (of China) Wangti, placed a magnetic figure with an extended arm, like the Astarte of the Phœnicians, on the front of carriages, the arm always turning and pointing to the south, which the Chinese regarded as the principal pole."—Atlantis, pp. 440–1.

The Chinese invented the mariner's compass eleven centuries before Christ. See Light in Darkness, by J. E. & A. H. Godbey, p. 289.

"The earliest references to the use of the compass are to be found in Chinese history. * * In the sixty-fourth year of the reign of Ho-ang-ti, 2634, B. C."—Encyclopedia Britannica.

Chambers gives it the same date and the Chinese the credit of its invention.

"The ancients discovered the rotundity of the earth, and the difference of local time, and of the hour of the day between places of different longitude; knew the causes and laws of eclipses and constructed tables which give the motion of the sun, moon and stars, and the annual revolution of the sun was mapped out and divided into twelve signs known as the zodiac, was preserved in the 'Almagest' of Ptolemy, a work which remained authority for sixteen hundred years."—Johnson's Universal Encyclopedia.

"The astronomical tables sent by Alexander the Great to Aristotle, show that observations had been taken by the Babylonians which reached to 2234 years B. C."—Encyclopedia Religious Knowledge, read page 163–5.

Mr. P. C. Truman, before the Shelby county (Iowa) Normal Institute, September 7th, 1876, said:

"Let us turn for a moment to our own continent and then I am done. When and by whom America was first settled is yet unknown. Geologists tell us it is the older continent, and some claim that it was first inhab-

ited.   This much we do know: Ages before Columbus
ever saw its shore, America contained great cities and
mighty empires.   When the Spaniards conquered Mexico and Central America, the ruins of a civilization,
long preceding that of the Aztecs, were hidden by the
forests of Yucatan and Honduras, and the natives of
those places had no tradition even of who had built or
destroyed them.   Scattered over the whole United
States are the remains of a people, perhaps as different
from the wild Indians as we are.   That they had attained a good degree of culture is abundantly proved;
that the country was thickly peopled is very evident,
but who they were, whence they came, and what convulsion of nature or politics swept them away, are un-
solved problems.   When the Spaniards over-ran Mexico
and Peru, they found those empires already in a decline.   A galloping consumption set in, and in about
two hundred years, those delightful specimens of christianity civilized them and their people from off the
face of the earth.   The whole history of the intercourse
of the White and Indian races, had been marked by
fraud, aggression and calculating cruelty on the one
side, and ineffectual resistance, often accompanied by
fiendish barbarity, on the other.   To this there are a
few pleasant exceptions, proving that it need not have
been.   The peaceful, honest followers of Penn were not
molested by the Indians while other colonies were continually at war with them.   The Toltecs and Mound
Builders have left written records, but their works are
found amid the forests of Central America and in the
mountains of Colorado.   Traces of their work and the
stone, bronze and copper tools with which that work
was done, are found in the copper mines of Lake Super-

ior and the desert of Arizona, in the mounds of Ohio
and the cliff built cities of New Mexico.   And the ruins
of Palenque and Chichen-Itza rival those of Nineveh
and Palmyra in magnificence and extent.   One by one
the facts are being gathered that will some day enable
us to write a history of these people that may be tolerably correct.   Still it must not be supposed that they
have left no other records.   The Spaniards found books,
written in the Toltec and Maya tongues, a few of which
have been preserved.   What fearful calamity so utterly
destroyed these people, we may never know.   They
perished centuries ago and the savage Indians took their
place."

CHAPTER XI.

DATES OF AMERICAN ANTIQUITIES.
WHEN PUBLISHED.

As to whether or not it was possible for Joseph
Smith to have read works of antiquity, and then have
written the Book of Mormon in conformity with the
findings of the explorers, the following is very interesting: Bancroft writes, "Since 1830 the veil has been
lifted from the principle ruins of ancient Maya works,
by the researches of Zalva, Waldec, Stephens, Catherwood, Norman, Fredderickstahl and Charney.   A general account of the antiquarian writings and explora-
tions of these gentlemen is given in the appended note,
—It will be noticed that all the authors mentioned who
write from actual observation, have confined their observations to from ONE to FOUR of the principal ruins,

whose existence was known previous to their visits, ex-
cepting Messrs. Stephens and Catherwood.   These gentlemen boldly left the beaten track and brought to the
knowledge of the world about FORTY ruined cities,
whose very existence had been previously UNKNOWN
even to the residents of the larger cities of the very
state in whose territory they lie. * * The visit of
these explorers was the first, and thus far proved, in
most cases, the last."—Native Races, Vol. 4, pp. 144–
46.

   Mr. David S. Banks, who went from New York to
Yucatan in the especial interest of certain departments
of scientific knowledge lets light shine upon several topics that are strong proofs of the correctness of the Book
of Mormon.   It will be remembered that Stephens, in
1842, gave the number of ruined cities at forty-two,
while this man gives an increased or corrected list in
1888, as follows: "There are between sixty and
seventy ruined cities in Yucatan, as far as they have
been discovered."—Leslie's Monthly, May, 1889, p.
547.

   Of Yucatan Ruins, Stephens says: "The ruins of
Mayapan cover a great plain, which was at that time so
overgrown that hardly any object was visible until we
were close upon it, and the undergrowth was so thick
that it was difficult to work our way through it.   Ours
was the first visit to examine these ruins.   For ages
they had been unnoticed, almost unknown, and left to
struggle with rank tropical vegetation."—Incidents of
Travel in Yucatan, Vol. 1, p. 131.

   Short says of Stephens and Catherwood: "These
indefatigable explorers examined about forty ruined
cities, nearly all of which were previously unknown to

others than the natives, and many of them were unknown at Merida, the capitol of the country."—American Antiquities, p. 347. (He dates Stephens' first
edition, 1843.)

Baldwin in his work issued 1871, says in its preface: "The purpose of this volume is to give a summary of what is known of American Antiquities. * *
Many of the more important of these works are either
in French or Spanish, or in great English quartos and
folios * * and not one of them attempts to give a com-
prehensive view of the whole subject."

Baldwin says of Central America: "Palacios, who
described Copan in 1576, may properly be called the
first explorer."—Ancient America, p. 102.

The discovery by Palacios was not published however until 1843, and not in English until 1860. See
Native Races, Vol. 4, p. 79, also American Encyclopedia, Article Squier.

In his "Origin American Antiquities," published in
1839, page eleven, Delafield says: "The antiquities of
America are an immense field hardly entered, abounding in promise of reward for the most devoted investigations."

Priest says in his book of 1838: "It yet remains
for America to awake her story from its oblivious sleep,
and tell the tale of her antiquities, the traits of nations,
coeval perhaps, with the oldest works of man this side
of the flood."—American Antiquities, p. 40.

Baldwin says: "One of the most learned writers
on American antiquities, a Frenchman, speaking of discoveries in Peru, exclaims, 'America is to be again discovered!' * * The gold hunting marauders who subju-
gated Mexico and Peru could be robbers and destroyers,

but they were not qualified in any respect to become intelligent students of American antiquity."—Ancient America, p. 13.

"But it remains for America to awake her story from sleep, to string lyre and nerve the pen, to tell the tale of her antiquities, as seen in the relics of nations, coeval, perhaps, with the oldest works of man."—Traditions of De-coo-dah by Wm. Pidgeon, (1853), p. 11.

Bancroft writes: "The only author who has attempted to treat of the subject of Central American Civilization, and antiquity comprehensively as a whole, is the Abbe Brasseur de Bourbourg."—Native Races, Vol. 2, p. 116. The work cited was first published in 1857–9. See American Encyclopedia, Vol. 3, p. 214.

He further writes: "Of all American peoples, the Quichees of Guatemala have left us the richest mythological legacy. Their description of the creation as given in the Popol Vuh, which may be called the national book of the Quichees, in its rude, strange eloquence and poetic originality, one of the rarest relics of aboriginal thought."—Native Races Pacific States, Vol. 3, pp. 42, 43.

"In Vienna in 1857, the book, now best known as the Popol Vuh, was FIRST brought to the notice of European Scholars."—Ibid., p. 42.

The Book of Mormon was published in 1830, and so gave the facts twenty-seven years BEFORE this last mentioned publication.

Bancroft writes: "For what is known of Copan, the world is indebted almost entirely to the works of the American traveler, Mr. John L. Stephens, and of his most skillful artist companion, Mr. F. Catherwood."—Native Races, Vol. 4, p. 81.

These gentlemen were sent out in 1839 by the United States government. Mr. Stephens wrote: "I shall make one remark in regard to the work of Mr. Waldec. which was published in folio in Paris in 1835, and except my own hurried notice, is the ONLY ACCOUNT that has ever been published of the ruins of Uxmal, Yucatan."—Incidents of Travel, Vol. 1, p. 297.

It is said that Humboldt whose work was published in 1809, wrote of the civilization of Central America, but Stephens did not so understand: "The first new light thrown upon this subject as regards Mexico was by the great Humboldt, who visited that country at a time when, by the jealous policy of the government it was almost as much closed against strangers as China is now. No man could have better deserved such fortune. * * Unfortunately, of the great cities beyond the Vale of Mexico, buried in forests, ruined, desolate, and without a name, Humboldt never heard, or, at least, he never visited them."—Incidents of Travel, Vol. 1, p. 98.

"The study of the great architectural works of the ancient Mexican and Peruvians led Humboldt to investigations of their languages, records, early culture and migrations."—American Encyclopedia, Vol. 9, p. 45.

Some, who are totally uninformed upon the subject, affirm that Kingsborough wrote upon Central American civilization before the publication of the Book of Mormon. In answer to this it is only necessary to state, that the earliest date given for the publication of Kingsborough's work, is 1830; the American Encyclopedia gives it as 1831. See Prescott's Conquest of Mexico, Vol. 1, p. 128; and American Encyclopedia, article Kingsborough.

CHAPTER XII.

JOSEPH SMITH'S OBJECT—A VISION.

"My object in going to inquire of the Lord, was to know which of all these sects was right, that I might know which to join. * * I asked the personages, who stood above me in the light, which of all these sects was right,—for at that time it had never entered my head that all were wrong,—and which I should join. I was answered that I should join none of them, for they were all wrong; and the personage who addressed me said that all their creeds were an abomination in his sight, that those professors were all corrupt, 'They draw near me with their lips, but their hearts are far from me;' 'They teach for doctrine the commandments of men,' 'having a form of godliness, but they deny the power thereof.' He again forbade me to join any of them."— Times and Seasons, Vol. 3, p. 727.

On the eve of September 21st, 1823, through fervent prayer, another vision was presented to Mr. Smith, and he gives it, in part, as follows: "After I had retired to my bed for the night, I betook myself to prayer and supplication to the Almighty God for forgiveness of all my sins and follies, and also for a manifestation to me, that I might know of my state and standing before him, for I had full confidence in obtaining a divine manifestation, as I had previously had one. While I was thus in the act of calling upon God, I discovered a

light appearing in the room, which continued to increase until the room was lighter than at noonday,
when immediately a personage appeared at my bedside,
standing in the air, for his feet did not touch the floor.
He had on a loose robe of most exquisite whiteness.   It
was a whiteness beyond anything earthly I had ever seen,
nor do I believe that any earthly thing could be made
to appear so exceedingly white and brilliant.   His
hands were naked, and his arms also a little above the
wrists; so, also, were his feet naked, as were his legs,
a little above the ankles.   His head and neck were also
bare.   I could discover that he had no other clothing
on but this robe, as it was open so that I could see into his bosom.   Not only was his robe exceedingly
white, but his whole person was glorious beyond description, and his countenance truly like lightning.
The room was exceedingly light, but not so very bright
as immediately around his person.   When I first looked
upon him I was afraid, but the fear soon left me.   He
called me by name, and said unto me, that he was a
messenger sent from the presence of God to me, and
that his name was Moroni; that God had a work for
me to do, and that my name should be had for good
and evil among all nations, kindreds and tongues; or
that it should be both good and evil spoken of among
all people.   He said there was a book deposited, written upon gold plates, giving an account of the former
inhabitants of this continent, and the source from
whence they sprang.   He also said that the fullness of
the everlasting gospel was contained in it, as delivered
by the Savior to the ancient inhabitants.   Also, that
there were two stones in silver bows, (and these stones,
fastened to a breastplate, constituted what is called the

Urim and Thummim) deposited with the plates, and the possession and use of these stones was what constituted seers in ancient or former times, and that God had prepared them for the purpose of translating the book."

"After telling me these things, he commenced quoting the prophecies of the Old Testament. He first quoted a part of the third chapter of Malachi, and he quoted, also, the fourth or last chapter of the same prophecy, though with a little variation from the way it reads in our Bible. Instead of quoting the first verse as it reads in our book, he quoted it thus: 'For behold, the day cometh, that shall burn as an oven, and all the proud, yea, and all that do wickedly, shall burn as stubble; for they that come shall burn them, saith the Lord of Hosts, that it shall leave them neither root nor branch.' And again, he quoted the fifth verse thus: 'Behold, I will reveal unto you the priesthood, by the hand of Elijah the prophet, before the coming of the great and dreadful day of the Lord.' He also quoted the next verse differently: 'And he shall plant in the hearts of the children the promises made to the fathers, and the hearts of the children shall turn to their fathers; if it were not so, the whole earth would be utterly wasted at his coming.' In addition to these, he quoted the eleventh chapter of Isaiah, saying that it was about to be fulfilled. He quoted, also, the third chapter of Acts, twenty-second and twenty-third verses, precisely as they stand in our New Testament. He said that that prophet was Christ; but the day had not yet come when 'they who would not hear his voice should be cut off from among the people,' but soon would come. He also quoted the second chapter of Joel, from the twenty-eighth verse to the last. He also said that this was not yet fulfilled, but was soon to be. And he further stated, the fullness of the Gentiles was soon to come in. He quoted many other passages of scripture, and offered many explanations which cannot be mentioned here. Again, he told me that when I got those plates of which he had spoken,—for the time that they should be obtained was not yet fulfilled,—I should not show them to any person; neither the breastplate with the Urim and Thummim; only to those to whom I should be commanded to show them. If I did, I should be destroyed. While he was conversing with me about the plates, the vision was opened to my mind, that I could see the place where the plates were deposited, and that so clearly and distinctly that I knew the place again when I visited it."—Times and Seasons, Vol. 3, p. 729.

CHAPTER XIII.

THE SEALED BOOK TO COME FORTH—FULFILLMENT OF PSALM 85 AND ISAIAH 29—PALESTINE RESTORED.

The Savior said (John 17: 17), "Thy word is truth."

The Psalmist said, "I will hear what the Lord will speak, for he will speak peace unto his people."—Ps. 85: 8. In verse eleven he says: "Truth shall spring out of the earth, and righteousness shall look down from heaven." Verse twelve states: "Yea the Lord shall give that which is good; and our land shall yield her increase."

Thus it will be seen (1) that the Lord was to speak unto his people; and (2) that associated with the Lord speaking, would be the coming forth of "truth," a record of God's "word," "out of the earth;" and (3) that at that time the Lord was to bless the land of Palestine, and give his people "that which is good," and the "land" which had been under the curse of sterility, was again to become fertile as in ancient times.

That "truth" should "spring out of the earth," it was necessary that it should have been reposed to its keeping, to come forth in the due time of the Lord. The Book of Mormon is God's word, "truth," as delivered to the ancient nations of America; and in its coming forth "out of the earth," clearly fulfills this prophecy of the "sweet singer of Israel."

The prophet Isaiah, in chapter twenty-nine, begins with vivid expressions of "woe," "distress," "heaviness," and "sorrow" to "Ariel, the city where David dwelt;" and in the latter clause of verse two, introduces that which says: "And it shall be unto me as Ariel." This that "shall be unto me as Ariel," is none other than another part of Israel, included in his prophecy, and not Jerusalem alone.   In chapter eighteen the prophet has described the Western continent both as to its form and location, — "Woe to the land shadowing with wings, which is beyond the rivers of Ethiopia." "And thou shalt be brought down, and shalt speak out of the ground, and thy speech shall be low out of the dust." (29: 4).   Being "brought down;" "speak out of the ground;" "and thy speech low out of the dust;" "whisper out of the dust," are strange particulars to be fulfilled in the history of the other Ariel, that people of whom the Savior spoke: "And other sheep I have which are not of this fold, [place] them also must I bring, and they shall hear my voice."—St. John 10: 16. This could only be accomplished by the coming forth

of the records of a people perished from the earth. Of
the people destroyed at Jerusalem, no record of which
we have any knowledge, was ever deposited in the
bosom of "mother earth;" and therefore, no record has
ever been recovered from the earth, concerning that
people and the times in which they lived. And now
the time is already past for the fulfillment of this prophecy, as we shall show later on.

The Israel of the Western continent, committed
their records to the earth; and that they have been
brought forth, is fully attested by evidence which can
never be impeached. The prophecies of David and
Isaiah relate to the same subject, and are as one in
their fulfillment, while Christ's definition of "truth" is
brought out in bold relief.

The people of to-day, "The day of His preparation," (see Nahum 2: 34), are presented with the record
and history of those who in ages past, flourished upon
the land "choice above all other lands." Verses five
and six deal with the distress and destruction to be visited upon that people. In verses seven and eight, the
"nations" who were to be arrayed against Ariel, or
"fight against Mount Zion," are represented as a hungry or thirsty man, who dreams of eating and drinking
only to awaken and "Behold he is faint, and his soul
hath appetite." These "nations" are estranged from
God; and although they make a great show that they
are on the Lord's side, and are fed with the manna from
heaven, yet it is only as a dream, it is not real. A mistaken, apostate christianity has been their heritage,
which will be confessed in that day yet to come.
Hence, Jeremiah prophesied: "Gentiles shall come unto thee from the ends of the earth and shall say, 'Surely

our fathers have inherited lies, vanity, and things wherein there is no profit.' "—16: 19.

The Lord states their condition in Isaiah 29: 9, as
being "Drunken but not with wine, they stagger but not
with strong drink." This evidently portrays their
spiritual condition, showing them to be spiritually
drunk, having imbibed of false doctrine and heresies,
partaking with the "great Babylon of the earth" "the
wine of the wrath of her fornication." They were to be
without present revelation from God; and to them there
was to be "No answer from God." See also Micah
3: 6, 7. The tenth verse (Isaiah 29) says: "For the
Lord hath poured out upon you the spirit of deep sleep,
and hath closed your eyes; the prophets and your rulers, the seers hath he covered." Truly their condition
must have been deplorable, to have been described as
drunken and sleepy, hungry and athirst. And yet this
was to be their sad state, and serves but to illustrate
the necessity of LIVING prophets, and teachers DIVINELY
APPOINTED to minister the word of life unto the people.
Verse eleven reads: "And the vision of all has become unto you, as the words of a book that is sealed,
which men deliver to one that is learned, saying, read
this I pray thee; and he saith, I cannot for it is sealed."
"The vision of all;" the writings of prophets and apostles as found in the Holy Scriptures, were to be possessed by that people, and to become unto them "as
the words of a book that is sealed." They were to be
without that inspiration of God (Job 32: 8) so necessary to understand the things of God, (see 1 Cor. 2:
11), and as a result were not to understand the things
written.

"The vision of all," (or scripture possessed by

them), being not understood, are compared unto another book, a book which they did not possess,—"The words of a book that is sealed." "These words," the prophet declares, "Men deliver unto one that is learned, saying, 'Read this I pray thee,' and he saith, I cannot, for it is sealed." A transcript of the hieroglyphics of a certain part of the Book of Mormon was prepared by Joseph Smith, and sent by Martin Harris to Prof. Anthon of New York. When informed as to the manner of Joseph Smith obtaining the "book," he said, when asked to translate, "I cannot, for it is sealed." Notice, that the "book" was not to be "delivered" "to one that is learned," but the "words" only, which was done when the transcript taken by Smith was delivered by Harris, as already described. Verse twelve: "And the book is delivered to him that is not learned, saying, Read this I pray thee, and he saith, I am not learned." To Joseph Smith was delivered the book; he was one "not learned." That he did have the records in his possession is attested by eight persons who SAW and handled them, whose testimony as also that of three others, was published in connection with the Book of Mormon. He complained to the Lord, saying, "I am not learned."

Verses thirteen and fourteen: "Fosasmuch as this people draw near me with their mouth, and with their lips do honor me, but have removed their heart far from me, and their fear toward me is taught by the precept of men: Therefore, behold I will proceed to do a marvelous work among this people, even a marvelous work and a wonder." It is clear that this "marvelous work" was not to be founded in the wisdom and precept of men, but in the wisdom and power of God. Therefore the unlearned was selected, and to "him" "was delivered" the "book." The Lord was to do the work, and this is accomplished by bestowing upon the "one not learned," power from God, with the use of the "Urim and Thummim," to "read" the "book that is sealed."

The worship of the times when this was to transpire, is described as of the "lip," "while the heart is removed far from me." The hungry, thirsty, dreamy, drunken condition, one of "deep sleep," is still upon the "nations." Human precepts (creeds) are substituted for the doctrine of Christ. The "marvelous work and a wonder," so introduced by God in the latter days, occasions not a little wondering and marveling, that "The wisdom of the wise men shall perish, and the understanding of the prudent men shall be hid."—v. 14.

And so we perceive another prophecy fulfilled. The efforts of the "wise" were to signally fail in their attempts to overthrow the work so introduced. Verses fifteen and sixteen are strong in condemnation of those who work in the dark, characterized as "Turning things upside down," opposing God's truth, perverting instead of receiving the way of truth. Verse seventeen is a veritable milestone, marking the fulfillment of prophecy: "Is it not yet a very little while, and Lebanon shall be turned into a fruitful field, and the fruitful field shall be esteemed as a forest." Only "a little while" after the fulfillment of the things foretold, and Lebanon or Palestine "shall be turned into a fruitful field."

Although century upon century should pass, and Palestine during this time should remain under the curse of barrenness and sterility; yet when the time appointed of God should have arrived, and the "little

while" elapsed, then the curse is to be removed, and the
"land of promise" shall again be a "fruitful field." In
1830 the Book of Mormon was published, fulfilling the
prophecy concerning the "words of the book that is
sealed" being "delivered by men to one that is learned;"
the book itself being delivered (not by man or men) to
"one not learned," and God's "marvelous work" introduced.

Louis Van Buren wrote, only a few years ago, an
account of his sojourn, and observations in Palestine:
"I arrived in Indiana a few days since, from the Eastern Continent. I stopped at Joppa nearly the whole
winter. For my part I was well pleased with the country. It is certainly a land of most wonderful fruitful-
ness, with a delightsome climate, producing everything,
if properly cultivated, and from two to three crops in a
year. They have grain, fruit and vegetables all the
year round; in fact I never was in such a country before. I have seen much good country in Europe and
America, but none to compare with Palestine; its fruit-
fulness is uncommon, and the climate the most delightsome; even in winter I did not see the least sort of
frost, and vegetables of every•sort were growing in perfection in gardens. It is a fact that the rain and dew
are restored; recently, in 1853, the former and the latter rain were restored, to the astonishment of the natives."— Louis Van Buren, Sen., Nov. 14th, A. D. 1867.

Thus it is seen that only twenty-three years had
passed after the publication of the Book of Mormon
before the long promised restoration came. According to Usher's Chronology, Isaiah made this prediction
two thousand, five hundred and sixty-five years before
its fulfillment. This restoration of Palestine and the

rebuilding of Jerusalem, was widely taught by the Latter Day Saints from the year 1830 down to the year 1853. They had faith in the immediate fulfillment of that promise, for they knew that the time was at hand. And now with pleasure they can point to the restoration and rebuilding of Jerusalem, and the events in the east which tend to push the sons of Abraham thither, and can say, "We told you so."

"It [Palestine] has the same bright sun and unclouded sky, as well as the early and latter rain, which, however, is diminished in quantity, owing to the destruction of trees."— Chambers' Encyclopedia, Vol. 7, p. 11. — Palestine.

"The result of Dr. Barclay's observations is to show that the greatest fall of rain at Jerusalem in a single year was eighty-five inches, and the smallest forty-four, the mean being 51 1-6. These figures will be best appreciated by recollecting that the average rain fall at London during the whole year is only twenty-five inches, and that in the wettest parts of the country, such as Cumberland and Devon, it rarely exceeds fifty inches. As in the time of our Savior, (Luke 12: 54), the rains come chiefly from the south or southwest; they commence at the end of October, or beginning of November, and continue with greater or lesser constancy till the end of February, or middle of March, and, occasionally, though rarely, till the end of April. Between April and November, there is, with the rarest exception, an uninterrupted period of fine weather, and skies without a cloud. During the summer the dews are very heavy, and often saturate the traveler's tent, as if a shower had passed over it. The nights, especially towards sunrise, are very cold, and thick fog or mists are common all over the country. Thunder storms of great violence, are frequent during the winter months."—Dictionary of Bible, by Wm. Smith, p. 636. —Art. Palestine.

In D A. Randall's Hand Writing of God, page nineteen, occurs his introduction to Dr. Barclay of the Disciple church and missionary to the land of Palestine, and resident of Jerusalem twenty years, but resident of Joppa at the time of Randall's visit. "The country about Joppa is certainly a most delightful one. Extensive plains covered with luxuriant vegetation stretched along the shore of the sea and far into the interior. Large orange groves were just yielding their luxuriant harvest of golden colored fruit. Such oranges I had never before seen and I had no idea that they ever grew to such a great size. The ground was dotted with flowers of every hue and the air was vocal with the music of birds."—Ibid., p. 23.

"Lydia or Ludd. It numbers about two thousand inhabitants, and is surrounded by beautiful groves, among which may be seen the olive, fig and pomegranate, etc."—Ibid., p. 24.

"Here, where we are now walking, and within the walls, are several large patches of ground upon which barley and wheat are growing. But a few weeks since the plow passed over that ground and the seed was scattered upon the furrowed soil, and close by it are great mounds of ruins covered with vegetation." (See Micah 3: 12)—Ibid., p. 60.

"This is about the closing up of the latter rains; after a few days they expect no more rain until the latter part of September or October."—Ibid., p. 261.

"The tall rank grass was waving among the stone,

and the ground had been plowed to the very foundation walls, and a crop of barley was rapidly approaching harvest."—Ibid., 271.

"The Baldwin Locomotive works in Philadelphia, has received the following note from its representative in Palestine:

'Hotel Jerusalem, Jaffa, October 3d, 1890.

'Gentlemen:—I am very glad to be able to report that we made a successful trial trip of the first engine (Jaffa) to-day. All Jaffa was out to see it, including the Turkish Governor and his court. It was estimated that at least ten thousand people were on the house-tops and along the line of the road, and over two-thirds of them never saw a locomotive before. Many of the Arab women moved their household effects along the line of the road several days ago, so as to be on hand when the great thing went along. Many flags were hoisted over public buildings in honor of the occasion. I got an American flag from the Consul and put it on the front bumper. The French engineers put two French flags on each corner of the cab, and we secured a Turkish one to put on the other corner of the bumper, and so we went up into town. I doubt if any other engine built by the works ever received so much attention as 8 24 D, 24, and as for me, well, I never expected people to regard me as the Arabs did today, and have been doing. They simply think I have been cutting and carving it out of a lot of railroad iron and boxes. They have a great respect for the French engineers, and think them very smart, but when it comes to making a machine such as they saw today, ' "they can't do it in France, they had to send to America for a man to make it." ' "—Hebrew Christian.

Rabbi F. De Sola Mendes, of New York City, contributing to the Patriot wrote: "The future of the Jews is inalienably and unalterably associated with Palestine, their own old home; let us turn thither. From time to time American readers have been familiar with newspaper statements of the enormous influx into Palestine of Russian and Roumanian Hebrew refugees. The scale of this immigration, although considerable, has by no means been as large as usually asserted; it is questionable whether there are today as many as seventy thousand Hebrews in all Syria, while Mr. Selah Merril, U. S. consul at Jerusalem, very recently reported their numbers as being only forty-three thousand, but this probably refers only to Palestine proper. Jerusalem, naturally, is the chief focus of this immigration, and all reports agree in placing her Jewish population today at about thirty thousand. This already makes the Holy City a Jewish one, seeing that that is considerably more than half the total population of the place. In Safed, too, more than half of the twenty-five thousand inhabitants are Jews, while in Tiberias, another important city, they number three thousand out of the total four thousand. In Hebron, on the other hand, they are only twelve hundred out of eight thousand. They have seventy synagogues, it is computed, and in Jerusalem several large hospitals and schools. The Rothschild Agricultural school at Jaffa, has for many years done much towards building up the real development of the country, by annually sending forth many well-equipped agricultural educators and farmers. This of course, is the pressing need of the land, to build up the waste places, to plant the desolate fields, and to restore the washed away soil to the mountain plateaus, whence

the unchecked and uncontrolled rains of centuries have
been allowed to flood it away. * * The screech of the
railroad whistle may be heard in Jaffa, on the two-
thirds finished road from that seaport to Jerusalem.
There is an electric light outside the Damascus gate at
the Holy City; the shadow of a telegraph pole falls
upon Jacob's well near Shechem, and a prosaic steam-
mill puffs hard day and night close by the ancient wall
of Nazareth. * * A very much more important railroad,
as far as the commerce of the country is concerned, is
that for which a concession has recently been granted,
from Haifa near Carmel, across the country to the
Hauran and Damascus. It will cross the plain of
Esdraelon, the upper Jordan, and the country to the
south of Mt. Hermon, the most fertile district of all
Syria. Its chief result will be the opening up of the
Hauran, an enormous wheatfield, as it were, south of
Hermon, some sixty miles by thirty in extent. The
traffic, on camel-back, is today already enormous, the
people, who are quite wealthy, importing all their
illuminating-oil, their iron, their lumber and their fruit
—there are no trees in the Hauran—in exchange for
their grain; what will it grow to when the iron horse is
ready to shoulder their loads? There is no sign of
impending change so potent as this new railroad, one
of whose termini will be under the shadow of hoary
Carmel by the sea, the other in venerable Damascus,
whose whistle will be heard in Nazareth and echo from
the shores of Galilee, and whose bridges will be flung
across the Kishon—"that venerable stream"—the
Jordan and the Pharphar. Eleven years ago, says a
recent traveler, the plain of Esdraelon was cultivated
only in small patches, the crops of which were pretty

regularly swept away by the marauding Bedaween of
East Jordan: now it is almost one unbroken sea of
wheat, owned and farmed by a wealthy Greek of
Beyrout. Wine growing too is being followed with
great success in the Lebanon, and the proverbial fig
tree will not be long in appearing. The Jews, of course,
are manfully taking their part in this transformation of
the land. Many colonies have been founded, with
varying success natural to a new occupation to new
men in a new country. * * With patience and perseverance these men will work on with God's blessings;
all true friends of Israel will watch their progress with
interest and concern, and hail each new enterprise
which looks to making loved Palestine's "wilderness
like an Eden, her deserts like the garden of the Lord."
"So shall joy and gladness be found therein once more,
thanksgiving and the voice of song."—Independent
Patriot, October 19, 1892.

Mr. E. Haldane contributing to the St. Louis
Republic wrote from Jaffa, December 10th, 1892: "An
English syndicate is now building a railway from Haifa
to Damascus. The cost of this Damascus road will be
about ten million dollars. The Jaffa road is to have a
branch to Gaza in ancient Philistia, and this will continue down to Egypt, with its probable terminous at
Port Said. This latter road will tap the great grain-
producing region of Southern Palestine and Upper
Egypt. As a result of all this railroad building the
whole of Syria is now experiencing such a "boom" as
has never before been felt in the East. The harvests
of the Hauran—where the finest wheat and barley in
the world are raised—now exceed two hundred thousand
tons of cereals, of which five eighths are exported, being

carried on camel-back.to Damascus, which adds fifty
per cent to the cost.   Caravans from Damascus, which,
with its population of three hundred thousand, is the
commercial center of Syria, travel through Mesopo-
tamia, by the Tigris and Euphrates, to Mosul, Bagdad
and Hilleh and to the most distant parts of Arabia,
Africa and Egypt.

"JAFFA, Palestine, December 3d, 1892.

"EDITORS HERALD:--In September last, the day
the first rain began, the wind and sea were high, and
the last boat load of passengers was swamped and most
of them drowned; little children with their parents.
The rain is still pouring with thunder and lightning.
The old Solomon's harbor is full and running over.
There were slight showers of rain all through the summer.   The people thought it would be unhealthy, but
it has been quite the contrary.   The rain is so heavy
that the houses are falling down, some also that have
been newly built, and the ovens also where the bread is
baked for market are broken down and cannot be
baked in at present, as it is still raining—pouring is the
word, for such a storm as this one.

"ABIGAIL YORK ALLEY "

"RAILROADS FOR PALESTINE.

"Formal announcement was made at London,
England, October 14th, that the contract for building
the much talked-of railroad from Haifa, in Syria, to
Damascus has been awarded to a Chicago firm, Huss
& Townsend, who have built the Mexican railroad also
for English capitalists.   Mr. Townsend said that the
equipment, engines and cars would probably be of
American make.   The contractors will sail for Haifa

on October 18th and will immediately begin work. They expect to complete the road in eighteen months. The project contemplates an ultimate extension of the road to India if Persian concessions can be obtained." —Independent Patriot, Oct. 19th, '93.

Joseph Smith affirmed that the angel said to him, "Jerusalem shall be inhabited as towns without walls for the multitude of men and cattle therein." Thus was fulfilled Zechariah 2: 4, applying it to modern times. Those ancient walls, destroyed by the Roman armies, were never to be rebuilt. The city, rebuilt, is "without walls," just as the prophet declared it would be. Verse eighteen, (Isa. 29), "In that day shall the deaf hear the words of the book, and the eyes of the blind shall see out of obscurity and out of darkness." This has had its literal fulfillment in the case of many through the blessings of the restored gospel.

Verse nineteen: "The meek also shall increase their joy in the Lord, and the poor among men shall rejoice in the Holy One of Israel." With the increasing light of the latter days, and the blessings of the gospel of Christ once more among men, the "meek" may "increase their joy in the Lord," and the "poor among men rejoice," because they again have the gospel of Christ in its simplicity declared unto them, "Not in word only, but also in power, and in the Holy Ghost, and in much assurance." The twentieth and twenty-first verses declare that the devices of the evil one shall be "brought to naught," the "scorner consumed," showing it to be a time of judgment. The twenty-second verse is a promise to the Hebrew. It is there stated that it is to be a time of returning favor for Jacob. "Jacob shall not now be ashamed, neither shall his face now wax pale." The long period of oppression, sorrow and affliction, visited upon them since their rejection of Jesus the Christ, is to be followed with a day of relaxation and liberty. Israel will once more enjoy his liberty among men, and the favor of God, ere they shall say in fulfillment of the Savior's words, "Ye shall no more see me till ye shall say, Blessed is he that cometh in the name of the Lord."

There has been a wonderful revolution of sentiment in favor of the Jews during this generation. And while all persecution has not ceased, yet so great has been its abatement, that many of that people have risen to positions of great honor and distinction, ranking among statesmen and figuring as leaders of the people. Surely the sons of Jacob are regaining favor among the nations, and this is in clear fulfillment of verse twenty-two.

In this connection we shall mention a few of that race who have received positions of political honor and distinction.

Disraeli, Premier of England, where, formerly, Hebrews were not permitted to own land. Solomon Hirsch was appointed minister to Turkey by President Harrison. Marcus Otterbourg, was the first American Hebrew to occupy the high office of Envoy Extraordinary and Minister Plenipotentiary, appointed by President Lincoln to Mexico. Oscar S. Straus, Minister to Turkey, by President Cleveland. Henry M. Phillips, one of the most distinguished members of the thirty-fifth Congress. Lewis C. Levin, who served in Congress three terms. E. B. Hart of the Congress of 1851. David Levy Youles, was for many years prior to the civil war, United States Senator from Florida. Isaac

Phillips, General Appraiser of the port of New York, which position he held fifteen years, was appointed by President Pierce. By appointment of President Grant, Dr. Herman Bendell, was Superintendent of Indian Affairs; and later, was Consul to Denmark. Henry M. Hymans, Lieutenant Governor of Louisiana. A host of others occupying places of distinction in the leading nations could have been given.

The return of Israel unto God is signified in the twenty-third verse, (Isa. 29), "They shall sanctify my name, and sanctify the Holy One of Jacob, and shall fear the God of Israel." The last verse of the chapter is as follows: "They also that erred in spirit shall come to understanding, and they that murmured shall learn doctrine." Under the ministry of the gospel of Jesus Christ as again restored, "the marvelous work and a wonder," the power of the Holy Ghost, and the record of the word, will be ample and sufficient to "try the spirits" which are abroad in the earth, and as a result, those who have "erred" need not continue therein, for to them special help is promised. "And they that murmured shall learn doctrine." This is to be fulfilled by reason of the flood of light to be ushered in, and the dawning of the latter day glory. With the records of both Judah and Joseph in their midst, matters of doctrine will have right solution, and the "faith once delivered" will be fully established, and a people prepared to meet the Christ when he comes to reign on the earth.

CHAPTER XIV.

AN ADMISSION.   WITNESSES TESTIFY.

PROF. ANTHON'S ADMISSION.

"Some years ago a plain, apparently simple hearted farmer, called on me with a note from Dr. Mitchell, of our city, now dead, requesting me to decipher, if possible, a paper which the farmer would hand me, and which Dr. Mitchell confessed he had been unable to understand.   When I asked the person who brought it how he obtained the writing, he gave me, as far as I now recollect [Note this language, 'As far as I now recollect'] the following account: A gold book consisting of a number of plates of gold fastened together in the shape of a book, by wires of the same metal, which had been dug up in the northern part of the state of New York, and along with the book an enormous pair of gold spectacles.   [Urim and Thummim]. These spectacles were so large that if a person attempted to look through them, his two eyes would have to be turned toward one of the glasses merely, the spectacles in question being altogether too large for the human face.   Whoever examined the plates through the spectacles was enabled to not only read them, but understand their meaning.   All of this knowledge, however, was confined at that time to the young man who had the trunk containing the plates and spectacles in his sole possession. He put on the spectacles, or rather looked through one of the glasses, and deciphered the characters in the book, and having committed some of them to paper, handed copies to a person outside. This paper was in fact a singular scroll. It consisted of all kinds of crooked characters, disposed in columns, and had evidently been prepared by some person who had before him at the time a book containing various alphabets, Greek and Hebrew letters, crosses and flourishes. Roman letters inverted or placed sideways, were ranged in perpendicular columns, and the whole ended in a rude delineation of a circle, decked with various strange marks, and evidently copied after the Mexican calendar given by Humboldt."—E. D. Howe's work, p. 272.

THE TESTIMONY OF THREE WITNESSES.

Be it known unto all nations, kindreds, tongues, and people, unto whom this work shall come, that we, through the grace of God the Father, and our Lord Jesus Christ, have seen the plates which contain this record, which is a record of the people of Nephi, and also of the Lamanites, their brethren, and also of the people of Jared, who came from the tower of which hath been spoken; and we also know that they have been translated by the gift and power of God, for his voice hath declared it unto us; wherefore we know of a surety, that the work is true. And we also testify that we have seen the engravings which are upon the plates, and they have been shown unto us by the power of God, and not of man. And we declare with words of

soberness, that an angel of God came down from
heaven, and he brought and laid before our eyes, that
we beheld and saw the plates, and the engravings
thereon; and we know that it is by the grace of God the
Father, and our Lord Jesus Christ, that we beheld and
bare record that these things are true; and it is marvelous in our eyes, nevertheless the voice of the Lord
commanded us that we should bear record of it; wherefore, to be obedient unto the commandments of God,
we bear testimony of these things.   And we know that
if we are faithful in Christ, we shall rid our garments of
the blood of all men, and be found spotless before the
judgment seat of Christ, and shall dwell with him
eternally in the heavens.   And the honor be to the
Father, and to the Son, and to the Holy Ghost, which
is one God.   Amen.

OLIVER COWDERY,
DAVID WHITMER,
MARTIN HARRIS.

THE TESTIMONY OF EIGHT WITNESSES.

Be it known unto all nations, kindreds, tongues
and people, unto whom this work shall come, that
Joseph Smith, Jr., the translator of this work, has
shown unto us the plates of which hath been spoken,
which have the appearance of gold; and as many of the
leaves as the said Smith has translated, we did handle
with our hands, and we also saw the engravings thereon,
all of which has the appearance of ancient work, and
of curious workmanship.   And this we bear record with
words of soberness, that the said Smith has shown unto
us, for we have seen and hefted, and know of a surety
that the said Smith has got the plates of which we have

spoken. And we give our names unto the world to witness unto the world that which we have seen, and we lie not, God bearing witness of it.

> CHRISTIAN WHITMER,
> JACOB WHITMER,
> PETER WHITMER, JR.,
> JOHN WHITMER,
> HIRAM PAGE,
> JOSEPH SMITH, SR.,
> HYRUM SMITH,
> SAMUEL H. SMITH.

DEATH OF THE THREE WITNESSES.

Oliver Cowdery died at Richmond, Missouri, March, 1850; his dying charge to David Whitmer, being, "Be true to our testimony, Brother David." This was related by Mr. Whitmer to the writer of this book, in company with Elder E. C. Briggs, in April, 1885, when visiting Mr. Whitmer.

Martin Harris died at Clarkston, Cache county, Utah, July, 1875. Answering the question of H. B. Emerson, of New Richmond, Ohio, "Did you go to England to lecture against Mormonism?" he said, "I answer emphatically, No, I did not; no man ever heard me in any way deny the truth of the Book of Mormon."

David Whitmer died at Richmond, Missouri, where he had lived HALF A CENTURY, January 25th, 1888. Of his death and the avowal of his testimony at that time, the Richmond Democrat, of January 26th, 1888, said: "On Sunday evening at 5:30, January 22d, 1888, Mr. Whitmer called his family and some friends to his bedside, and addressing himself to the attending physician, said, 'Dr. Buchanan, I want you to say whether or not, I am in my right mind, before I give my dying testimony.' The doctor answered, 'Yes, you are in your

right mind, for I have just had a conversation with you.'
He then addressed himself to all around his bedside in
these words, 'Now you must all be faithful in Christ:
I want to say to all of you that the Bible, and the record
of the Nephites (Book of Mormon) is true, so you can
say that you have heard me bear my testimony on my
death-bed.'"

The Globe-Democrat of January 25th, 1888, states
of Mr. Whitmer's death: "A night or two since he
called his physician, Dr. Buchanan, to his side and told
him that his testimony as recorded in the Book of
Mormon was true."

"We the undersigned citizens of Richmond, Ray
county, Missouri, where David Whitmer, Sr., has
resided since the year A. D. 1838, certify that we have
been long and intimately acquainted with him and know
him to be a man of the highest integrity, and of un-
doubted truth and veracity:" A .W. Doniphan; G. W.
Dunn, Judge of the Fifth Judicial Circuit; T. D. Wood-
son, President of Ray County Savings Bank; J. T.
Child, Editor of Conservator; H. C. Garner, Cashier of
Ray County Savings Bank; W. A. Holman, County
Treasurer; J. S. Hughes, Banker; James Hughes, Banker;
D. P. Whitmer, Attorney at Law; Jas. W. Black, Attorney
at Law; L. C. Cantwell, Postmaster; Geo. I. Wasson,
Mayor; Jas. A. Davis, County Collector; C. J. Hughes,
Probate Judge and Presiding Justice of Ray County Court;
George W. Trigg, County Clerk; W. W. Mosby, M. D.;
Thos. McGinnis, ex-Sherriff Ray County; J. P. Quesen-
berry, Merchant; W. R. Holman, Furniture Merchant;
Lewis Slaughter, Recorder of Deeds; Geo. W. Buch-
anan, M. D.; A. K. Reyburn.

Given at Richmond, Mo., this March 19th, A. D. 1881.

CHAPTER XV.
CONCLUSIONS.

Now, dear reader, we solicit your candid attention, while we proceed with our statement of conclusions upon some of the many evidences presented in this work.

At the time of the coming forth of the Book of Mormon very little was known of American antiquities; but since then, interest has been awakened and effort stimulated, which have resulted in a flood of light being thrown upon the great past of ancient America. The treasure-house has been unlocked, and the remains and monuments of her ancient civilizations now tell the story of those past ages.

The students of American antiquities will find, upon a careful examination, that no discovery has thus far been made which, in a single instance, contradicts the record of America's great and glorious past, as found in the Book of Mormon.

The Book of Mormon contains the record of a people who came to the Western continent from the tower of Babel at the confusion of tongues. Fortunately for the believers in the authority of the Bible, there is in the Book of Genesis, an historical statement which fully warrants the statement of the Book of Mormon. See Gen. 11: 9.

The labors of the student of ethnology and aboriginal traditions, have resulted in finding the statements, both of Genesis and the Book of Mormon, confirmed by the clearly defined traditions of the aborigines of the Central American states. This corroboration of history and tradition, especially where the existence of one had nothing to do with the creation of the other, is but a link in the chain of facts with which the Book of Mormon is vindicated.

The Book of Mormon affirms that two Hebraic colonies came to America from Jerusalem about six hundred years before the Christian era. Its statement is also in harmony with special promises and prophecies delivered by the olden Israelitish prophets concerning the colonization of a distant land by a portion of the house of Israel. (See Gen. 49: 22–26; Zeph. 3: 10). In this case also, now that the record attests the fulfillment of those prophetic promises made to ancient Israel, we have ample vindication of that Spirit which gave the "sure word of prophecy" unto His people in all the ages. The antiquarian comes to the front confirming the statement of prophecy, and the book which is the subject of this work. We are confronted with the indisputable evidence of the Hebrew language, as found upon tablets discovered in mounds and tumuli where they were deposited in the ages long ago. Tablets and ancient parchment containing parts of the Jewish scriptures and Mosaic Law have been found, which confirm the statement of the Book of Mormon, that there was an Hebrew colonization, and that they brought their customs and religion, and also their sacred books with them when coming to this land. In this we have a striking fulfillment of ancient prophecy, and a

strong endorsement of the book which records its fulfillment.   The use of stone tablets and parchment for the
purposes of record are of ancient custom with Israel,
and their discovery in America, employing the language
and the religion of that people, are strong evidences
that their authors were of Israel, just as stated in the
Book of Mormon.

The writers of the Book of Mormon affirm that
they made records upon metallic sheets or plates, as is
instanced in the golden plates from which the book
itself was translated.   At the time of the publication of
that book there had been no discovery of an ancient
writing upon a metallic sheet or plate in all America,
save that alone made by Joseph Smith concerning the
plates of the Book of Mormon.   The wise and learned
scouted the idea, not supposing for a moment that time
in its developments would confirm the statements of the
unlearned Smith, and the record of the Book of Mormon.   And yet in the order of events calculated alike
to confound the unbelieving scoffer and to inspire faith
in those who accepted that book as containing a true
record, only thirteen years elapsed before the discovery
of what are known as the Kinderhook plates.   They
were of brass and covered with hieroglyphics.   Only a
few years ago there was a remarkable find in Ohio,
when a large number of copper plates were unearthed,
and these also were covered with hieroglyphical characters.   And only about twenty years ago there were
found in old Mexico, quite a number of earthenware
plates also covered with engravings.   And it would
seem that while the work of exploration proceeds stimulated by the thirst for discovery by those engaged in it,
the providence of "Him who doeth all things well," is

appropriating their labors to confirm the claims of the book, now unsealed. In this last cited proof, we have a clear case in confirmation of the Book of Mormon.

That book of ancient story affirms the ancient existence and use of domestic animals, such as the horse and the ox, upon the American continent. In 1830, when that publication first appeared, the idea of the horse or the ox having existed upon this land anciently was considered by men of education and learning, as simply ridiculous; for it was believed that such animals were first introduced by the Europeans after the year 1492. But in this particular, as also in others, the antiquarian serenely puts in an appearance and gives a good eye-opener, effectually exploding the popular error, and fully establishing the fact that the domestic animals named, did flourish in the ages long ago upon the American continent. Thus we perceive that the wisdom of the wise, when contradicting the Book of Mormon, is brought to naught, while the statements of that book are corroborated and sustained as the years roll by. The Book of Mormon clearly affirms that in the bye-gone ages there were two distinct civilizations upon this land. And now, after sixty-two years have passed since the first publications of that work, and during which time the work of exploration has been pushed by hundreds and thousands of able men, the conclusion generally reached is, that in the ages past there were two distinct peoples and civilizations upon the American continent. And so it is, that as knowledge increases and the curtain of the past is lifted and the remains of the great past are exposed to view, that one by one the statements of the Book of Mormon are verified and proved to be true.

It has ever been the privilege of God's people to have their prayers, when made in righteousness, heard and answered by the Giver of all good. In this the unchangeable character of God is asserted, and his people are furnished a basis upon which to exercise faith in his word. If the ancient people of America were favored of God, and records were kept among them of their experiences from time to time, it is not unreasonable that some of their records, under divine providence, should be preserved for the enlightenment and blessing of mankind. A revelation such as the Book of Mormon claims to be, is neither unreasonable nor unscriptural, but as shown in these pages, it is both reasonable and scriptural, and therefore, worthy of our belief.

In its fulfillment of the twenty-ninth chapter of Isaiah, the Book of Mormon has as clear a case in vindication of prophecy as was ever known among men. Even those remarkable prophecies detailing the events in the life of the great Nazarine, are not more lucid and explicit than are those of Isaiah 29, and Psalms 85, in their application to the coming forth of a record of truth, a book to be unsealed. The thirty-seventh chapter of Ezekiel is full of significance, pointing to the coming of another record, "The Stick of Joseph," and its being "joined" in its use with the "Stick of Judah." The Book of Mormon alone fulfills the express terms of prophecy concerning the "sealed book" and the prophecies we have cited, and so stands as a strong witness attesting the divinity of those ancient prophecies.

It will doubtless be asked: What benefit to the believer in Christ is the Book of Mormon? We answer:

1st, It gives additional witness concerning Jesus the Christ. 2d, It speaks in great plainness upon doctrine, forever setting at rest matters of doctrine in dispute among the various sects of Christendom. 3d, It contains many "precious promises" unto God's people, and like "All scripture, is given by inspiration of God, and is profitable for doctrine, for reproof, for correction, for instruction in righteousness, that the man of God may be perfect, thoroughly furnished unto all good works."—2 Tim. 3: 16, 17.

We now invite attention to the witnesses whose testimony is published in the Book of Mormon, which they gave to the world concerning the plates from which the book was translated, and the visitation of the angel of God who affirmed that the record so translated was true. The testimony of eight persons who saw and handled the plates while they were yet in the possession of the one who translated them, has never been impeached. Those men while they lived, constantly re-affirmed their original testimony. Their lives gave evidence of their sincerity which must be regarded as the test of truth, and all died in the faith of the Book of Mormon.

The testimony of the three special witnesses, namely: Oliver Cowdery, Martin Harris and David Whitmer, is of great significance in its relation to the coming forth of the book so attested. They testify: 1st, That an holy angel brought unto them the plates of the Book of Mormon, and permitted them to handle them and see them: 2nd, That the angel bore testimony identifying the plates as those from which the Book of Mormon had been translated, and certified to the correctness and truth of the translation so made.

Upon an examination of the Book of Mormon it is found that it contains a prophecy concerning this occurrence,—the testimony of the three witnesses. · See Book of Mormon, page 100. Joseph Smith had also received an especial revelation in which it was asserted that the Lord would raise up three witnesses to whom would be shown those plates in a most remarkable way. —See Doctrine and Covenants, page 69. The testimony of these men not only attests the truthfullness of the Book of Mormon, but also furnishes a most signal instance in the fulfillment of prophecy. In the year 1838 there was an estrangement between the three witnesses and the prophet, and under the pressure of the fiery trial and bitter persecution visited upon the Saints, these men ceased to hold membership in the church, and remained aloof during the remainder of the prophet's life. It certainly is most reasonable, that if there had been a collusion between these men to give false testimony to the world concerning the angel's testimony and the plates of the Book of Mormon, that when they ceased to be friends, and these witnesses were no more members of the church, they would have renounced their testimony, and have pronounced Joseph Smith to have been only a scheming imposter. It is, however, notorious that during their long and eventful lives, these men ever declared that Joseph Smith was a true prophet, and that their testimony concerning the Book of Mormon was true. They had affirmed an occurrence—a fact; and the years that followed, furnished conclusive evidence that they were sincere in the testimony so given to the world. As men of sound minds, if they were sincere in their statement of the alleged fact, and their statements all agree, the conclusion is inevitable, that

they told the truth.   Upon their death-beds, they
re affirmed their testimony, and passed peacefully away.

Coincident with the publication of the Book of
Mormon was the founding anew of the church afterward
known as the Church of Jesus Christ of Latter Day
Saints.   The authority to preach the gospel and ad-
minister its ordinances had been restored to the earth,
and as a result, the church with the gifts and blessings
as of old, was again among men.   Tongues, prophecy,
interpretation of tongues, healings, and other gifts
named in the twelfth chapter of first Corinthians, were
among the blessed experiences of the faithful and true
of ''like precious faith.''   Experiences and scenes like
those of the day of Pentecost, are testified of by men
and women from all parts of the earth.   This universal
testimony and witness of the Holy Ghost are surely the
seal of the Almighty to the divinity of the Book of
Mormon and the church of the last days.   The restoration of the ''former and latter rain'' to the land of Palestine, just as predicted by the Prince-Prophet of Israel,
coming as it does in the time of the coming forth of the
''sealed book,'' now that the book is unsealed and published to the nations, and the ''marvelous work and a
wonder'' established among men, shows quite conclusively that the time is fulfilled, and the events foretold
have truly come to pass.

In the doctrine and promise, the Book of Mormon
is in harmony with all other authoritative declarations
of ''law and testimony,'' and therefore, as tried by the
divine standard, stands approved.   In James 1: 5, is a
choice promise to those who will seek the Lord for
guidance and light.   In the Book of Mormon, on page
544, is a promise fraught with importance to those who

love the Lord and his truth. It is there promised that if the people to whom the Book of Mormon should go, will seek the Lord for witness and testimony concerning it, that God will hear them, and the Holy Ghost WILL ATTEST ITS TRUTH. Dear reader, will you not accept this TEST, and so "PROVE ALL THINGS AND HOLD FAST TO THAT WHICH IS GOOD?"

May the loving Father bless you in your search for truth, and ultimately grant you "abundant entrance" into the mansions of everlasting rest.

PART II.

Twelve Works Against Mormonism

REVIEWED

IN COMPARISON WITH THEMSELVES AND EACH OTHER.

BRADEN'S MISTAKES.—OTHER CONTRADICTORY STATE-
MENTS.—SIX UNITED STATES SCHOOL HISTORIES
REVIEWED IN COMPARISON WITH EACH OTHER AND
FACTS. — FOUR LEADING ENCYCLOPEDIAS WITH
THEIR RE-ISSUES, EXAMINED IN COMPARISON AND
WITH FACTS.—ENCYCLOPEDIA, OFFICIAL AND PRESS
REFERENCES RELATIVE TO THE REORGANIZED
CHURCH OF JESUS CHRIST OF LATTER DAY SAINTS.

"Oh! * * that mine adversary had written a book,"
—Job 31: 35.

Job, a man of God, knew the adversary's book,
when examined, would defeat its aim, with those of true
mind and heart. Let us examine some of the works on
Mormonism from this standpoint. E. D. Howe of
Painsville, Ohio, (about ten miles from Kirtland), wrote
and published the first, entitled "Mormonism Unveiled."

On page 27 he represents Nephi as making plates in the wilderness with no ore. Book of Mormon, Palmyra Edition, page 43, shows the plates were made after the people arrived upon this continent, and after they had found ore with many other things.

Howe, same page: "Has a commandment from the Lord to make plates for the special purpose of making a record of his own ministry and his own people."

Book of Mormon, P. E., page 17: "I have received a commandment from the Lord that I should make these plates for the special purpose that there should be an account engraven of the ministry of my people."

Howe again: "Our hero introduces himself as a minister."

Book of Mormon, P. E., page 17: "And now I, Nephi, proceed to give an account upon these plates and of my proceedings, and my reign and ministry."

Howe, page 32: "It brought them all safely on the borders of the Red sea with the exception of Ishmael."

Book of Mormon, P. E., page 42: "And we did sojourn for the space of many years, yea, even eight years, in the wilderness. And we did come to the land which we call Bountiful, because of its much fruit, and we beheld the sea, which we called Ireantum, which, being interpreted, is many waters." Notice there is no Red sea in it.

Howe, page 35: "Whether the ship was propelled by oars, or by a current, or by the wind, or by the power of the spindle, we can not inform our readers, for it is not stated."

Book of Mormon, P. E., page 48:   "And it came
to pass that after we had all gone down into the ship
and taken with us our provisions and things which had
been commanded us, we did put forth into the sea, and
were driven forth before the wind towards the promised
land."

Howe, page 42:   "The Nephites warred with each
other until they exterminated the whole race except
three, who were immortalized."

Book of Mormon, P. E., pages 493–496:   "Yea,
even all my people, save it were those TWENTY and FOUR
who were with me, and also a FEW who had ESCAPED
into the south countries, and a FEW who had DISSENTED
over unto the Lamanites, had fallen and their flesh and
bones and blood, lay upon the face of the earth."

"Howe, page 52:   "We are likewise told in the
same discourse that the plates or book would be sealed
up, and should finally be found by an unlearned man,
who should see them and show them to three others."

Here is found the great bug-bear sought to be kept
before the people to deceive.   How different, however,
it is from the true reading.

Book of Mormon, P. E., page 110:   "Wherefore,
at that day when the book shall be delivered unto the
man of whom I have spoken, the book shall be hid from
the eyes of the world, that the eyes of none shall behold it, save it be that three witnesses shall behold it,
by the power of God, beside him to whom the book
shall be delivered, and they shall testify to the truth of
the book and the things therein.   And there is none
others which shall view it, save it be a few, according to
the will of God, to bear testimony of his word unto
the children of men."

Howe, page 77: "Smith used a stone in a hat for the purpose of translating the plates. The spectacles (Urim and Thummim) and plates were found together, but were taken from him and hid up again before he had translated one word, and he has never seen them since." "This is Smith's own story."

Pearl of Great Price, page 53, says: "By the wisdom of God (the plates, Urim and Thummim and breastplate) remained safe in my hands until I had accomplished by them what was required at my hand, when, according to arrangements, the messenger called for them; I delivered them up to him and he has them in his charge until this day being the second day of May, 1838."

Ibid., page 46, Oliver Cowdery wrote: "Day after day I continued, uninterrupted, to write from his mouth as he translated with the Urim and Thummim, or, as the Nephites would have said, Interpreters, the history or record called the Book of Mormon."

Howe, page 89: "The whole record being handed down and altered according to our manner of speech."

Book of Mormon, P. E., page 538: "And now we have written this record according to our knowledge in the characters, which are called among us, reformed Egyptian, being handed down and altered by us according to our manner of speech." The characters were altered, not the record.

Howe, page 90: "God marched before them in a cloud."

Book of Mormon, P. E., pages 451-2: "The Lord did go before them, and talked to them while he stood in a cloud, and gave directions whither they should travel."

Howe, page 124: "Even their wine they used for communion they were ordered to make from cider and other materials."

Book of Doctrine and Covenants, page 112: "You shall not purchase wine, neither strong drink from your enemies, wherefore you shall partake of none save it is made new among you." Cider and other materials are not mentioned.

Howe, page 129: "If thou lovest me, thou shalt serve me and keep my commandments, and thou shalt consecrate all thy properties, that which thou hast, unto me, with a covenant and a deed which can not be broken."

Book of Doctrine and Covenants, page 143, from which the above is garbled, reads: "If thou lovest me, thou shalt serve me and keep all my commandments. And behold, thou wilt remember the poor, and consecrate of thy properties for their support that which thou hast to impart unto them, with a covenant and a deed which cannot be broken, and inasmuch as you impart of your substance unto the poor, ye will do it unto me."

The foregoing is ample to show Howe to be utterly unreliable. Also that the work he assailed could not be defeated with truth, hence his only resource to vilify. The copious affidavits to be found in Howe's work and copied into many others, sometimes in varied form, are of the same stamp. One who will falsify a record so widely published as the Book of Mormon, as shown, will not fail to manufacture anything he may need to accomplish his purpose; such was Howe's work—"Mormonism Unveiled."

FOLLOWING the inscription of title page of Mrs. Maria Ward's expose of Mormonism, are a few of her glaring lying blunders, that show clearly her work is simply trash.

"FEMALE LIFE AMONG THE MORMONS.

"A NARRATIVE OF MANY YEARS' PERSONAL EXPERIENCE, BY THE WIFE OF A MORMON ELDER, RECENTLY FROM UTAH.   NEW YORK, 1855."

Mrs. Ward, relating her capture by Ward, says on page 12: "I became immediately sensible of some unaccountable influence drawing my sympathies towards him. In vain I struggled to break the spell. I was like a fluttering bird before the gaze of the serpent-charmer."

On page 417, treating of the same influence again, she says: "I learned the whole affair in my inter-course with the elders. I was present when Smith instructed Mr. Ward in the art."

On page 18, of eavesdropping when a miracle was to be performed, she says: "Perhaps it was a breach of hospitality, but my curiosity overcame my discre-tion. I applied the key, the bolt flew back, and the door swung open. I now perceived that this was the entrance to a long hall or passage, with doors on either side, communicating with other rooms. I advanced to one of them, and plainly perceived the glimmering of light through the crevices, and heard the indistinct murmur of voices."

On page 209, she is very much horrified. " 'But, Mrs. Stillman,' I began, for my mind rather recoiled from so dishonorable an act as private listening, 'is there no other way by which your curiosity could be satisfied?' "

But on page 60, she advertises her method thus: "The place of our encampment was on the border of a wood, near the banks of a limpid stream. I had wandered off by myself, and sat down on a fallen log behind a clump of elders and laurels, yet in plain view of the encampment, and where I could see all that was going on without being seen."

On page 137, Joseph Smith's death is described as seen by Mrs. Ward: " 'This is for my wife, my poor, forsaken Laura,' said Clarke, as he raised the gleaming tube of death to his eye. It exploded. I heard a wild and piercing screech, and saw Smith fall from the horse."

And on page 147, Mrs. Ward's High Priestess, Mrs. Bradish, says: "On that dreadful night," she said, "when these eyes beheld the fall of our holy prophet, when he tumbled from his horse."

On page 176, a raft built as follows, using ropes, chains, planks, etc., as if in New York city, when hundreds of miles from any such supplies, and far to the west on their journey. "The raft was soon constructed. It consisted of middling-sized logs, bound together by very strong ropes and chains, on which thick planks were laid, and fastened with iron spikes."

See what a time Mrs. Ward had with Buffaloes and grass on pages 191–2: "One morning we came unexpectedly on an immense drove of buffalo, which were swarming, as far as the eye could reach, over the plains, where they had left SCARCELY A BLADE OF GRASS remaining. In the presence of such a huge mass of animated beings, the beholder feels overcome by a strange emotion of grandeur. The continuous undulating motion, the dull, confused noise, unlike any other, and so admitting no comparison, struck us with awe and astonishment. Here a cow, separated a little from the others, stood quietly suckling her calf; there a huge bull would be ROLLING AND TUMBLING IN THE GRASS; and, not far off, clouds of dust would prove the existence of an obstinately contested fight."

On page 254, Mrs. Ward kindly gives us a combination affair, dry rivers, luxuriant flowers, no insects except a troop of wild horses. She says: "That, however, was only the beginning of sorrow, for in a few days we entered a sandy and barren region, where, to our other ills and inconveniences, that most intolerable of all, the want of water, was added. The streams were all dried up, the rivers disappeared from their channels, there was neither rain nor dew. But, though the air seemed intensely hot, and the sky exhibited not a trace of clouds, there was a softness in the atmosphere at night, a resplendent glory in the stars, altogether incomprehensible and most delightful. And this region, otherwise so sterile, was filled with flowers of the richest perfume and the brightest colors. In many places, where it would seem, from the gravelly, sandy nature of the soil, that no plant whatever could take root, cactuses, literally covered with a profusion of large crimson flowers, thrived luxuriantly, thus presenting a remarkable contrast to the surrounding desolation. For one of the remarkable characteristics of this place, was the utter absence of animal life. Not a bird visited these resplendent blossoms, not a butterfly or insect enlivened the solitude. Neither hares nor pheasants lurked beneath their coverts. Even the

Indians seemed to avoid the country.   Once, and once
only, we caught the glimpse of a troop of wild horses,
skirting the horizon.   It was only a glimpse, and yet I
shall ever remember the graceful agility of their mo-
tions, and the sleek sparkle of their glossy sides.   But
sadder sights than these awaited us.   I had descended
from the wagon to walk, in order that I might examine
the beautiful flowers.   I was particularly charmed by
two or three huge plants of the cactus species, which
had grown so close together that they appeared compact.   They were, at least, ninety feet in circumference,
and large scarlet blossoms depended from the branches.
But, while stooping to gather a bouquet, my fingers
inadvertently touched a relic, the sight of which filled
me with horror.   It was a human skeleton."

EXTRACTS from the work of Mrs. C. V. Waite, who
was wife of Chief Justice C. B. Waite, who served in
Utah when Mrs. Waite wrote, in 1866.   She has been
very much more fair than most others, only a fragment
of one of her books was at hand in the arranging of
this which did not contain the contradictions so common to other works on the subject.

"THE MORMON PROPHET AND HIS HAREM.

"BY MRS. C. V. WAITE.   FIFTH EDITION, REVISED AND EN-
LARGED.   CHICAGO; CINCINNATI; 1867."

On page 13, Mrs. Waite mentions Brigham Young
in the ascending scale officially, and suggests his zeal
to be worthy of a "better cause."   She says: "In
1835, on the 14th of February, at Kirtland, Brigham
Young was ordained one of the newly-organized quorum

of the Twelve Apostles.   Armed with his new power.
and fired with a zeal worthy of a better cause, he went
forth, and preached and proselyted with marked success.   Thomas B. Marsh having apostatized, Brigham
was chosen to succeed him, as President of the Twelve
Apostles, in 1836."

On page 18, of the usurpation of leadership by Brigham, she says: "Young was now ready to enact another
scene in this Mormon drama.   He was ruling the church
in the capacity of President of the Twelve Apostles.
He desired greater power; he wished to occupy the
place of the Prophet of the Lord.   This was the more
difficult, as the people venerated the memory of Joseph
Smith, sanctified as it was by the remembrance of his
cruel and untimely death.   Brigham knew well the
extent of this feeling, and that it would be impossible
to supplant Joseph in their affections, and extremely
difficult to occupy his position.   But his plans de-
manded that he should be in form what he was in fact,
—the absolute head of the church.   He resolved to
execute a brilliant coup d'etat, and risk the consequences."

Page 92 says: "It may be well here to remark,
for the benefit of the tender-footed upon this subject,
that polygamy is no part of the Mormon religion, so
far as the same has any history, and can be distinguished from the personal edicts of Brigham Young.
It is not only not permitted but explicitly condemned
in the 'Book of Mormon' and the 'Book of Doctrine
and Covenants,' which are the Old and New Testaments of Mormonism."

Having treated on the Morris movement, the work
of the Reorganized Church is thus set forth on pages

142–147:   "The next movement and one which promises seriously to interfere with the schemes of Brigham
Young, is under the auspices of the Mormon Church
East, or the 'Josephites,' as they are called, in contra-
distinction to the 'Brighamites.'

"Joseph Smith, the son of the Prophet, resides at
Nauvoo, in Illinois, near where his father was put to
death.   He claims to be the head of the true Mormon
Church, and of course repudiates Young for the same
position.   He is opposed to polygamy, is loyal to the
Government and laws of the United States, and is said
to be a good and worthy citizen.

"For several years there have been indications of
a 'breaking up' among the followers of the Pretender,
Brigham, and a rallying around the standard of the
legitimate House of Joseph.   In the States, those who
have gone back to their first love are to be numbered
by thousands.

"In Utah the progress of disintegration, and of
secession from the church as there organized, is slower,
and accompanied by more danger.

"But in July, 1863, the 'fulness of time' having
come, the movement was commenced in earnest, and a
system of proselyting inaugurated, which has already
drawn hundreds of deluded people back to their duty
to themselves and their country, and which even now
threatens the power of Brigham so strongly that it seems
almost tottering to its fall.

"During the latter part of the month mentioned,
E. C. Briggs and Alexander McCord, two missionaries,
sent by the Church East, for that purpose, arrived in
Salt Lake, and announced themselves as harbingers of
a better gospel,—as messengers of the true Church of

Christ on earth. Taking their lives in their hands, they had crossed the Plains alone, and the Lord had protected and sustained them.

"It may be supposed that their arrival caused considerable excitement at Salt Lake City.

"Briggs called on Young and acquainted him with the nature of his 'mission.' The Prophet became very angry; refused him the use of the Tabernacle, or any other building in the city; forbade him preaching to the people and said if he remained in the city, he (Young) would not be responsible for his personal safety. Briggs declined to avail himself of this polite hint to leave, and notwithstanding these thunders from the Vatican, he went boldly to work, and 'daily ceased not to teach and preach Jesus Christ.'

"He talked with the people, visited them at their houses, prayed with them, and sang with them.

"The effect was electrical. Singly, by dozens, and by scores, the people began to fall off from the great apostasy, and to return to the mother-church. Persecution commenced from the first day of his labors. He and McCord were forbidden all the houses of the city, by an order of Brigham, which none dared to disobey. One house, that of a gentile, was still open to them, and there they held their meetings, which were well attended.

"Before spring their numbers had increased to over three hundred. About half of that number returned across the Plains in the spring of 1864, and so strong was the excitement, and so bitter the persecution and enmity of the 'Saints' toward this comparatively hand ful of seceders from Brigham's authority and dominions, that Gen. Connor deemed it necessary and advisable to send a strong escort with them as far as Green River, about 145 miles.

"Besides this number who departed for the region of the rising sun, large numbers of the westward-bound emigration were stopped, and having their eyes opened by missionaries of the same stamp, were induced to withhold their steps, at least until another season.

"The Josephites in Salt Lake, although the subjects of bitter and unrelenting persecution from the Mormons, found favor and protection from Gen. Connor and the military under his command.

"They will doubtless continue to flourish and increase, and it is possible that in this way Utah may be brought to loyalty and good citizenship, without bloodshed or commotion."

Of those seeking release from Utah Mormon bondage, page 210 says: "To such, the new preachers sent by the 'Josephites,' to bring the people back to virtue, to loyalty, and to the original Mormon religion, appear as angels from heaven, and hence the ready assent given to their teachings, and the rapid defection from the established church."

Of reformatory influences and showing that her best appreciation is bestowed elsewhere than Mormonism, page 299 says: "Among the agencies already at work to accomplish this desirable end, and to redeem Utah from her enthrallment, may be mentioned the discovery of mines of precious metals, and the large influx of miners,—the preaching not only of a purer Mormon faith, under the auspices of Joseph Smith, Jr., but the promulgation of the Gospel itself, and of the principles of Christianity in their purity, by Rev. Norman Mc-Leod, a Congregational minister of great boldness and talent, who is now firmly established in the Territory."

Of the time previous to 1852, page 172 says·
"Previous to the year 1852, it was also an orthodox
principle of the Mormon religion, that a man should
have but one wife, to whom he should be true and
faithful."

Page 176 says: "But the greatest change of all in
the Mormon religion, made by Brigham Young, was
the introduction and establishment of polygamy.   This
was no part of the Mormon system of religion as
originally established.   On the contrary it was expressly
repudiated by all the Mormon writers and speakers,
previous to 1852 and in Europe for some years afterward.

"The Mormon religion was founded by Joseph
Smith and his coadjutors, and the principles and doctrines of the religion were, in the first instance, such as
they established.   The Book of Mormon is the historical foundation, corresponding with the Old Testament
of the Christian Bible.   Afterward, a volume of revelations to Smith and others was collected and published,
called the Book of Doctrine and Covenants.   This corresponds to the Christian's New Testament.   It may be
safely asserted, therefore, that previous to the innovations of Young, the Mormon religion was embodied in
these two volumes.   Their authority in the church is
universal and unquestioned.

"Let us examine these volumes, and see whether
they teach or countenance polygamy.

"The Book of Mormon nowhere contains a word
in favor of it."

Treating on this, ten citations are given from Book
of Mormon and the Doctrine and Covenants, page 178,

gives this as one: "As if to place this matter beyond any question, we have the following still more explicit testimony, on pages 115 and 118:

" 'And now it came to pass that the people of Nephi, under the reign of the second king, began to grow hard in their hearts and indulge themselves somewhat in wicked·practices, such as like unto David of old, desiring many wives and concubines, and also Solomon his son.'

" 'The word of God burdens me because of your grosser crimes. For behold, thus saith the Lord, this people begin to wax in iniquity; they understand not the Scriptures; for they seek to excuse themselves in committing whoredoms, because of the things which were written concerning David, and Solomon his son. Behold David and Solomon truly had many wives and concubines, which thing was abominable before me, saith the Lord; wherefore, thus saith the Lord, I have led this people forth out of the land of Jerusalem, by the power of mine arm, that I might raise up unto me a righteous branch from the fruit of the loins of Joseph. Wherefore, I, the Lord God, will not suffer that this people shall do like unto them of old. Wherefore, my brethren, hear me, and hearken to the word of the Lord; for there shall not any man among you have, save it be one wife; and concubines he shall have none; for I, the Lord God, delighteth in the chastity of women.   And whoredoms are an abomination before me; thus saith the Lord of Hosts.'— Jacob, 1st and 2d chapters, Book of Mormon.

"Here it is stated, as coming from God himself, that the polygamy and concubinage of David and Solomon were abominable before the Lord.   And yet we every day hear David and Solomon, as well as Abraham, Jacob, and others, cited by those practicing polygamy, as their illustrious prototypes, whose example is worthy of all imitation."

Page 180 says: "Let us now turn to the Book of Doctrine and Covenants, and see if we can find in that volume any authority for polygamy.   The following passages will determine the question:

" 'Thou shalt love thy wife with all thy heart, and shalt cleave unto her, and none else; and he that looketh upon a women to lust after her, shall deny the faith, and shall not have the spirit; and if he repents not he shall be cast out.'

"Again.   In 1845, the year after Smith's death, an Appendix was authoritatively added to the Book of Doctrine and Covenants, containing the following, which is extracted from the section entitled 'Marriage':

" '2.   Marriage should be celebrated with prayer and thanksgiving; and at the solemnization, the persons to be married standing together,' etc., 'he [the person officiating] shall say, calling each by their names, "you both mutually agree to be each other's companion, husband and wife, observing the legal rights belonging to this condition; that is, keeping yourselves wholly for each other, and from all others, during your lives."   And when they have answered "yes," he shall pronounce them "husband and wife," in the name of the Lord Jesus Christ, and by virtue of the laws of the country, and authority vested in him.' * *

" '4. * * Inasmuch as this church has been reproached with the crime of fornication and polygamy;

we declare that we believe that one man should have one wife; and one woman but one husband, except in case of death, when either is at liberty to marry again.'

"Can anything be more explicit than this?   Polygamy is not only expressly repudiated by the church, but is classed by the side of fornication as a crime.

"Thus we find that polygamy is contrary to both books of the Mormon Bible.   That it is, in fact, strongly condemned in those volumes.

"It is, therefore, no part of the Mormon religion, as given to the world by Joseph Smith."

Pages 247–249, give the several denials of polygamy of Joseph and Hyrum, Pratt, Spencer, Taylor, etc., up to 1850.

Page 172 says of Brigham's Theology, or Utah Mormonism: "The doctrines taught and practiced by the present head of the Mormon Church differ so much from the previously established tenants of the church, that they require a separate consideration.   One of the most important innovations upon the established doctrines of the church, is in relation to the Godhead.   In April, 1852, Brigham put forth the startling doctrine that Adam is God, and to be recognized and honored as such!   This announcement created some consternation among the Mormon theologians and some had the courage to oppose it."

Page 175 says: "Another doctrine of a startling character, promulgated by one of Young's counsellors and endorsed by him, is that of human sacrifice for the remission of sins.

"It was first announced by Jedediah M. Grant, Second Counsellor to the President, in the following language:

" 'Brethren and sisters, we want you to repent and forsake your sins.   And you who have committed sins that cannot be forgiven through baptism, let your blood be shed, and let the smoke ascend, that the incense thereof may come up before God as an atonement for your sins, and that the sinners in Zion· may be afraid.' —Deseret News, October 1, 1856.

"Again:

" 'We have been trying long enough with this people, and I go in for letting the sword of the Almighty be unsheathed, not only in word, but in deed.'—Ibid.

"In accordance with such bloody teaching, it is said that an altar of sacrifice was actually built by Grant, in the temple block, upon which these human sacrifices were to be made.   On the 21st of September, 1856, Grant said:

" 'I say there are men and women here that I would advise to go to the President immediately, and ask him to appoint a committee to attend to their case; and then let a place be selected, and let that committee shed their blood.'—Ibid., Vol. VI, p. 235."

Brigham is also quoted at length from Deseret News, October 1, 1856.

P. TUCKER'S "RISE AND PROGRESS OF MORMONISM" EXAMINED.

There are numerous publications abroad in the land that claim to give the history of the Church of Jesus Christ of Latter Day Saints, but which are in reality but the histories of the false reports that have been circulated by opposers of the work, and therefore only calculated to mislead the public mind, in reference to the rise of the Church, its origin, doctrine and practice, its aims, policy and objects.

It is not our object to enter into an examination of all these various works referred to, but to make a slight investigation of the one designated in our caption. It was written as late as 1867; at least was published in that year, and the writer had the advantage of similar works published prior to that date. Our apology for examining this work, is: The writer was a resident of Palmyra, N. Y., the place where the work began, about the time of the rise of the Church, and was acquainted (or claimed to have been) with the Smith family, Harris, Cowdery, and all the "Pioneer Mormons," and with all the important events connected with the "Advent of Mormonism." Let us examine these claims, and if we shall discover that "would-be witnesses" fail to give us a truthful relation of things they claim to see, then beware of the writings of those "far away."

We begin this review by reference to a statement found in the preface of Mr. Tucker's work, and which is as follows:

"The facts and reminiscences contained in this volume, based upon the author's personal knowledge and information, are produced to fill the blank and supply the omitted chapters in Mormon history," and "this truthful narrative is necessary to the completion of the history from the foundation of the institution."

We wish these statements to be borne in mind, for if they are true, we shall find that the author "personally knows" some very opposite things, that the sources of his "information" are very conflicting and contradictory, even amounting to "it is believed," "I have heard," and "it is thought," etc.

As testimony of the authenticity of the work, Mr. Tucker, on page five, cites names to the number of ten, and as an evidence of the strength of the evidence of his witnesses, inserts a letter from Mr. Thurlow Weed, some time of Rochester, N. Y., in which is found this statement: "The character you have given 'Joe Smith,' his family and associates, corresponds with what I have often heard from the old citizens of Palmyra." "Often heard." This needs no comment. In the first two chapters of the work we are treated to a pretty full history of the stories then current, (but these did not happen to be known till about 1827), concerning the boyhood days of Joseph Smith, and his father's family. Of all this, however, he could have had no knowledge till the tenth year of Smith's age, as he did not reside in Palmyra till of that age. Beside, there is nothing in the after years of Joseph's life to warrant the statements made by Mr. Tucker. He tells us, however, on page seventeen of the work, that as Joseph "further advanced in reading and knowledge, he assumed a spiritual or religious turn of mind, and frequently perused the Bible, becoming quite familiar with portions thereof, both of the Old and New Testaments."

But Mr. Tucker fearing he had said too much in Joseph's favor, immediately proceeds to kill the strength of the foregoing statement, by telling us on the eighteenth page, that: "In unbelief, theory and practice, the Smith family * * were unqualified Atheists." This latter saying not only contradicts the former one, but also the public record of their lives, as attested by their works, their friends and their foes. This illustrates the utter regardlessness, as to truth, of Mr.

Tucker in his pretended history of those he writes of.

In chapter two of Mr. Tucker's work, is a detailed account of some of the false stories that were manufactured by the enemies of the work, about the "fortune-telling," "money-digging" schemes of Joseph, all concocted to falsify and ridicule the fact of his having labored for one Mr. Stoal, of a neighboring county to Wayne, who believed there was money or silver on his farm, and who employed Joseph, in company with others, in digging for it. Why not brand the others as "money-diggers?" Nay, all the gold and silver miners of the "Great West?" Mr. Stoal failed to find the supposed treasure, and hence the failures of Joseph's "schemes!"

But this "long-continued" "career" of Smith's "failures" of "seven or eight years," all sprung out of a "curious shaped" "stone," found in digging a well for Mr. Clark Chase, in the year 1819, of which Joseph became possessed at the time—this was the "fortune-stone"— the "acorn" from which the Mormon tree grew.

On pages twenty-four and twenty-five is a lengthy description of one of Joseph's "money-digging," night scenes, said to have taken place by "lantern-light." He now "assumes a mysterious air," employs the "miraculous stone," goes to neighbor Stafford, who is "a respectable farmer in comfortable worldly circumstances," who supplies the "black sheep," the blood of which is to encircle that spot where the treasure lies buried in the earth. All being now in readiness, Joseph and his dupes repair to the spot, and the digging begins. All is silent, no one daring to speak! But bye and bye some one in a moment of forgetfulness speaks, the spell is broken, the treasure vanishes, and the work

ceases!   A retrospect of the locality shows that the
sheep's carcase is gone, investigation reveals that J.
Smith, Sen., has taken it to his house, "reduced to
mutton" for family use.   The above is only illustrative
of the many, and in all such work respectable farmers,
such as Harris and Stafford; with school teachers, such
as O. Cowdery, are engaged!   Does it seem reasonable
that respectable farmers and school teachers would be
duped in this way out of their sleep, property and
honesty?   And lawyers too! ?   But Mr. Tucker has not
informed us whether he was present as one of Joseph's
chief managers, or one of his dupes!   Probably the
latter, that is, if he knows these things to be true whereof he writes.   Mr. Tucker spoils all these stories, however, when he tells us, on page twenty-seven, that these
"failures" were of "seven or eight years" duration.
Can it be possible that men of sense and education could
thus be duped, and led, and deceived in such a manner for a period of seven or eight years?   Think of this,
ye respectable farmers, everywhere.   Could you be
made to believe that men of your class could be
deceived in this manner, by experiences not of a mystic
or spiritual character, but of a natural, physical character?   What utter nonsense!   If any body can be found
silly enough to believe these stories, then, in the language of Mr. Tucker, "The fools are not all dead yet."
I much prefer to believe in the doctrine of the minister-
ing of angels in this age of the world.

Mr. Tucker goes back to the pretended "little
stone," as a basis on which to novelize and ridicule the
Urim and Thummim.   And in attempting to account
for its non-existence in 1827, says: "This spectacle
pretension, is believed to have been purely an after-

thought, for it was not heard of outside of the Smith family for a considerable period subsequent to the first story." Yes, "it is believed," and we are called on to receive this belief as evidence.

There is no reason whatever for believing that these said-to-be first stories – false stories— had any existence till after the real events thus counterfeited by the false, had really transpired, and thus these pretended forethoughts, are in reality the after-thoughts, not of Joseph, or his opposers.   If the best evidence of the best witness is belief only, what of the testimony of a "far off" writer.

On pages 38 and 39, is enumerated the names of some thirty-one persons "and the remainder of the Smith family," with the statement, "It is believed that this list embraces all the persons residing at or near the prime seat of the Mormon advent, who from first to last made a profession of belief either in the money-digging, or Golden Bible finding pretensions of Joseph Smith, Jun." Another instance of "it is believed," but the writer does not tell us who it is believed by; does not even say whether he believes it or not.   But this kind of evidence seems to be characteristic of "the author's personal knowledge" of the things he writes concerning.   Belief is not evidence, either legal or historical, hence is no decision of this question.

On page 33, Mr. Tucker avers that it is further "believed" that the development of the Book of Mormon or the "plates" "was also a secondary invention."   By this it may be clearly seen that the very best evidence, that the most accredited historian on the negative side of this question concerning the

Urim and Thummim and the Book of Mormon is in possession of, is mere belief, and belief only. These examples serve to illustrate "the author's personal knowledge" of the historical "facts" he pretends to relate.

In dealing with this question the author encounters the plain, straightforward, unequivocal testimony of twelve witnesses to the veritable existence of the plates, and not being able to impeach their evidence by reference to character, proceeds to manufacture "another theory" as a basis for their testimony which he divulges at length on pages 74 and 75, entitled the "Glyph" theory; that is: As similar plates to those described by the witness in some respects, are referred to by Professor Rafinesque in his Atlantic Journal for 1832, and others found in Pike county, Illinois, in 1836.   "Smith may have obtained through Rigdon (the literary genius behind the screen) one of these glyphs, which resemble so nearly his description of the book he pretended to find on Mormon Hill. For the credit of human character, it is better at any rate to presume this, and that the eleven ignorant witnesses were deceived by appearances, than to conclude that they willfully committed such gross moral perjury before high heaven, as their solemn averments imply."

From this statement we learn that even Mr. Tucker had too much respect for the "moral" character of the witnesses to believe they would knowingly testify of things they knew not, and tries to apologize for their testimony on other grounds, as above stated.   This ought to have its due weight with those who consider this author as good authority.   But the testimony of the eleven witnesses was published to the world in 1830, and those plates described by Professor Rafinesque were not discovered till 1832, and those of Illinois in 1836. This "Glyph" theory will not answer, and this Mr. Tucker admits on page 112. He says, in speaking of the origin of the Book of Mormon, "It," the Glyph theory, "can in no wise apply in this case." And last, but not least, he only "presumes" all this "for the credit of human character." When we remember that Mr. Tucker was a resident of Palmyra in 1830, and had ample opportunity to investigate these events in detail, and that this was the best explanation he was able to give, as a result of his own investigation, what of the explanation of those "from afar?"

Mr Tucker, however, repudiates his own "Glyph" theory, as we have seen, to make room for the introduction of the "Spaulding Story" theory, as gathered from books that had been published prior to his own; thus manifesting his determination to write a book at all hazards, all this exemplary of "the author's personal knowledge."

In presenting his claims to our consideration of his rendering of the "Spaulding Story," he informs us that his data are "derived from the declarations of Mrs. Spaulding herself, as in 1831 and subsequently." Page 124. Our author anticipates the current date of the story, however, by telling us that, "Sidney Rigdon," who on pages 28 and 46, is styled "a mysterious stranger," frequently visited at Joseph's house between the years 1820-27, planning the arrangements to be subsequently developed. That these visits were "the subject of inquiry and conjecture by observers, from whom was withheld all explanation of his identity, or purpose." If these visits were subjects "of enquiry and conjecture" and "all explanation

of identity and purpose" was "withheld," how does
Mr. Tucker know that they were plotting this great
delusion during these years? More especially, if,
as he says on page 121, "they were mutually sworn" to
"secrecy and falsehood." How does he know that this
"mysterious stranger" was Rigdon, if "all explanation
of his identity was withheld?"

All this is mere "conjecture" with him, as with
other "observers." As to Rigdon's whereabouts from
the time of his birth till 1827, yes, 1830, the following
from the Family Record of Rigdon's father, is quite
satisfactory: "He returned to Pittsburgh in the winter of 1821 and '22, and took the care of the First Regular Baptist Church, and there continued to preach
until the Baptist Association met in Pittsburgh in 1824
Rev. Williams (at which time they brought some
charges against him for not being sound in the faith)
brought him to trial, but denied him the liberty of
speaking in self-defence, and he declared a non-fellow-
ship with them, and began to preach Campbellism.
And he and those that joined with him got the liberty
of the Court House; there they held their meetings,
and he and his brother-in-law, Mr. Brooks, followed
the tanning business till the winter of r827 and '28,
when he (S. Rigdon) moved somewhere into the Western Reserve of Ohio, and there continued to preach
till the Latter Day Saints came to that part of the
country, when he joined them and continued to be an
Elder in that Church (of Latter Day Saints, called
Mormons)." This is confirmed by Carvil Rigdon and
Peter Boyer, whose characters are attested by five
others, two of whom are members of the Old Regular
Baptist Church.

But, as Mr. Tucker admits that "the bearing of these circumstances (of the visits of the mysterious stranger to Joseph Smith during the years 1820–27) upon any important question, can only be left to reasonable conjecture in reference to the subsequent developments," we need not devote further space to a refutation of this assumption. Page 48.

We are told on pages 122 and 123, that Spaulding took his manuscript to a Mr. Patterson of Pittsburg, a printer, for publication. Patterson did not print it. In 1816 "it was reclaimed by the author, who in that year removed to Amity, Washington county, N. Y., where he died in 1827." But this same Mrs. Spaulding, who supplies the above data, says in her Boston letter, published in the Episcopal Recorder: "At length the manuscript was returned to the author, and soon after we removed to Amity, Washington county, Pa., where Mr. Spaulding deceased in 1816." Mr. Tucker further says, page 123, that "one Sidney Rigdon" was in the office of Patterson in 1816, "and the probable solution of the mystery of the Book of Mormon is found in the fact that he had made a copy of Spaulding's manuscript, and communicated information of the existence of the fictitious record to Joseph Smith, Jun." Also, page 125 "Rigdon was in possession of a copy of this manuscript before he had heard of Smith's money-digging delusions." But, we ask, What object had Rigdon in making "a copy" of this romance ere he became acquainted with Smith and his designs touching the establishment of a church? An answer is unneccessary. Rev. Samuel Williams of Pittsburgh, a bitter opponent of the Latter Day Saints, on the twenty-second page of his Mormonism Exposed; says: "Rigdon came to this city and connected himself with the First Regular Baptist Church on the 28th of January, 1822."

Dr. Hulbert, an apostate from the Church of Latter Day Saints, said in 1834, on the 289th page of his History of Mormonism: "Now, as Spaulding's book can nowhere be found, or anything heard of it after being carried to this establishment, there is the strongest presumption that it remained there in seclusion till about the year 1823 or 1824, at which time Sidney Rigdon located himself in that city."

Rigdon's Family Record says he went to Pittsburg in the "winter of 1822 and '23." Hence, Rigdon was not in Pittsburgh for eight years after the manuscript was taken to Amity by its author, and therefore had no opportunity of copying it, and Mr. Tucker's "fact" is a false one. Now, while Mrs. Spaulding tells Mr. Tucker that the manuscript was reclaimed by the author in 1816, she informs Dr. Hulbert that she "was unable to tell whether it was ever returned or not from this office."—Tucker, page 123; Howe, page 287.

Our reason for introducing the testimony of Howe, is that Mrs. Spaulding's statements are the basis of his data likewise, and no two persons whose writing we have yet consulted, render her story alike. And this fact demonstrates that the sources of their information are not to be relied on. And further, shows this Spaulding Story to be a mere conjuration by the enemies of the work of God.

Again, Mr. Tucker says, page 123: "The manuscript remained in the widow's possession until it was missed or stolen from a trunk in Otsego county, where she had removed about the time the Book of Mormon began to be publicly spoken of." Howe says: "She was unable to tell whether it was ever returned or not from this office." In her Boston letter Mrs. Spaulding says:

"The manuscript then (1816) fell into my hands and was carefully preserved. It has frequently been examined by my daughter [who was five years old when the manuscript was written in 1809–10, see Haven's letter in the Quincy (Ill.) Whig, and was twelve years old when she read it in 1816 or 1817], Mrs. McKinstery, of Monson, Massachusetts, with whom I now reside, and by other friends. After the Book of Mormon came out a copy of it was taken to New Salem. * * The excitement became so great in New Salem that the inhabitants had a meeting, and deputed Dr. Philastus Hulbert, to repair to this place and obtain from me the original manuscript of Mr. Spaulding, for the purpose of comparing it with the Mormon Bible, to satisfy their own minds and to prevent their friends from embracing an error so delusive. This was in the year 1834. Dr. Hulbert brought with him an introduction and request for the manuscript signed by Messrs. Henry Lake, Aaron Wright and others, with all of whom I was acquainted, as they were my old neighbors when I resided at New Salem."

Can any one tell from the three foregoing statements whether the manuscript was stolen, remained at Patterson's office, or whether it was preserved carefully by Spaulding's widow till 1834. Yet these authors all claim that the widow Spaulding is their authority for the three contradictory stories. How many Spaulding stories are there as origins of the Book of Mormon?

Would not any judge, justice or jury in all the land dismiss such a witness as the above testimony shows Mrs. Spaulding to be, from the court and reject the evidence as unworthy of credence?   It seems so to us.

Now this whole story of Rigdon's copying the manuscript seems to contradict what Mr. Tucker had before said on page 36:   "The manuscripts were in the handwriting of one Oliver Cowdery."   The reason assigned was "Cowdery had been a school-master, and was the only man in the band who could make a copy for the printer."

Thus it seems, the more we investigate this Spaulding Story, as to its giving rise to, or relation to the Book of Mormon, the greater the humbuggery of the story appears.   And Mr. Tucker's efforts relative to this, like those of his predecessors, amount to nothing against the work.

On pages 55 and 56, in referring to the printing of the Book of Mormon, Mr. Tucker tells us that: "The first and second books of Nephi and some other portions of the forthcoming revelations were printed in sheets; and armed with a copy of these, Smith commenced other preparations for a mission to Pennsylvania, where he had some relatives residing, and where the before mentioned Rev. Sidney Rigdon was then (1829) residing, or temporarily sojourning." Mr. Tucker is not certain about where Rigdon then resided, but bye and bye he grows more positive, and on page 76, he tells: "He was a backsliding clergyman of the Baptist persuasion, and at the period referred to (1830) was the principle preacher of a sort of religious society calling themselves 'Reformers,' or 'Disciples,' at Mentor, Ohio, near Kirtland."   While this latter statement seems to harmonize with and support the "Family Record" of Rigdon, it surely contradicts and invalidates the former one, and still further illustrates the utter unreliability of Mr. Tucker's history of the "Rise and Progress of Mormonism."

Again, on page 76: "This man Rigdon now [1830, see page 126] appeared as the first regular Mormon preacher in Palmyra." Now as the Church was organized on the 6th of April, and a conference was held in June, 1830, near Palmyra, and as Joseph Smith, Oliver Cowdery and others took missions from this conference, and they had all preached at Palmyra, how could Rigdon appear "as the first regular Mormon preacher at Palmyra?" More especially, since Mr. Tucker himself informs us on page eighty-two, that: "In the summer of 1830 the founders of the Mormon Church then remaining at the scene of its birthplace * * went to Mentor, Ohio, the residence of Rigdon, and of Parley P. Pratt, his friend and co-worker." "Near this place is Kirtland, where there were a few families belonging to Rigdon's congregation. * * Seventeen of these people, men and women, readily espoused the new revelation, and were immersed by Cowdery in one night."

We learn by these statements, first, that Rigdon resided in Ohio, instead of Pennsylvania, in 1829 and 1830; second, that instead of preaching the Mormon faith at Palmyra then, he was a pastor of a congregation of "Disciples" at Mentor, Ohio; that seventeen of his congregation were baptized by Cowdery, when on his mission west, in the latter part of 1830.

On page 56, Mr. Tucker speaks further of Smith's visit to northern Pennsylvania, as before referred

to, and says: "The result was, that in November,
[1829, see page 55], Smith went to northern Pennsylvania, as previously appointed, when he married
the daughter of Isaac Hale, and was baptized after the
Mormon ritual—Rigdon being the 'match-maker' and
officiating 'clergyman' in these celebrations."

As to Joseph's marriage, Mr. Tucker falsifies in
three points, viz: Joseph was married by Squire Tarbell, in South Bainbridge, Chenango county, New
York, January 18th, 1827.   See birth and marriage
record of Joseph Smith, Sen., as published in "Joseph
Smith the Prophet," page 40; printed 1853; written
by Joseph's mother.

Mrs. Emma Smith, one of the parties to the marriage under consideration, about three months prior to
her death, in reply to the following question: "Who
performed the marriage ceremony for Joseph Smith and
Emma Hale? When? Where?" as propounded by her
own son, Joseph Smith, now of Plano, Illinois, answered: "I was married at South Bainbridge, New
York, at the house of Squire Tarbell, by him, when I
was in my twenty-second or twenty-third year."   (See
the Saints' Herald, number for October 1st, 1879).
As to Joseph's baptism, by Oliver Cowdery, in May,
1829.   See "Pearl of Great Price," page 45; "Joseph
Smith the Prophet," page 131.   Now while these works
cited place the date of Joseph's baptism in May, 1829,
Mr. Tucker says it was subsequent to November of that
year; and while they say Cowdery officiated, he says
Rigdon baptized him.   One is the evidence of Smith
and Cowdery; the other is according to the "information" of Mr. Tucker.   How creditable the sources of
Mr. Tucker's information!

Mr. Tucker is not satisfied with having made false and contradictory statements concerning the foregoing subjects and characters, but proceeds to falsify and misrepresent the plain, unequivocal record and historical statements of the Book of Mormon itself, and hence on page 35 of his work, in referring to the translation of the Book of Mormon, says: "These translations purported to relate to the history of scattered tribes of the earth, chiefly Nephites and Lamanites, who, after the confusion of tongues at the tower of Babel, had been directed by the Lord across the sea to this then wilderness land, where they mostly perished by wars among themselves, and by famine and pestilence, and from whose remnants sprang our North American Indians." Now, while it is true that the Book represents that the Aborigines of America sprang from the Lamanites alone, it does not say that the Nephites and Lamanites "had been directed by the Lord across the sea," at any time, or from any place. The progenitors of the Nephites and Lamanites never had been at the tower of Babel, so far as is now known to us through any record whatever. And we believe this statement of Mr. Tucker to be a willful misrepresentation of the record, just like hundreds of other subjects he refers to, as we are able to make manifest.

Our reason for so believing, is because he has devoted the greater part of three or four chapters of his work to extracts from the Book of Mormon itself, and in making his selections and arranging them, it is plainly manifest that he was not ignorant of its contents. Moreover, some of the very extracts which he gives are from the Books of Nephi, and contain the history of the progenitors of the Nephites and Lamanites; of their exodus from Jerusalem, about six hundred years before Christ, as may be seen by referring to the eighty-sixth and eighty-seventh pages of the work. When a pretended author knowingly and willfully misrepresents and falsifies a plain matter of record like this, can we accept as valid and true his writings on any subject treated of by him? Enough has been culled from the work already, to arouse the suspicions of those who have trusted his veracity, and to create doubt in their minds as to his honesty as a historian. His testimony should be discredited and rejected.

On the fifty eighth page, Mr. Tucker, in giving an account of the organization of the Church, says: "This ceremony, conducted with apparent seriousness by the prophet, supported on the right and left by Cowdery and Harris—of which it is now too late to write the full particulars from memory—took place at the dwelling-house of Joseph Smith, Sen., in the month of June, 1830. There was no praying, singing or preaching attempted, but Joseph gave various readings and interpretations of the new Bible. The senior Smith was installed as Patriarch and President of the Church of Jesus Christ of Latter Day Saints."

A glance at the above statement will detect no less than three falsities. First, the Church, instead of being organized in the month of June, was organized April the 6th, 1830. But we are sure that Mr. Tucker means to tell us and have us to understand that this organization that was affected in June, was the first and original organization of the Church, for on the next—the fifty-ninth page—he styles it "this incipient church inauguration;" and on the next, or sixtieth page, "this preliminary launching of the Mormon ship" Zion—"this

primeval foundation." Now if our author was at Palmyra when the "incipient" organization of the Church
was effected, April 6th, 1830, and was not aware of it,
nor had he learned it after thirty-seven anniversary
conferences had convened, all on April 6th, in com-
memoration of the "incipient" organization, what does
the authenticity of his history amount to?   Secondly,
"No praying, singing or preaching was attempted" on
this occasion.   This meeting referred to was the first
conference ever held by the Church, and the thought
expressed by our author (?) is altogether an unreasonable one.   There were more than thirty persons present
at this meeting, according to Mr. Tucker himself.   And
the idea that a conference would be held and no praying, singing, or preaching even attempted, is evidently
untrue.   Yet, he describes to us that "Cowdery and
Harris" were ordained to office, by laying on of hands,
and that other "ceremonious observances" were attended to.   These other ceremonies are not described,
but had they been, would no doubt have contradicted
the statement referred to, that there was neither prayer
nor song.   Thirdly, "The senior Smith was installed
Patriarch and President of the Church of Jesus Christ
of Latter Day Saints."   How this statement could be
made by Mr. Tucker, with the history of the Church,
for and against it, for thirty-seven years before him,
we are unable to explain, unless it be his desire willfully
to misrepresent and falsify.   Those who are acquainted
to any extent whatever, with the history of the rise of
the Church, are aware that this is a clear mistake.

On page 130, Mr. Tucker repeats this same story:
"Joseph Smith, Sen., the first Patriarch and President
of the Church;" but, on pages 134 and 135, he informs

us better, and contradicting the former statements, tells us: "Joseph Smith, Jun., was the first President;" and after quoting from some of the early revelations of Joseph, as now found in the Book of Doctrine and Covenants to prove this, says in conclusion: "By these exalted authorities, the prophet becomes the president of the Church." This surely entitles our author (?) to valid authenticity!

For the sake of consistency, we must quote once more from page 35: "These translations purported to relate to the history of scattered tribes of the earth, chiefly 'Nephites' and 'Lamanites,' who, after the confusion of tongues at the tower of Babel, had been directed by the Lord across the sea to this then wilderness land." And to the above annex as a part of a summary, as given on page 85: "The reader will discover a chain of events, incidents, episodes, perils, and tribulations, by wilderness and by sea, constituting the story of immigration by various Israelitish tribes, with their brazen and golden records, from the beginning of their journeyings at Jerusalem, to the consummation of the same in the promised land."

The Nephites and Lamanites referred to in the first quotation, are the descendants of but a part of ONE Israelitish tribe, that came from Jerusalem, six hundred years before Christ, instead of from Babel, after the confusion of tongues. Both of these statements misrepresent the claims of the Book of Mormon in some points, while they contradict each other in others; at the same time they manifest the utter unscrupulousness of the writer, as well as his disregard as to whether he states the facts in the case or not. A writer that will falsify the historic statements of a record, will give false renderings as to its origin.

We now call attention to a lengthy statement found on page 125, where, in referring to the coming forth forth, printing, and other circumstances connected with the publication of the Book of Mormon, says:

"Indeed, it is apparent from the MARKED CHANGES IN STYLE OF COMPOSITION occurring in numbers of instances, that EMENDATIONS AND ADDITIONS WERE MADE by some other than the original writer's hand. Then, too, the verbose title-page—the 'preface' in regard to the translations lost by the incendiarism of Mrs. Harris— the testimonies of witnesses, and the long line of revelations that followed—WHICH ARE NOT PRESUMED TO HAVE BEEN COMPOSED BY THE ILLITERATE SMITH, BUT BY RIGDON DURING SMITH'S LIFE-TIME—all these are strong corrob orative considerations connected with the proofs that Rigdon supplied the literary aliment needed in conforming the Spaulding production to the grand co-partnership Mormon speculation. And it is not known that he has ever disclaimed the part that for more than thirty years has been publicly assigned to him in the great plagiarism and imposture."

We have emphasized some words in the foregoing, and wish them to be considered. The "unity" of "style of composition" that characterizes the Book of Mormon, all through it, has been urged by many as an objection, when it is considered that it is a compilation of many books, written by as many different writers, or nearly so. But this objection has been answered by the fact that the compilation was effected mainly by one man. And were it not for this latter fact, the objection would be a valid one. The "emendations" referred to, are simply an abridgement and

condensation of the parts not compiled by the compiler.   As to the additions which our author (?) supposes
to be found in the books, just the opposite is true, for
instead of adding to the writings of those he compiled,
the compiler condensed and abridged much of their
writings, and what the compiler has said of himself, is
no addition to their writings.   As to "the title," "preface," "testimony of the witnesses," "lost translations"
and the "long line of revelations," their writing, or
composition, Mr. Tucker presumes they were written,
not by "Smith, but by Rigdon, during Smith's life-
time."   As all this is presumption with no evidence to
sustain it, it needs no refutation.   Mr. Tucker does
not claim to have been informed of all this, much less
to have "personal knowledge of it."   This presumption
is said to be a "strong corroborative consideration connected with the proof that Rigdon supplied the literary
aliment needed in conforming the Spaulding production
to the grand co-partnership Mormon speculation."
The "proofs" that the above allegation is true, have
been examined and compared, and have been found to
be contradictory and false; and this presumptive aux-
iliary to the "proof" is as true as the proof has been
found to be.   In relation to the last sentence of this
quotation, we say most emphatically that "it is known"
that Rigdon "had disclaimed," and most positively
denied "the part that for more than thirty years has
been publicly assigned to him in the great plagiarism
and imposture," that he is said, (though not proved),
to have committed, in connection with the origin of
the Book of Mormon.   As evidence of this, see his
letter written to Messrs Bartlett and Sullivan, Editors
of some periodical, on the 27th of May, 1839.   This

letter was reprinted, and published as late as 1843 or 1844; and was also inserted in another work published as a "History of the Mormons," and is recorded on pages 45–48. The title page of this latter history was torn off ere it came into our possession, hence we know not the author's name, but it was written subsequent to 1849, as it contains a lengthy article from a correspondent of the New York Tribune, from Salt Lake City, July 8th, 1849, which stands on pages 310–314. This proves that Mr. Tucker writes falsely in regard to Sidney Rigdon. And we scarce believe that, when collating data for his work, he was ignorant of all this.

Mr. Rigdon says: "If I were to say that I ever heard of the Rev. Solomon Spaulding and his wife, until Dr. P. Hulbert wrote his lie about me, I should be a liar like unto themselves. Why was not the testimony of Mr. Patterson obtained to give force to this shameful tale of lies? The only reason is, he was not a fit tool for them to work with; he would not lie for them; if he were called on, he would testify to what I have here said."

Mr. Tucker gives a very lengthy account of the troubles of the Saints, while in the State of Missouri; of the arbitrations of the Saints and citizens; of the riotous scenes that followed; and on page 161, says: "Riotous scenes of violence followed. The printing office was destroyed, several of the 'saints' were tarred and feathered, and others were killed and wounded while defending their rights." He concludes his story of these events on page 166, as follows: "Perhaps the occasion should not pass without the remark, that by enlightened people the Mormons were regarded as the victims of misguided vengeance in Missouri. The ruffianly violence they encountered at the hands of lawless mobs, in several instances eventuating in deliberate murder, finds no extenuation in any alleged provocation. The due process of law might have afforded adequate redress for the criminalities of which they should be found guilty on legal trial. Such was the view of the subject rightly taken by the people. of Illinois and of the world, though it may have been wrongfully applied in favor of the persecuted."

When it is remembered that the data used by Mr. Tucker, as the basis of his history of these Missouri scenes, are the statements of the civil and military officers of the state, uttered during the 'excitement of those times, the foregoing are peculiarly strange admissions to be made by one so bitterly opposed to the Church as Mr. Tucker was. That the unparalleled persecutions of the Saints was brought on by "lawless mobs" is surely more than was aimed to be said, and ought to be duly considered by those who hold to Mr. Tucker as authority.

"The due process of law," is all the Saints ever asked at the hands of the officers of the Government, as their entreaties and "petitions," and "memorials" to the State and United States Governments will show. And the only reply ever received to these written instruments, were, by Missouri, "You must be exterminated;" by the Union, "Your cause is just, but we can do nothing for you."

But the testimonies of the opposing side of this question, as on others, is contradictory and conflicting. Hence, page 162, speaking of the efforts of the Saints to obtain redress for their wrongs, says: "In

the interim, the Governor of the State was appealed to
by the Mormons for redress, and he advised them to
apply to the courts," and in their efforts to carry out
this advice, and urging their suits in the courts, "a
further lawless violence was thus provoked."   And on
page 165, represents Gov. Boggs as saying to the Legislature of Missouri, in 1840:   "These people had vio-
lated the laws of the land by open force and armed
resistence to them; they had undertaken, without the
aid of the civil authority, to redress their real or fancied
grievances."

One or the other of these statements is untrue, for
they are opposed to each other, and an honest historian
would have ascertained which was true and left the false
statement out, if he wished to be believed.

On page 164, Mr. Tucker represents General
Clark as writing to Gov. Boggs, in 1838:   "There is
no crime from treason down to petit larceny, but these
people, or a majority of them, have been guilty of."

Now as to the truthfulness of this communication
we can better judge, by a comparison of this with a
statement uttered by this same Gen. Clark in his address to the Mormons, about the year 1838, which says:
"Another thing yet remains for you to comply with—
that is, that you leave the State forthwith; and whatever your feelings concerning this affair, whatever your
innocence, it is nothing to me.   General Lucas, who is
equal in authority with me, has made this treaty with
you, I am determined to see it carried out."—History
of the Mormons, page 111.   A treaty has been entered
into between the Saints and Gen. Lucas, and Gen.
Clark was to see it carried out.   As to the innocency
of the Saints, this was nothing to him; thus admitting

that he knows nothing of their innocence or guilt.   But
of their innocency he cares not; he simply is determined
to carry out the treaty of Gen. Lucas.

Mr. Tucker's work is mainly a revision of previously printed works, as is manifest from his reference to
subjects treated of by Howe and others; not only in
regard to the Spaulding story, but the history of Mrs.
Waite is cited; as also introduction to Wright & Co's
New York edition of the Book of Mormon, and a
lengthy article written by Ex-Gov. S. S. Harding
expressly for this work.   And, hence, a refutation of
the false statements made in this work, is an answer to
all the works referred to by Mr. Tucker.

In view of the above, we see why the forged, or
pretended affidavit, as gotten up by Howe, is referred
to by Mr. Tucker on the 128th page of his work,
and fathered on to one Peter Ingersoll.   Now we are
credibly informed that this same Peter Ingersoll lives in
Lapeer county, Michigan, and solemnly denies ever
making oath to the subject referred to, or any other
subject connected with the faith of the Saints.   This
affidavit is ''Dated Palmyra, Wayne county, New York,
December 2d, 1833, certified by Thomas T. Baldwin,
Judge of Wayne county, to have been sworn to before
him according to law, 9th day of December, 1833.''

In 1833, there was no such office as Judge of
''County Court.''   Circuit Courts, Courts of Oyer and
Terminer, Common Pleas and General Sessions were
held for every county, but there was no ''County
Court.''   For these latter statements we are indebted to
a ''Mr. W. W.,'' of Boyne, Michigan, December 6th,
1876.

This pretended affidavit, manufactured by Dr. Hul-

bert alias Howe, is used by Mr. Tucker as evidence
against the Saints in his efforts to degrade their character, and is only another evidence of the utter
unscrupulousness of Mr. Tucker, as to the truth or
falsity of what he uses as evidence against those he
opposes.

An occasional anecdote characterizes the work of
Mr. Tucker, but these are the statements only of "fun-
loving dare-devils" and "notorious wags," and we are
inclined to the idea that the greater part of his data is
from a like source.   See pages 31 and 80.

The "Rise and Progress of Mormonism" contains
a lengthy history of the Utah apostates, and the pretended revelation on polygamy, accepting at the same
time the assumption that it was developed by Joseph
Smith.   As to this assumption, the only evidence
ever produced to sustain it is the word of Brigham
Young, and his word only; and though he claims that
it was in existence as early as 1843, and that Emma
Smith, Joseph's wife, burned the original revelation, he
(Brigham) preserved a copy of it, but never considered
it expedient to present it to the Church, or bring it to
light, till 1852, which he then did at a special conference in Salt Lake City, asking that it be received as authority.   As to the burning of the original, Mrs. Emma
Smith says, "This is a lie, made out of whole cloth."
This she said as late as 1867.   And in the same conversation with Elder J. W. Briggs, now of Iowa, in
1867, in reply to the question, "Did you ever see that
document [the pretended revelation] in manuscript or
previous to its publication by Pratt?" (1852).   Answer
by Mrs. Bidamon, (Smith), "I never did."   This conversation is found on page 7, of "A Criticism upon

the so called Revelation, of 1843," by J. W. Briggs.
And he that fabricates a falsehood in regard to the pretended history of a pretended revelation, would do the
same in regard to its pretended origin.   There is no
evidence that such an instrument of writing as this pretended revelation is, ever came through, or originated
with Joseph Smith.   We challenge any credible evidence.

Mr Tucker is not satisfied with charging Joseph
with having originated polygamy, but also with practicing the doctrine; with having "forty wives all told."
Just as well tell a big lie as a little one, while he is
about it.   But there is not one word of evidence of the
truthfulness of this on record anywhere.   As our reply
to this charge will conclude our investigation and expos-
ition of Mr. Tucker's work, we shall not amplify to any
great extent, — shall not here introduce the many negative proofs, as found in the Book of Mormon and Doctrine and Covenants, as these, with others, are extensively circulated through the medium of the tracts published by the Church, also the Saints' Herald.   We
shall, however, append a few questions, as propounded
to Mrs. Emma Bidamon, formerly Smith, by her son,
Joseph, about three months prior to her death, and
her answers, "whereby though she being dead, yet
speaketh."

"QUESTION.—'What of spiritual wifery?'

"ANSWER.—'There was no revelation on either
polygamy or spiritual wifery.   No such thing as polygamy, or spiritual wifery, was taught, either publicly
or privately, before my husband's death, that I now
have, or ever had any knowledge of.'

"Q.—'Did he not have other wives than yourself?'

"A.—'He had no other wife but me; nor did he to my knowledge ever have.'

"Q.—'Did he not hold marital relation with other women than yourself?'

"A.—'He did not have improper relations with any woman that ever came to my knowledge.' "—The Saints' Herald, Oct. 1st, 1879.

This testimony was borne by Sister Emma, to her own son, only about three months before her death, and is now recorded, and consequently is of force. Just prior to death is the wrong time of one's life to bear false witness and deny the wrong done during life, or to conceal the wrongs of others with whom they have been connected.   This testimony, therefore, should, with all honest people, be an end of controversy relative to this subject, and forever close the mouths of "false accusers" "of the brethren."

As we have reviewed the modern historical part of this work, except that part which relates to the people of Utah, and as we are not "set for the defense" of those in apostasy, we now submit our efforts to a candid public, asking a patient hearing, and a faithful comparison of this our review with the "work reviewed."   C. SCOTT.

LAWRENCE, Michigan, Nov. 14th, 1879.

The above lengthy expose is inserted for the reason that Tucker was a resident of Palmyra, New York, and had access to the entire work of both Hulbert and Howe, as well as others, up to 1867, when his work was issued.

LIFE IN UTAH;

OR THE MYSTERIES AND CRIMES OF MORMONISM,

BY J. H. BEADLE, 1870.

"Several works have appeared, purporting to be exposures of the secret rites and mysteries of this strange sect, but none have been complete, and few authentic. The high praise which this work has received from members of Congress, and Government officials to whom it was submitted, and by whom its publication was urged as a duty to the country, stamps it as no ordinary work, but as one of the most powerful and thrilling books ever published."

After giving items of Joseph Smith's birth, etc., Beadle says, on page 22: "Almost innumerable are the stories of his youth, giving bright promise of future rascality. But many of them depend on little more than popular report, and we can only receive as authentic those events which rest upon the sworn testimony of reliable men who were his neighbors."

Connecting Smith and Rigdon and alleging Solomon Spaulding's manuscript was stolen of Mrs. Spaulding says, page 22: "She thinks it was stolen from her trunk. Thus far all is clear. * *"

How is that for sworn evidence? Of the evidence setting forth that the Book of Mormon was made up from Spaulding's manuscript. Beadle on page 32, says: "Suffice it to say, that while it is of moral force sufficient to convince most minds, it is yet not such proof as would establish the fact beyond all doubt, or convict Smith and Rigdon of theft and forgery in a court of justice."

Mr. Beadle's sworn testimony seems to be lacking! But let Mr. Beadle speak again; page 27 says: "The 'Book of Mormon' was first given to the world early in 1830, when three thousand volumes were published, under contract, by Mr. Pomeroy Tucker, then proprietor of a paper in the county."

On page 33, Beadle says: "In August of 1830, Parley P. Pratt, a young Campbellite preacher, came on a visit especially to hear of the new faith, and was at once converted, and soon after, Sidney Rigdon appeared as a leading Mormon."

And on page 34: "Rigdon had previously collected a band of nearly one hundred persons, who called themselves Disciples, mostly seceders from other denominations, holding to a literal and rapid fulfillment of the prophecies, very fanatical and looking daily for 'some great event to occur.' Many of these adopted the new faith at once, and a church of thirty was organized."

In the light of the preceding, how does this sound from page 32: "The best evidence furthermore shows, that Sidney Rigdon was the prime mover in the fraud, and that Joe Smith was conveniently put forward as the Prophet."

Mrs. Emma Smith is written of on page 33: "She became thoroughly disgusted at her husband's religion while in Nauvoo, and expressed no particular regret at his death; she refused to emigrate to Utah, but apostatized and married a Gentile, and is rather

popular as land-lady of the old Mansion House, at
Nauvoo." She never wavered, raised her family in
the faith, and she died firm in it in 1879.

Beadle disposes of Cowdery, Harris and Whitmer,
the three witnesses, thus, on page 26. Cowdery: "He
led a rambling life for many years, and died a short
time since a miserable drunkard " He died reaffirming his testimony in a most solemn manner, in February,
1850, at Richmond, Missouri, which was twenty years
before Beadle wrote.

Harris next: "He continued with the Mormons
till his means were exhausted, and, having quarrelled
with Joe Smith, in Missouri, returned to his old residence in New York." Harris died in Utah, also
reaffirming his testimony at time of his death in 1875.

"Of David Whitmer little is known. He dropped
out of the Mormon community, in one of the 'drives'
in Missouri, and settled in that State." Yes, Mr.
Beadle knew or wrote little. Whitmer lived at Richmond, Missouri, from 1838 to January 25th, 1888, was
often interviewed by the press of various leading cities.
Mrs. Smith, Cowdery, Harris and Whitmer are wantonly
misrepresented in his alleged authentic work!

Page 48 says: "Joe Smith, Hyrum Smith, and
forty others were held for trial, and the militia officers
forthwith organized a Court Martial and condemned
several of them to be shot. But General Doniphan,
a sound lawyer and brave man, by a firm use of his
authority and influence, prevented this foolishly illegal
action. The prisoners were taken before the nearest
Circuit Judge and put upon trial 'for treason, murder,
robbery, arson, larceny, and breach of the peace.'
They could not well have been tried for more, but it

seems by the evidence that many of them were guilty
on most of the charges. They were committed to jail
to await their final trial. The evidence in the case was
printed by order of the Missouri legislature, and presents a singular instance of how a few knaves may lead
to their destruction a whole people, if sufficiently ignorant and fanatical."

Page 50 says: "The Missourians found, in the
meantime, that they had 'caught an elephant;' they had
Joe Smith, his brother Hyrum, and forty others in jail
on a multitude of charges, but many of the witnesses
were gone, the trial would have been long and expen-
sive, and it was probably the best policy to get them
all out of the State in such a way that none would
re-enter it, rather than condemn a few to the peniten-
tiary."

What difference, Mr. Beadle, about witnesses gone,
with evidence printed by order of legislature? Hard
to make a case against an innocent people.

Page 58: "A city rose as if by magic. Temporary in character as most of the buildings were, rude
log houses or frame shanties, they served to shelter the
rapidly gathering Saints. The first house on the new
site was erected June 11, 1839, and in eighteen months
thereafter, there were two thousand dwellings besides
school houses and other public buildings * * The
temporary buildings, in no long time, gave way to more
permanent buildings; improvements multiplied on every
hand, and Joe Smith had almost daily revelations
directing how every work should be carried on."

Compare with preceding, this, page 74: "Two
years had not elapsed since the first fugitives arrived at
Nauvoo before the Mormons outnumbered the old

settlers. * * None of the promised advantages had accrued from the settlement of the Mormons among them. They had created but little trade or commerce, had made no improvement of the rapids, had established no manufactories, erected no school houses, organized no institutions for instruction, and made no provision for the support of the poor."

Beadle, quoting Gov. Ford, on page 98, says: "Justice, however, requires me here to say, that upon such investigation as I then could make, the charge of promiscuous stealing appeared to be exaggerated."

Ford again, page 111: "The Mormons had been represented to me as a lawless, infatuated and fanatical people, not governed by the ordinary motives which influence the rest of mankind."

Another statement of his, page 98: "But the great cause of popular fury was, that the Mormons at several preceding elections had cast their vote as a unit, thereby making the fact apparent, that no one could aspire to the honors or offices of the country within the sphere of their influence, without their approbation and votes."

It was similar in Missouri. Beadle says, page 39: "In April, 1833, a number of Missourians came together in Independence, and decided that 'means of defence ought to be taken,' but determined upon nothing. The first June number of the 'Morning and Evening Star' contained an intemperate article, headed, 'Free People of Color,' which excited the wrath of the old citizens against the Mormons, as 'abolitionists,' and was answered by a small pamphlet, headed, 'Beware of False Prophets.' As summer advanced, it appeared that the Mormons would be sufficiently numerous to carry the county at the August election, and this roused all the fears of the old settlers afresh. Without apparent concert, an armed mob of three hundred assembled at Independence, tore down the newspaper office, tarred and feathered several of the Saints, whipped two of them a little, and ordered all to leave the county."

¶ Page 116 says: "The spiritual wives of the dead Prophet filled the city with their cries, but his lawful wife Emma, was quiet and resigned."

Dr. B. W. Richmond, an eye witness, and not a Mormon, said of Emma Smith: "Six times she attempted to see the bodies, and six times she was removed in the arms of her two attendants."—Herald, January 1, 1876.

Page 82 contains: "So completely had Joe's head been turned and so wild and visionary had he become, that it was not without reason that his wife, only a few years after his death, published a statement in the 'Quincy Whig' that she had no belief in his prophetic character, and considered his pretended revelations the emanations of a diseased mind."   She did nothing of the kind, or more than one expose of Mormonism would have published it; why does not Mr. Beadle furnish it?

Page 375 says: "Joseph Smith had a dozen spiritual wives; but three sons survived him – all of his legal wife "   Strange that an even dozen were not prolific!

Of Joseph Smith's fortune, reputed to be a million, that accumulated from sale of land, Beadle gives one use he put it to on page 428:   "With this he paid all his old debts in Ohio." * *

Mr. Beadle divides time on page 351:   "I.   The

monogamic period: from its origin till 1843, during which time all their publications and sermons were opposed to polygamy in their tone. II. The transition period: from 1843 till 1852, when polygamy was secretly taught and extended, but openly denied and condemned. III. The polygamic period: from 1852 to the present, in all which time polygamy has been avowed and defended as an essential part of Mormon religion."

Page 347 says: "So the doctrine was more and more openly discussed, and finally, on the 29th of August, 1852, it was publicly announced by Brigham Young, in a meeting at Salt Lake City, where the revelation was for the first time publicly read and pronounced valid."

Page 429: "In 1860, young Smith was 'called as a Prophet' and the 'Re-organized Church' was set up, with head-quarters at Plano, Illinois. They number twenty or thirty thousand in the West, and have flourishing missions in Great Britain and Scandinavia. In July, 1863, E. C. Briggs and Alex. McCord, their first missionaries to Utah, reached Salt Lake and created quite a sensation; Brigham intimated to them that their lives were in danger, and refused them the use of any public building in the city. But General Connor was then in command at Camp Douglas, with a small provost guard in the city, and the Brighamites dared not try violence; Briggs visited the people at their homes and preached wherever Gentiles would open their houses to him, and soon had many converts. Nearly two hundred of these left the territory in 1864, under a military escort furnished by General Connor, and since that time many more have left Utah, and their missions there include over five hundred members.

See how Mr. Beadle plies his pen on the fly question! Verily he is a great writer and discloses often how
authentic his book is.   Pages 217 and 251.   "On the
morning of August 28th, 1868, from the heights east of
Green River, then the eastern boundary of the Territory, I took my first view of Utah.   At the end of two
weeks in Salt Lake City my impressions are, on the
whole, rather favorable.   I find the city quiet, apparently in good order, neat and pleasant to dwell in "

Pages 472 and 162:   "In Salt Lake City, the flies
are probably worse, both as to number and peculiarities, than in any other city in America, but fortunately
their time is very short.   During the spring and early
summer they are rarely seen; in August they begin to
multiply, 'coming in with the emigration,' according to
local phrase, meaning the Mormon emigrants, who formerly completed the journey across the plains by the
latter part of July.   From the middle of August till
cool weather they are perfectly fearful, certainly much
worse than they need be if proper cleanliness were
practiced; large, flat-headed, light-winged and awkward,
they light and crawl over the person in the most annoy-
ing manner, not yielding, like 'Gentile flies,' to a light
brush or switch, but requiring literally to be swept off.
No other part of the Territory I have visited, is half so
bad in this respect as Salt Lake City, and the southern
valleys seem peculiarly free from this pest."

"The Secrets of the Great City" (New York) published two years before Beadle's work, or in 1868, contains a cut entitled "Noon Day Prayer meeting, at the
Wickedest Man's Dance House," which Mr. Beadle
reproduced in his work between pages 248–9, and en-

titled it "Mormon Missionaries Preaching to the Mormons." This piece of piracy is quite fitting to his
work as a whole. If this man is not the ten cent novel
writer, he should join him, if falsifying is a success.
"Members of congress and government officials" must
have been very proud of this book! See title page!

————

EXAMINATION of Mr. T. B. H. Stenhouse's Book.
He was twenty-five years a Mormon. He cites five
pages of authorities consulted, some of which contain
thirty-eight to the page. The inscription of his title
page is:

"THE ROCKY MOUNTAIN SAINTS.

"A FULL AND COMPLETE HISTORY OF THE MORMONS FROM
THE FIRST VISION OF JOSEPH SMITH TO THE LAST
COURTSHIP OF BRIGHAM YOUNG. BY T. B.
H. STENHOUSE. D. APPLETON &
CO., NEW YORK, 1873."

Stenhouse, page 1: "The faith of the Latter Day
Saints was in the beginning strictly confined to Biblical
doctrines, and the preaching of the first elders was
something like a resuscitation of the dispensation committed to the apostolic fisherman of Galilee."

Page 4: "The reader will readily perceive from
the following chapters that Mormonism has contained
within itself the elements of a sincere faith." * *

Page 6: "The polygamic faith contended for today was not in the original programme, neither has it
contributed to create the power that now reigns in
Utah."

On page 184 Mr. Stenhouse refers to John C. Bennett and his book "Mormonism Exposed," thus: "There is, no doubt, much truth in Bennett's book, 'Mormonism Exposed,' but no statement that he makes can be received with confidence. * * He (Bennett) states that he never was a believer, but only assumed the faith in order to become thoroughly initiated, and qualify himself for its exposure."

Mr. Stenhouse then confirms his words with Gov. Ford in his "History of Illinois." Page 263: "This Bennett was probably the greatest scamp in the western country. I have made particular enquiries concerning him, and have traced him in several places in which he had lived before he joined the Mormons, in Ohio, Indiana and Illinois, and he was everywhere accounted the same debauched, unprincipled, and profligate character."

If Bennett is not to be believed, how about Stenhouse? who claims in his introductory pages, fellowship "over a quarter of a century," * * "familiar intimacy with the apostles and leading elders, and for a dozen years had daily intercourse with Brigham Young." Why did he not quit sooner?

On page 193, Mr. Stenhouse charges Brigham with the preservation of falsehood a "quarter of a century," which he seems to think too long. "Brigham is peculiarly unctuous in confessing other men's sins to the public, but his own are never mentioned. It would have been equally proper for him on this occasion to have explained why he, for nearly a quarter of a century, had preserved that falsehood in the 'Book of Covenants,' [monogamic marriage regulation.—AUTHOR] notwithstanding the opportunities he had of removing

it in the several editions of the book that have been
published under his Presidency.   Why does not the
good Mr. Stenhouse explain his "quarter of a century
membership?"

Page 472, Mr. Stenhouse says: "The believers in
the new faith were organized in 1830; they were only
six in number, but they were full of their mission, and,
in their way, wholly devoted to Christ.   Their heroism
in the proclamation of their doctrines never was sur-
passed in any age or in any country, by any other disciples or missionaries of any faith.   They were pure in
thought, and burned with zeal for the redemption of
mankind."

On page 194, Mr. Stenhouse says: "Joseph Smith
and Oliver Cowdery must, as early as the first year
of the church, have contemplated * * polygamy."
While on page 6, already given, he says: "The
polygamic faith contended for today was not in the
original programme."   Mr. Stenhouse having testified
on both sides, is impeached and out of court.

Page 196, Mr. Stenhouse says: "It is not a little
singular that the most forcible arguments that have yet
been adduced against Mormon polygamy are those furnished by the pens of the three sons of Joseph Smith?"

Then occurs a memorial of which Mr. Stenhouse
says: "The name of the oldest son of the prophet is
found at the head."

Of the polygamic revelation, Mr. Stenhouse says, on
pages 201 and 202:   "Had this revelation been presented to the Mormons with the 'first principles' taught
by the elders, not one in ten thousand among them
would have accepted it as an emanation from Jesus
Christ."

"On the first of January, 1853, it was published in the Star.   It fell like a thunderbolt upon the Saints, and fearfully shattered the mission."

Page 202:   "The statistical reports of the mission in the British Islands, June 30, 1853, show that the enormous number of one thousand, seven hundred and seventy-six persons were excommunicated there during the first six months of the preaching of polygamy."

Page 208 says of Sidney Rigdon: "All through his trial, those who knew him before he was a Mormon, spoke of him in such a manner as leaves no room to doubt Rigdon's own sincerity in the Mormon faith, and his total ignorance of the existence of Joseph Smith and the Book of Mormon till after that work had been published."

Page 212 says of Wm. B. Smith, quoting the Clayton County, Iowa Journal: "He served two years as a soldier in helping to put down the rebellion.   In 1841–2 * * in legislature of Illinois * * a farmer in the vicinity of Elkader and upon Sundays occasionally preaching.   As a man, he is candid, honest and upright —a citizen of whom rumor speaks no evil, * * a faithful expounder of Mormonism while he deprecates polygamy."

On page 204, Mr. Stenhouse says: "Unfortunately, however, for the peace and unity of the Church, in all the multitude of his sayings and doings he made no direct and open preparation for the presidency of the Church in case of his death, and thus his martyrdom wrought confusion among the disciples."

On page 628:   "From the death of the founder of Mormonism, the Saints had had their attention RIVETED on 'the seed' of the Prophet, and expected that some day the young man Joseph would be the head of the Church.   Brigham had fostered this faith in the Saints for some years, but when in 1860 young Joseph was chosen President of the Reorganized Church and publicly denounced Brigham * * David H. was to be the man." How did it happen that the Saints had their attention RIVETED on the seed of the Prophet, and expected that some day the young man Joseph would be the head of the church?

The reader is referred to Judge Philips' decision on the Temple Lot case, March 3, 1894, where he sets forth how plainly Joseph Smith predicted his successor.

On page 639, Mr. Stenhouse says: "The names of Godbe, Harrison, Tullidge, Stenhouse and three others—not rebels—were called, and, as all these gentlemen were absent, Brigham in his anger, moved that they all be 'disfellowshipped' from the church, and the following brief notification was sent each:

" 'SALT LAKE CITY, Oct. 16th, 1869.

" 'DEAR BROTHER:—I hereby inform you that a motion was made, seconded, and carried by a unanimous vote of the School of the Prophets today, that you be disfellowshipped from the church until you appear in the School and give satisfactory reasons for your irregular attendance there.

" 'Your brother in the gospel,

" 'GEO. STODDARD, Secretary.'

"On the Saturday following, the rebels appeared in the School."

Mr. Stenhouse continues: "Never before had there been such a scene in the 'Old Tabernacle.'   Mr. Godbe frankly stated his position, and Brigham fol-

lowed him with aggravating mimicry, turning everything into ridicule.   Mr. Harrison threw caution to the
winds, and answered the insinuations of the Prophet
defiantly.   It was a squally time, and not without apprehension of danger."   Why did Mr. Stenhouse keep
still?

Page 642 says: "To all this add that Elders
Godbe, Harrison, Kelsey, Tullidge, Sherman, Lawrence, and others had a living faith to preach—that
which the people knew to be the original faith of the
founder of Mormonism, and 'the gifts' came back
again."

Is it not a little strange that after the "quarter of a
century" "fellowship" that Mr. Stenhouse neither reports himself as helping to beard the lion in his den,
or with the others who rebelled, preaching the "living
faith?"   How else could he exhibit true manhood?
Perhaps he was practicing as stated in the next quotation.

Page 665:   "Furthermore, though he (Stenhouse)
had daily intercourse with Brigham Young, his family
and his immediate friends, not a single thing that ever
transpired in Brigham's office or house, in his presence,
has been alluded to.   On all that he saw or heard while
Brigham's guest, or when with him in the capacity of
friend a STUDIED SILENCE HAS BEEN MAINTAINED."

The readers' attention is called to the fact, that
while Stenhouse culls from more works and documents
by far than the average writer, and while his wife
expatiates much on his paper and editorship in Salt
Lake City, not a scintilla of evidence is given of his
denouncing Brighamism, or of having supported those
who broke away from the terrible iniquity before his

book appeared. All he says relating to his having been a Mormon and leaving it is, that he has "outgrown the past," and the reference he makes of his being "cut off."

Page 588: "It was the author's intention when he commenced this work to give a complete expose of polygamy, exhibiting that institution in all its bearings and influences upon the social life of the people of Utah, but an unlooked for incident induced Mrs. Stenhouse to publish what she knew of polygamy. Had that book been written by any other authoress, reference would have unquestionably been made to it in this work; the author, therefore, sees no impropriety in acknowledging that his wife has produced a work which only a woman could write, and superior to anything which he himself could offer to the public, and he refers the reader to 'A lady's life among the Mormons' (Russell Bros., New York) as a full and unreserved Expose of Polygamy in Utah." Let the reader here refer back to his title page where his work is stated as full and complete from first vision of Joseph Smith to last courtship of Brigham Young.

The work of Mrs. Stenhouse, here referred to, was her first; the one we review hereafter is her perfected work, of 1876, which was three years after that of Mr. Stenhouse. Of the first, he said, it was "SUPERIOR TO ANYTHING which he himself could offer to the "public."

Stenhouse, in his forty-ninth chapter, devotes thirty-four pages to an expose of the Book of Mormon, and follows the beaten trail of the ridiculous quibbling that has been doled out by all his predecessors, even denying, as usual, on page 532, elephants, horses, asses, etc., as having existence on this continent ages ago, as claimed in Book of Mormon. It is no small compli-

ment to that book that after his "over a quarter of a
century fellowship" in the church, he dare not make an
attack from the standpoint of MORALS or DOCTRINE
found therein.   Can the book be entirely human and
its doctrines and morals beyond attack?   The concession by failing so to attack, is strong evidence in its
favor.   All who have tried to expose it have quibbled
over its literary inelegance as viewed by them.

"TELL IT ALL.

"THE STORY OF A LIFE'S EXPERIENCE IN MORMONISM, BY MRS. T. B. H. STENHOUSE.   A. D. WORTHING-TON & CO., PUBLISHERS, 1876."

A preface, written by Mrs. Harriet Beecher Stowe,
contains the following sentences: "In these pages, a
woman, a wife and mother, speaks of the sorrows and
oppressions of which she has been the witness and the
victim. * * It is no sensational story, but a plain,
unvarnished tale of truth, stranger and sadder than fiction."

The closing sentence or phrase of her own preface
is: "I have told the truth, the whole truth and nothing but the truth."

The entire preface is a lamentation over the un-
truthfulness of nearly all the works on Mormonism which
had been written before hers.   If any reliable works
had been written they were either out of date or were
only partial accounts, in her estimation.

The opening sentence of chapter one is: "The
story which I propose to tell in these pages is a plain,

unexaggerated record of facts which have come immediately under my own notice, or which I have myself
personally experienced."

Of early preaching in England, she says: "Their
first teaching had been a mixture of Bible texts about the
last days, and arguments about the millenium, the return
of the Jews to Palestine, the resurrection of the dead
and a new revelation and a new prophet."—p. 41.

Read this in connection: "Mormonism was bold
then in Europe, it had no American history to meet in
those days. * * The saving love of Christ, the glory
and fullness of the everlasting gospel, the gifts and
graces of the Spirit, together with repentance, baptism
and faith, were the points upon which the Mormons
touched, and who can wonder that with such topics as
these, and fortifying every statement with powerful
and numerous texts of Scripture, they should captivate
the minds of religiously inclined people."—p. 48.

"Controversy would arise, and his appeal (that of
missionary) to Scripture, literally interpreted, was
almost invariably triumphant."—p. 56.

"A person who has never attended a Mormon
meeting can form no idea of the joyous spirit which
seemed to animate every one present. I am not, of
course, speaking of modern meetings, but of meetings
as they used to be."—p. 57.

Of meetings in the old room in England: "Never
did I experience so rapt a feeling of communion with
'the armies of heaven' as I felt in that unadorned meeting room, surrounded by those plain but earnest and
united people."—p. 59.

On the 6th of February, 1850, * * I was married
to * * Elder Stenhouse."—p. 72.

"Not long after my marriage I saw a miracle performed—a real true miracle. Let not the reader smile,
or think that I am only jesting, for I am quite in earnest, and mean what I say.   I saw a sick person who
for years had been confined to her bed, her limbs distorted and her back bent, * * I saw them annoint her,
and lay hands upon her, and pray most fervently, and
I saw the same decrepit old woman walking and singing and praising God.   If that was not a miracle I
should like to know what is"—p. 74.

Compare the following with the above: "After
this I saw plenty * * of miracles. * * That they were
miracles in the sense in which we generally use, that
term, I do not for a moment believe, but I think that
in cases where the efforts of the elders were successful,
scientific enquiry would readily show that the effects
were only natural results of natural causes.   One
brother, a deacon in the church, was suddenly attacked
with cholera.   He sent immediately for Elder Stenhouse. * * In the case of the deacon to whom I have
just alluded, the experiment was successful."—p. 86.

"On the following day, an enthusiastic sister came
running to Elder Stenhouse for him to come and lay
hands upon her husband who had also been attacked
by cholera. * * Elder Stenhouse laid hands upon him
in the usual way, but instead of commanding the
disease to depart as it was expected he would, he prayed
that the afflicted brother * * might pass away in peace.
The head of the dying man instantly fell back upon his
pillow, and all was over."—p. 87.

Of a sick child: "My husband complied, and began by praying that the child might rest well, when
suddenly, as if by an irresistible impulse he implored

that the child might die easily and without pain. * *
In a moment we knew that the child was dying * *
peacefully, as if he were going to sleep."—p. 88.

Mrs. Stenhouse does not tell us if scientific enquiry
would discover why Elder Stenhouse was so moved in
these two cases. But she does say: "There are
moments of our life when silence is better than speech,
and it is safer to trust in the mercy of God than try to
shape our own destiny."—p. 94. Why not use scientific enquiry, Mrs. Stenhouse?

On page 120 she gives a personal experience of
extremity, and says: "We realized literally the necessity of trusting to God's daily mercies for our daily
bread, * * our only hope."

"Never, till the possibility that polygamy might
some day be acknowledged by the church, began to be
whispered * * did a solitary doubt respecting my religion itself intrude upon my mind."—p. 139.

Pages 143–149 recite a sickly tale of Mrs. Stenhouse theoretically accepting the doctrine of polygamy
and how she and Madame Baliff taught it. She says:
"That God had sent the revelation I never questioned,
and all rebellion to his will I knew to be sinful."

Compare with the above this: "About this time
I procured a copy of the revelation * * and read it
through carefully and calmly, from beginning to end.
The reader may, perhaps, remember that when a copy
of it was first given me, in Switzerland, years before, I
was so angry and indignant that when I had got only
partly through it, I cast it from me in disgust as an out-
rage upon all that was good and true. From that time,
although I had heard portions of it quoted and read, I
had never perused it as a whole."—p. 541. Yet she

and Madame Baliff had taught the doctrine of polygamy!

On page 132 she relates the first appearance of the revelation in the Millenial Star, January, 1853.   Of it she says: "I retired to my own chamber.   There, for the first time I read that document, * *

Pages 135–138 contain the revelation, then follows: "And this was the revelation—this mass of confusion, cunning, absurdity, falsehood and bad grammar!" Yet she had taught it, had no doubt but that God gave it, had not read it, and then again tells us she had.

"New Year's we set foot upon the shore of the New World."—p. 178.   (Jan. 1, 1856).

Having reached Utah, she says: "The Tabernacle services seemed to me as strange as the women. * * As for the spirituality and devotional feeling which characterized our meetings in England, they were conspicuous only by their absence and many devout Saints * * feel as if they had come to witness a puppet show, rather than attend a religious meeting."—p. 251.

"My own experience as a Mormon woman leads me to form anything but a flattering opinion of the Mormon stories told by Gentile pens."—p. 258.

"I do not think Brigham Young a wicked man or an imposter in the sense in which those words are ordinarily used; * * ."—p. 266.

Compare this with the above: "The innocent blood which cries for vengeance against Brigham Young and some of the leaders * * is sufficient to weigh the purest spirit which stands before the throne of God down to the nethermost abyss of hell."—p. 365.

Pages 304–308 are devoted to scenes and conditions in Missouri and Illinois where she does not claim to have been at all, yet the opening sentence of the

book says: "Facts which have come immediately
under my own notice, or which I have myself experienced."   Now listen!   "One instance I can give from
my own personal knowledge."—p. 319.   She promised
they all should be.

"Shortly after our arrival in Salt Lake City, we
visited President Young, who received us very gracious-
ly, and appointed an early day for us to dine with him.
On that occasion * * we passed an exceedingly
pleasant evening."—p. 263.

Compare this: "It was with the greatest.difficulty
that I could control my feelings sufficiently to call upon
any family where there was more than one wife."—
p. 345.

And this: "When I first knew Bro. Brigham,
poor man, he had only sixteen living with him in Salt
Lake City, and even now he has no more than nineteen! * * Eliza Ann has run away."—p. 276.

"My husband gave no signs of apostasy, and, as a
Saint, I knew he would never think of undertaking anything without the permission of Bro. Brigham."—p. 511.

Regarding Stenhouse's visits east: "After these
visits his editorials took a more liberal turn."—p. 544.

"My husband's paper was silent upon the subject,
and in consequence he was suspected of being in league
with the enemy."—p. 577.

"The change from Methodism to Mormonism, as it
was first presented to the world, was nothing near so
great, as the departure which Brigham has made from
the original faith of the Saints."—p. 614.

"In the preceding pages I have endeavored to
present to the reader the story of my life's experience
in Mormonism and polygamy, and to place before him

a truthful picture of the doctrine of the Saints."—
p. 618.

She proceeds again to lament the unreliability of
others, as she had done in her preface, and then says:
"I have told my story simply but truthfully."—p. 620.

Again she weaves in the phrase "all too true!"
Again, "I have most scrupulously kept to the very letter
of the truth."--p. 620.

That she told much truth is granted.   That she
was most reckless and contradicted herself often is as
clear as the noonday sun.   She emerges from the mael-
strom of pollution—polygamy; intends to make some
money: panders to the prejudice of the world, and
attempts to down the early part of the latter day
work as a farce, as well as her late experience in Utah.
Let the reader calmly think over all that Mrs. Harriet
Beecher Stowe subscribed to and vouched for, referring to the book as "a plain, unvarnished tale of truth,
stranger and sadder than fiction."   Mr. Stenhouse had
a very large idea of the gullibility of the people, when
he wrote of Mrs. Stenhouse's book, that it was "superior
to anything he could offer to the public."

"WIFE NUMBER NINETEEN;

"OR, THE STORY OF A LIFE IN BONDAGE.   BY ANN
ELIZA YOUNG, 1876."

"All the events which I shall relate will be some
of my own personal experiences, or the experience of
those so closely connected with me that they have
fallen directly under my observation, and for whose
truth I can vouch without hesitation. * * I was born

at Nauvoo, Illinois, on the 13th of September, 1844."
—p. 32.

Speaking of her father she says: "He first heard the
Mormon doctrine preached in 1833. * * Joseph Smith
had given the Book of Mormon to the world, and had
announced himself as another Messiah."—p. 33. Why
did not Eliza give us some evidence on this? It is
basely false.

Speaking of the Kirtland bank matter she says:
"But, as usual, he eluded the officers of justice, and all
attempts to arrest him were unavailing."—p. 41.

"Others had him arrested every little while! It is
a matter of official record that he was several times
arrested but not proven guilty as charged."—p. 41.

Eliza tells of being told by a "person:" "At one
time he was himself sent by the prophet to steal lumber
for coffins. He went with a party of men down the
river, loaded a raft with lumber from a Gentile saw-
mill, and brought it up to the city of the Saints."—p. 52.

In the light of extract from page 33 she can VOUCH
for this THIEF. Just how the raft was taken UP THE
RIVER OVER THE RAPIDS she does not say. The reader
should remember, however, it was for coffins.

Eliza says: "I feel that I must pay this tribute to
the Mormon people. Naturally, they were a law-abiding, peace-loving, intensely religious people."—p. 58.

Compare the above with: "Although its founder
arrogated to it the title of the 'Church of Jesus Christ,'
there is nothing Christ-like in its teachings or in its
practice."—p. 59.

And with this: "They applied oil, and laid
hands' on all sick persons, without regard to their ail-
ments."—p. 124. See Mark 16: 18 and James 5: 14,

whether this was Christ-like in teaching or practice? See first few pages of both Mr. and Mrs. Stenhouse's books, as examined in this part of this work.

"The first PUBLIC announcement Joseph ever made of his belief in the plurality of wives was at Nauvoo in 1840."—p. 67. This is a base lie, all his work proves the opposite as seen in the evidence and decision of the recent Temple lot case.

Compare this with the last citation: "So intense was the feeling that in the Summer of 1843, the prophet, moved by pressure * * was compelled to intrench himself behind a * * revelation. * * It was at first only communicated to a chosen few. * *. Young delivered it to the world in 1852."—pp. 76, 77. Joseph had preached it in 1840 by PUBLIC ANNOUNCEMENT, but now it was restricted to a "chosen few." Pooh!

"Joseph Smith had been assassinated the previous July."—p. 89. Ignorance or stupidity, which? It was June 27, 1844. On page 64 she gives a cut view of the assassination as unreal as her date. The building still stands and is properly given by Beadle; having seen it, I know. (R. E.)

Of house furnishing: "It was the very cheapest pine furniture which could be bought in the city, and the crockery was dishes that Brigham had left when he sold the Globe bakery."—p. 458.

Selling furniture: "Arrangements having been previously made, three furniture vans came at the same time, and in forty minutes my entire household goods were in charge of the auctioneer. They were sold the next day, and I realized three hundred and eighty dollars from the sale."—p. 546. Eliza tried to start herself out with funds, at any rate!

"MORMONISM UNVEILED;

"OR, THE LIFE AND CONFESSIONS OF JOHN D. LEE."

A book, bearing the above title is now going the rounds, and the enemies of the latter day work think they have now found the weapon which shall forever demolish "Mormonism" as a whole, and many, though refusing to accept the testimony of honest, law abiding citizens in regard to "Mormonism," are ready to swallow with greediness every statement that militates against the people they have tried so long, but in vain, to overthrow; though it proceeds from a culprit who has been executed for his crimes.   This work is published by Bryan, Brand & Co., St. Louis, Missouri, who claim to have received the manuscript from Wm. W. Bishop, of Pioche, Nevada, Lee's confidential attorney, in whose hand the history and confession had been placed by Lee himself, prior to his execution.

I had repeatedly been informed that a perusal of this work would satisfy me that "Mormonism" was a fraud from its inception; but at the risk of having my faith shaken I concluded to examine the work, and my conclusion is, it will not do to rely on as evidence. For the benefit of those who may be trying to get at the truth of the matter, and those who may feel scared about the book, I will give my reasons for the above conclusion.

Under the head of "How I First Heard of the Doctrine of Polygamy," Lee is made to say that while acting as police in the city of Nauvoo, he was ordered by the Chief of Police to guard the house of a widow and knock down a man who was in the habit of spending his nights there. Lee reported the order to Hyrum Smith, and says, "Hyrum then told me that the man that I was ordered to attack was Howard Egan, and that he had been sealed to Mrs. Clawson, and that their marriage was A MOST HOLY ONE; that it was in accordance with a REVELATION that the prophet had recently received direct from God. He then explained to me fully the doctrine of polygamy, and wherein it was permitted, and why it was right." (Page 288).

Again, he is made to say: "During the winter (of 1844), Joseph, the prophet, set a man by the name of Sidney Hay Jacobs, [Henry Jacobs.—ED.], to select from the Old Bible such scriptures as pertained to polygamy, or celestial marriage, and to write it in a pamphlet form, and to advocate the doctrine. This he did as a feeler among the people to pave the way for celestial marriage. * * The excitement among the people became so great that the subject was laid before the prophet. No one was more opposed to it than his brother Hyrum who denounced it as from beneath." (Page 146).

Here Lee is made to say, that when he first heard of polygamy it was explained to him by Hyrum, and declared to be "most holy." Again, when polygamy was first introduced Hyrum "denounced it as from beneath." Which of these statements is true? Both can not be. If it be argued that he first denounced it, and then when the revelation was given, he advocated, we answer that Lee has Hyrum denouncing it as late as the winter of 1844, and it is claimed that the revelation was given the 12th day of July, 1843. Moreover, if

Lee had never heard of it until explained to him by Hyrum, how did he know that he had before denounced it?   I see no way of harmonizing the passages, and must, therefore, reject one or both.

Again, he says: "In less than one year after I first learned the will of the Lord concerning the marriage of the Saints, I was the husband of nine wives." (Page 288).   On page 166, he tells us that his second wife, Nancy Bean, was sealed to him in the winter of 1845.   So, according to his own statement, he had but one wife in the days of the martyrs, as they were killed the 27th day of June, 1844.

On page 168 he tells us: "About the 1st of December, 1845, we commenced fitting up the rooms for giving endowments."   Now notice, that more than seventeen months had elapsed since the death of Hyrum Smith, yet he goes on to tell us that: "In the Temple I took three more wives - Martha Berry, Polly Ann Workman and Delethea Morris."   On page 289, he gives us the order in which he took his wives, and says: "Polly Ann Workman was eighth, and Martha Berry ninth."   Now, these women were not sealed to him until more than seventeen months after the death of Hyrum, yet Lee was the husband of "nine wives" "in less than one year" from the time he first heard the doctrine, and Hyrum first explained it to him, and it took these wives to complete the nine.

> "O, what a tangled web they weave
> Who practice solely to deceive!"

Again, he says, on page 289, "In 1847, while at Council Bluffs, Brigham Young sealed to me three women in one night, viz., Nancy Armstrong, Polly V. Young and Louisa Young   Next I was sealed to * *

Emeline Vaughn;" but on page 199 he says the next
(after these three) was "Emeline Woolsey."   And on
page 199 he says Emeline Woolsey was his thirteenth
wife, but on page 289 he says Louisa Young was number thirteen.

In giving the number of his wives on page 289, he
does not mention Emeline Woolsey; I suppose he had
forgotten her.   Well, just as I expected, polygamy
causes a man to forget his wife!

On page 184, he states that in 1844, prior to
Joseph Smith being nominated for the Presidency of
the United States, he wrote to Martin Van Buren, also
to Wm. H. Harrison, asking them their "views in
regard to the grievances and wrongs of the Mormon
people," should they be elected.   Did not Lee know
that Martin Van Buren took his seat in 1837, served
his time, and retired from office three years before this,
and that General Harrison took his seat 4th of March,
1841, and died a month later?   Comment is useless.

On page 134, in speaking of his travels in Tennessee, in connection with Elder Twist, in 1842 or 1843,
he says: "While we were in Memphis, General Wm.
Henry Harrison, then a candidate for President,
arrived, and a great political meeting of the Whig party
was held in the open air."

Well, General Harrison may have been a candidate for President after his death, but this is the first
intimation I ever had of it.

He states that Lyman Wight was one of the Twelve
before the difficulty commenced in Missouri, in 1838,
(see p. 56), which is not so, as David Patten was killed
during the trouble, and Lyman Wight was ordained in
his stead.

On page 135 he says that at Memphis, Tennessee, they "took passage in a new steamer that was owned in Nashville, and was then making its first trip from Nashville to New Orleans. The boat got into a race with the Eclipse, another fine boat. * * I threw off * * and our boat soon left the Eclipse far in the rear. The steamers parted at the mouth of the Ohio."

Now this boat was on its way from "Nashville to New Orleans;" after passing Memphis, Tenn., it got into a race with the Eclipse, and parted company with her at the mouth of the Ohio. I wish some of those who are so much carried away with "Lee's, Confession," would tell us how a steamer can pass the mo th of the Ohio, between Memphis and New Orleans. I confess I can not understand it.

On page 137, he tells us that he used "the Masonic sign of distress" while in trouble in Tennessee; then on page 144 he gives us an account of joining the Masonic order after he had returned to Nauvoo. Is it reason_able to suppose that he understood and used Masonic signs before he was a Mason?

On page 51, he says that the first sermon that he "ever heard concerning Mormonism" was in 1837, and on page 35, he says he was baptized June 17th, 1838, in Abrosia, Davies county, Missouri. This would do very well, but he spoils it all by saying on page 279, "I have been with the Church since the dark days in Jackson county. Now every one acquainted with the history of the Church knows that they left Jackson county the autumn of 1833. So if Lee never heard a sermon "concerning Mormonism" till 1837, his statement that he had "been with the Church since the dark days in Jackson county," must be a mistake to say the least of it.

On page 120, he says, the "plates containing the Book of Mormon, and God's will, * * were taken to Professor Anthon of New York City, for translation." Now it has never been claimed by those connected with this affair that the plates were taken to Prof. Anthon; on the contrary, Joseph Smith was forbidden to show them to any only a few that were chosen to bear testimony, and their names may be found in connection with the Book of Mormon. A few of the characters were transcribed and sent to Professor Anthon, and that is all that was claimed by Joseph Smith who sent them, or Martin Harris who carried them, or by Professor Anthon himself. And the Prophet Isaiah only predicts that "the words of the book" should be sent to him that is learned. (Isa. 29).

Again he says, on page 184: "While there, (St. Joseph, Mo.) I met Luke Johnson, one of the witnesses to the Book of Mormon. I had a curiosity to talk with him concerning the same. We took a walk down on the river bank. I asked him if the statement he signed about seeing the angel and the plates was true. If he did see the plates from which the Book of Mormon was printed or translated. He said it was true."

Now every one who knows anything about the Book of Mormon or its history, knows that Luke Johnson was not one of the witnesses. But three (besides Joseph Smith) testify to having seen the "angel," viz: Oliver Cowdery, David Whitmer and Martin Harris. Luke Johnson did not even testify to having seen the plates, and according to history he did not see them.

I am tempted right here to say I do not believe Lee ever wrote the book bearing his name, for he must have known that Luke Johnson was not one of the witnesses to the Book of Mormon; he must also have known that the claim had never been made that the plates were taken to Professor Anthon.

But whether Lee, Bishop or the publishers are responsible for these statements it does not change the FACT that the book is UNRELIABLE. While l have no sympathy with the works of darkness in Utah, my faith in original "Mormonism" is unshaken by the perusal of the work; and while I sincerely hope that all those engaged in the "Mountain Meadow Massacre," and crimes of like nature, may be overtaken and punished according to their crime, I can have but little confidence in "Mormonism Unveiled, or the Life and Confessions of John D. Lee."

HEMAN C. SMITH.

GARLAND, Alabama, Sept. 11th, 1878.

————

"HISTORY OF THE MORMONS, OR LATTER DAY SAINTS.

"FROM THEIR ORIGIN TO THE PRESENT TIME. BY SAMUEL M. SMUCKER, A. M. HURST & CO., PUBLISHERS, 122 NASSAU STREET, NEW YORK. COPYRIGHT 1881."

Having reached page 36, the errand of Harris to Professor Anthon is taken up, and while all parties concerned, Anthon included, say a paper was shown him, Mr. Smucker on page 37, says: "Submitted the plates to him." "Professor had seen the plates." While so much is put in, from Anthon's letter is withheld the phrases: "And which Dr. M. confessed he had been unable to understand." The other being: "As far as

I now recollect."—Howe's Book, page 272, is the first appearance of it in print.

The following except emphasized words appear on pages 36 and 37.

"He was at once captivated by the doctrines and pretensions of Joseph, and lent the 'prophet' the sum of fifty dollars to enable him to publish his new Bible. Joseph, though asked by Martin Harris to show the plates, refused, on the pretence that he was not pure of heart enough to be allowed a sight of such treasures; but he generously made a transcript of a portion of them upon paper, which he told him to submit to any learned scholar in the world, if he wished to be satisfied. Martin Harris was an earnest man, and he set out from Palmyra to New York, to visit Professor Anthon, a gentleman of the highest reputation, both in America and Europe, and well known for his valuable and correct editions of the classics. He found the Professor, and submitted the plates to him. The Mormons at this time were too insignificant to excite attention, and the result of Martin Harris' interview with the learned man was not known until three or four years afterwards, when a report having been spread abroad by the Mormons that the Professor had seen the plates, and pronounced the inscriptions to be in the Egyptian character, that gentleman was requested by a letter directed to him by M. E. D. Howe, of Painesville, Ohio, to declare whether such was the fact?   Professor Anthon returned the following answer, detailing his interview with the simple-minded Martin Harris:

" 'NEW YORK, Feb. 17, 1834.

" 'DEAR SIR:— I received your letter of the 9th, and lose no time in making a reply.   The whole story about my pronouncing the Mormonite inscription to be "Reformed Egyptian Hieroglyphics," is perfectly false. Some years ago a plain, apparently simple-hearted, farmer called on me with a note from Dr. Mitchell, of our city, now dead, requesting me to decipher, if possible, a paper which the farmer would hand me, AND WHICH DR. M. CONFESSED HE HAD BEEN UNABLE TO UNDERSTAND. Upon examining the paper in question, I soon came to the conclusion that it was all a trick, perhaps a hoax. When I asked the person who brought it how he obtained the writing, he gave me, AS FAR AS I NOW RECOLLECT, the following account: A "gold book," consisting of a number of plates fastened together by wires of the same material, had been dug up in the northern part of the State of New York, and along with it an enormous pair of "spectacles!" These spectacles were so large, that if any person attempted to look through them, his two eyes would look through one glass only, the spectacles in question being altogether too large for the human face. "Whoever," he said, "examined the plates through the glasses was enabled, not only to read them, but fully to understand their meaning." * *

" 'This paper, in question, was in fact a singular scroll. It consisted of all kinds of crooked characters, disposed in columns, and had evidently been prepared by some person who had before him at the time a book containing various alphabets, Greek and Hebrew letters, crosses and flourishes; Roman letters inverted or placed sideways, were arranged and placed in perpendicular columns, and the whole ended in a rude delineation of a circle, divided into various compartments, decked with various strange marks, and evidently copied after the Mexican Calendar, given by Humboldt, but copied in such a way as not to betray the source whence it was derived.' "

Of matters in Missouri, page 89 says: "The Lieutenant-Governor of the state of Missouri, Lilburn W. Boggs—a man who from thenceforward appears to have pursued the Mormons with unrelenting hostility—was in the immediate neighborhood of the riot, but declined to take any part in preserving the peace."

Of the situation at Nauvoo, Smucker, on page 128, says: "The organization of the sect began to be more fully and admirably developed, and the Mormons were' even at this early period of their career, a pre-eminently industrious, frugal, and pains-taking people.   They felt the advantages of co-operation.   Though robbed and plundered, they did not lose their time in vain repinings, but set themselves to repair the calamities they had suffered.   The needy were aided by the more affluent in the purchase of land, and in the plenishing of their farms; and the inducements which they held out to skilled mechanics and others to join them, were not merely of a religious and spiritual, but of a social and worldly character.   The Mormons as a body understood the dignity and the holiness of hard work, and they practiced to the fullest extent the duty of self-reliance."

Pages 110, 111 gives this: "The following address, which is of itself sufficient evidence of the cruelty and injustice with which the sect was treated, was delivered at Far West by Major-General Clark to the Mormons, after they had surrendered their arms, and declared themselves prisoners of war:

" 'Gentlemen,—You whose names are not attached

to this list of names, will now have the privilege of going to your fields to obtain corn for your families,
wood, etc. Those that are now taken will go from
thence to prison, be tried, and receive the due merit of
their crimes; but you are now at liberty, all but such
as charges may be hereafter preferred against. It now
devolves upon you to fulfill the treaty that you have
entered into, the leading items of which I now lay before you. The first of these you have already complied with, which is, that you deliver up your leading
men to be tried according to law. Second, that you
deliver up your arms—this has been attended to. The
third is, that you sign over your properties to defray
the expenses of the war—this you have also done.
Another thing yet remains for you to comply with—that
is, that you leave the state forthwith; and whatever
your feelings concerning this affair, whatever your innocence, it is nothing to me. General Lucas, who is
equal in authority with me, has made this treaty with
you. I am determined to see it executed. The orders
of the Governor to me were, that you should be exterminated, and not allowed to continue in the state; and
had your leader not been given up, and the treaty complied with, before this, you and your families would
have been destroyed, and your houses in ashes.

" 'There is a discretionary power vested in my
hands, which I shall try to exercise for a season. I did
not say that you shall go now, but you must not think
of staying here another season, or of putting in crops,
for the moment you do, the citizens will be upon you.
I am determined to see the Governor's message fulfilled,
but shall not come upon you immediately—do not
think that I shall act as I have done any more—but if

I have to come again, because the treaty which you
have made here shall be broken, you need not expect
any mercy, but extermination; for I am determined the
Governor's order shall be executed.   As for your leaders, do not once think—do not imagine for a moment—
do not let it enter your mind—that they will be delivered, or that you will see their faces again, for their
fate is fixed, their die is cast, their doom is sealed.' "

Mr. Smucker gives a preacher's account of the
"prophet" in the pulpit, on page 151:   "Another account of Joseph was published about the same time by
a Methodist preacher of the name of Prior.

" 'I will not attempt,' said this writer, 'to describe
the various feelings of my bosom as I took my seat in
a conspicuous place in the congregation, who were
waiting in breathless silence for his appearance. While
he tarried, I had plenty of time to revolve in my mind
the character and common report of that truly singular
personage.   I fancied that I should behold a counte-
ance sad and sorrowful, yet containing the fiery marks
of rage and exasperation.   I supposed that I should be
enabled to discover in him some of those thoughtful
and reserved features, those mystic and sarcastic
glances, which I had fancied the ancient sages to possess.   I expected to see that fearful, faltering look of
conscious shame, which, from what I had heard of him,
he might be expected to evince.   He appeared at last;
but how was I disappointed, when instead of the heads
and horns of the beast and false prophet, I beheld only
the appearance of a common man of tolerably large
proportions.   I was sadly disappointed, and thought
that, although his appearance could not be wrested to
indicate anything against him, yet he would manifest

all I had heard of him when he began to preach. I sat uneasily, and watched him closely. He commenced preaching, not from the Boook of Mormon, however, but from the Bible; the first chapter of the first of Peter was his text. He commenced calmly, and continued dispassionately to pursue his subject, while I sat in breathless silence, waiting to hear that foul aspersion of the other sects, that diabolical disposition of revenge, and to hear that rancorous denunciation of every individual but a Mormon. I waited in vain; I listened with surprise; I sat uneasy in my seat, and could hardly persuade myself but that he had been apprised of my presence, and so ordered his discourse on my account, that I might not be able to find fault with it, for instead of a jumbled jargon of half connected sentences, and a volley of imprecations, and diabolical and malignant denunciations heaped upon the heads of all who differed from him, and the dreadful twisting and wresting of the Scriptures to suit his own peculiar views, and attempts to weave a web of dark and mystic sophistry around the gospel truths, which I had anticipated, he glided along through a very interesting and elaborate discourse with all the care and happy facility of one who was well aware of his important station, and his duty to God and man.' "

On page 152, he describes Nauvoo: "At length the city burst upon my sight. Instead of seeing a few miserable log cabins and mud hovels, which I had expected to find, I was surprised to see one of the most romantic looking places that I had visited in the west The buildings, though many of them were small, and of wood, yet bore the marks of neatness which I have not seen equaled in the country."

Another item of Prior's account, on page 155: "I passed on into the more active parts of the city, looking into every street and lane to observe all that was passing.   I found all the people engaged in some useful and healthy employment.   The place was alive with business — much more so than any place I have visited since the hard times commenced.   I sought in vain for anything that bore the marks of immorality, but was both astonished and highly pleased at my ill success. I could see no loungers about the streets nor any drunkards about the taverns.   I did not meet with those distorted features of ruffians, or with the ill-bred and impudent.   I heard not an oath in the place, I saw not a gloomy countenance; all were cheerful, polite, and industrious."

An Englishman's letter, given by Smucker, furnishes the following on page 159:   "I have witnessed the Mormons in their assemblies on a Sunday, and I know not where a similar scene could be effected or produced.   With respect to the teachings of the Prophet, I must say that there are some things hard to be understood, but he invariably supports himself from our good old Bible.   Peace and harmony reign in the city.   The drunkard is scarcely ever seen, as in other cities, neither does the awful imprecation or profane oath strike upon your ear; but, while all is storm and tempest and confusion abroad respecting the Mormons, all is peace and harmony at home."

Col. Kane, brother of the arctic explorer, is quoted by Mrs. Smucker on page 236, thus: "I can scarcely describe the gratification I felt in associating again with persons who were almost all of Eastern American origin —persons of refined and cleanly habits and decent language—and in observing their peculiar and interesting mode of life, while every day seemed to bring with it its own especial incidents, fruitful in the illustration of habits and character. It was during the period of which I have just spoken, that the Mormon battalion of five hundred and twenty men was recruited and marched for the Pacific coast."

Again, of sportive scenes on the Missouri River, on page 248: "But in the hours after hours that I have watched this sport at the ferry-side, I never heard an oath, or the language of quarrel, or knew it provoked the least sign of ill-feeling."

Mr. Smucker's first of two accounts of the introduction of polygamy or spiritual wifery, occurs on page 161: "The power and influence of Joseph were too great not to excite envy, and Sidney Rigdon did great mischief by introducing a novelty called the 'spiritual wife' doctrine. This caused great scandal, both among the Mormons and among their enemies."

Of Joseph Smith's attitude on the matter occurs the following, page 171: "Joseph would not tolerate this scandal, and every offender was forthwith excommunicated, and publicly declared to be cut off from the church."

Page 172: "The Mormons then, and ever since, have indignantly denied the truth of this particular charge; and of all the charges brought against Joseph as regards a plurality of wives—and in especial reference to the 'spiritual wife' doctrine—they allege what appears from his whole career to be most probable, that he was at all times most anxious to preserve the church free from taint, and to exclude adulterers, seducers, and persons of immoral lives."

Page 174:   "If is utterly incredible that Joseph Smith, who, great impostor as he was, never missed an opportunity to denounce seducers and adulterers as unfit to enter into his church, should have been concerned directly or indirectly in proceedings like these, though it is scarcely surprising that when such stories had been circulated by men whom the 'Prophet' had thwarted or reprimanded, there should have been found some persons willing to credit them."

Pages 382–384 contain the leading quotations on the matter from the Doctrine and Covenants, showing the strict monogamic rule.   On page 384 is found: "And if they are to be judged by their writings, we may assume that their efforts are continually directed towards the attainment of a higher system of morality than that commonly in vogue."

On page 379 is found: "We must remember, too, that Smith, universally, in all his letters, revelations, and speeches, denounced adultery and fornication. Subject as all founders of religious systems are to calumny, we cannot resist the doubt that there may have been misrepresentation and exaggeration, both as to the character of Joseph Smith and the cause of his untimely end."

After all this, Mr. Smucker gives us the second account of the introduction of polygamy on page 413: "The prominent and peculiar feature in this part of their system, is the defence and prevalence of polygamy, which Joe Smith first introduced, at the commencement of his career, and which has ever since prevailed among his followers."

And on page 416:   "Joe Smith had over forty wives at Nauvoo, and yet the number of his offspring fell far short of even that of Young."

A statement about Oliver Cowdery on page 375, says: "Thus, we learn from an obituary in the Millennial Star (July 1st, 1850), that one of the 'three witnesses' has lately died. Elder Wallace informs us, that Oliver Cowdery died last February, of consumption. Brother Cowdery is one of the 'THREE WITNESSES' to the BOOK of MORMON. For rebellious conduct he was expelled from the Church some years since. Although he stood aloof from the Church for several years, he never, in a single instance, cast the least doubt on the truth of his former testimony. Sometime in 1847 or 1848, he sought to be re-admitted to the fellowship of the Saints. His return to the fold was hailed with great joy by the Saints, who still remembered him with kindly recollection, as one who had suffered much in the first rise of the Church."

Mr. Smucker, in his book, has dealt more fairly than many others, but, like most all who have exposed Mormonism, he has not failed to expose himself.

AN EXAMINATION OF REV. M. T. LAMB'S GOLDEN BIBLE.

ISSUED 1886 BY WARD AND DRUMMAND, NEW YORK.

Preface, page 12, he says: "The book is not written for literary critics. It makes no pretensions whatever to any literary excellence."

Page 14 of the preface, he says: "The author desires to acknowledge his great obligations to Dr. Brisbin of Philadelphia, and Dr. Augustus Le Plongeon of Brooklyn, two of the most accomplished antiquarians now living, for valuable suggestions in their special

lines of study.   Also to Rev. H. G. Weston, D. D.,
President of Crozier Theological Seminary; Rev. T. J.
Morgan, Principal of the State Normal School, Providence, Rhode Island; Rev. J. W. Wilmarth, D. D., of
Philadelphia; Rev. A. J. Rowlands, D. D., of Baltimore; Rev. G. F. Genung, of New London City, and
Rev. T. F. Day, of the Presbyterian Board of Utah, for
valuable criticisms and suggestions.   And especially to
the Rev. G. W. Hervey, D. D., of New York, for a
careful and painstaking examination of the entire
work.''

No literary merit after all this flourish of titles!
just think!   One almost feels dizzy passing over such a
list.   Then Mr. Lamb thinks a book may have merit
other than literary merit.   Why then does he use nearly
all his precious space trying to defeat the Book of
Mormon from a literary point of view, and that, too, in
the face of the fact that it nowhere claims elegance in
that line, but, on its opening page statement, signed
Moroni, says: ''And now if there are faults they are
the mistakes of men.''   Why does not Mr. Lamb attack
the doctrines and morals set forth in it?   If it is entirely human as he claims, in its origin, it would be easy to
make an inroad upon it.

Pages 1 and 2 he proceeds: ''It is claimed for the
Book of Mormon that it is superior to the Bible in
several particulars: It was translated by Divine inspiration, the Bible was not.   The translation of the
Bible was the work of fallible men, and therefore liable
to many errors; the Book of Mormon was translated
through the 'Urim and Thummim,' helped by an angel
sent from heaven, and therefore free from the errors
that necessarily attach to a human translation.''   The

phrase "helped by an angel sent down from heaven," is a deliberate falsehood of Mr. Lamb's.

On page 2, he quotes from the testimony of the three witnesses to the Book of Mormon: "And we know also that they have been translated by the gift and power of God, for his voice hath declared it unto us, wherefore we know of a certainty that the work is true." This was not strong enough in its claim of divine aid. Mr. Lamb takes the pains to add an angel by way of help.

Then on pages 2, 9, 10, 240 and 241 he gives us eight extracts from accounts of the translation, not one of which connects angel help with the translating.

A ninth extract occurs on page 240, where other matters are treated of, but not one word said about translating; in this one an angel is mentioned.

On page 3, Mr. Lamb quotes from the Book of Mormon: "For behold they have taken away from the gospel of the Lamb many parts which are plain and most precious." Which refers to the Bible as it is, having passed through many changes during the ages. Does the building up and tearing down of creeds, the existence of all the various sects, argue such a condition of the Bible? or, does Mr. Lamb wish to plead guilty for himself and all the rest that they conflict of preference?

Mr. Lamb says, on page 5: "It professes two things—first to be a true record or history of three different colonies that came over from the old world to this country in ancient times, and lived and flourished here for a period of twenty-five hundred years   Second, It professes to contain the fullness of the gospel of Christ, a fuller and more complete presentation of the plan of salvation than is found in the Bible, either in the Old or New Testament." Does Mr. Lamb examine the book on these facts, its history and doctrine? Whether it is more clear on points of doctrine than the Bible? What its moral tone is? HE DOES NOT.

After making and exploding a few bubbles, Mr. Lamb says on page 11: "But after a careful study of the book, a conscientious and painstaking examination of all the evidences he has been able to gather both for and against it, the author of these pages has been forced to reject every one of the above claims. He is compelled to believe that no such people as are described in the Book of Mormon ever lived upon this continent. * * In short, that no such civilization, Christian or otherwise. as is described in the Book of Mormon, ever had an existence upon either North or South America."

This sweeping statement he seems to have forgotten; page 268 says: "We should, therefore, certainly expect to find, in every portion of both continents, the same evidences of an ancient civilization as are found in Central America."

Again, on page 272: "Remains of antiquity have been so well preserved * * upon paper and parchment, hundreds of ancient books and manuscripts were found well preserved at the time of the Spanish conquest, three hundred years ago." Mr. Lamb!! Listen!!!

"Oh what a tangled web they weave,
Who practice solely to deceive."

You are down and out of court on your own evidence.

Mr. Lamb adds to his own impeachment in his eighth chapter, pages 253–283. Why does he do so after a "painstaking examination of all the evidence on both sides."

On pages 11 and 12 he says: "On the contrary, the book is altogether, and in every part of it, except so much as is borrowed from the Bible, a modern fabrication. * * In the discussion of this important question, the author proposes to say nothing whatever of the various theories that have been propounded to account for the origin of the book. * * There is, as the author conceives, a far more direct and satisfactory method of reaching a conclusion—that is, by an examination of the book itself."

Into this examination Mr. Lamb plunges, using the most of the space from page 12 to 253 to show the LITERARY INELEGANCE of the Book of Mormon. Yet Moroni on the opening page says: "And now if there are faults they are the mistakes of men." The same is expressed in other words on pages 44, 495 and 500. (Small print edition). Mr. Lamb claims no literary merit for his own book, but thinks its merits as to facts, all right. Why is not the Book of Mormon rated in the same way? Mr. Lamb is a preacher; wonder if he ever read, "Whatsoever ye would that men should do to you do ye even so to them?" Are all the books of the Bible of the same literary merit? Is that of the unlearned Peter, an humble fisherman, as elegant as that of the learned Paul or Luke? Is Peter's writing less inspired because he was not a polished scholar? Pshaw! shame on any man that takes such position.

Read the following: "Companion to the Revised Version of the New Testament," by Alexander Roberts, D. D., page 1. "The number of various readings in the New Testament has been differently estimated at different times. Nor could this have been otherwise. Every new manuscript which is discovered increases the amount, and every more accurate examination of already known manuscripts tends to the same result. Hence, while the varieties of reading in the New Testament were reckoned at about thirty thousand in the last century, they are generally referred to as amounting to no less than one hundred and fifty thousand at the present day." Mr. Lamb should put a stop to such work, for his ideas of grammar and rhetoric would not admit of the differences existing, and that would spoil their inspiration.

Jared's barges do not escape Mr. Lamb's scrutiny, with their "hole in the bottom, and hole in the top." Ridicule of that feature of their construction has been exploded a hundred times; it being shown that vessels are now so constructed. See citations from Philadelphia Record, December 13, 1891, and Globe Democrat, February 3, 1889, in chapter 3 of Book Unsealed, or visit any prominent life-saving station. Mr. Lamb, evidently for the want of something better, gives us alternately his ignorance and pusillanimity.

On pages 209, 210, 211, three pages, he gives fifty-two quotations from the Book of Mormon, but does not cite a page from where taken. Then triumphantly asserts "No advance upon the Bible whatever." Why did he not give the pages from where taken so the impartial reader could examine for himself? Simply because his misrepresentation would thereby be laid bare.

On pages 208, 209, he says: "The Book of Mormon has nothing whatever upon the subject of 'Laying on of hands,' 'Christ's second coming,' his 'Millennial reign,' the subject of 'marriage,' except the prohibition of polygamy already noticed, 'tithing,' the 'Sabbath'

and 'baptism for the dead.' Have we a Mormon
reader who can believe that any book could contain the
'Fullness of the Gospel' without a word upon either of
the above subjects? These are all very important subjects; with the Latter Day Saints they are fundamental,
and yet here this Golden Bible is ENTIRELY SILENT."
To show how UTTERLY FALSE the preceding is, a few
of many citations are given.

Book of Mormon, Alma 4: 1, says: "And now it
came to pass that after Alma had made an end of speaking unto the people of the church, which was established in the city of Zarehemla, he ordained priests and
elders, by laying on his hands according to the order
of God, to preside and watch over the church."
Moroni 2: 1: "Ye shall have power that on whom ye
shall lay your hands, ye shall give the Holy Ghost; and
in my name ye shall give it." Also Moroni 3: 1. On
millennium, see Nephi 10: 1; Ether 6: 1, and Nephi 9: 9.
On tithing, see Alma 10: 1; Jacob 2: 5; Mosiah 9: 9,
and Nephi 11: 3-7. On Sabbath, see Jarom 1: 3;
Mosiah 9: 9; 7: 21. Mr. Lamb could not have written
a more glaring falsehood.

On page 219, Mr. Lamb treats of modern words
used in Book of Mormon, and because it contains such,
concludes it is a modern production. If some of
Adam's writing should be found and translated into our
language it would contain modern words and therefore
be untrue according to Mr. Lamb's wonderful logic!
The one hundred and fifty thousand various readings
cited by Mr. Roberts, of the New Testament, evidently have several modern words! What TRANSLATED
work would not, Mr. Lamb?

On page 235, Mr. Lamb tells us Harvey discovered

the "circulation of the blood about the year 1619 A.
D., and the fact that the skin has pores could not have
been known * * until after the invention of the micro-
scope." Wonderful logic, Mr. Lamb! Was any body
permitted to sweat before the invention of the micro-
scope? We suppose Mr. Lamb would say no. And
therefore Jesus never "sweat as it were great drops of
blood."—Bible. The foregoing is Mr. Lamb's hard
hit at the Book of Mormon, stating with respect to Jesus,
"blood cometh from every pore." It is a fair sample
of both the man and his book as to merit. In his ninth
chapter "American Antiquities versus the Book of
Mormon," he says: "The Mound Builders of the Ohio
and the Mississippi valleys do not represent the oldest,
but the youngest, by far the younger of the two civilizations already mentioned." Mr. Lamb has forgotten
again that he denied "civilization, christian or otherwise," to have an "existence either upon North or
South America." But why did he not give book and
page where he found what he states about Mound-
Builders.

Bancroft, Short, Baldwin and many others, in
fact nearly all writers on American antiquity accord to
the Mound Builders, the earlier settlement. But then,
Mr. Lamb "examined all the evidences on both sides."
To misrepresent facts in a collossal manner seems to
be his ambition.

On page 257, Mr. Lamb begins to annihilate
"Smith's reformed Egyptian," and on page 260, says:
"Unfortunately for the claims of the Book of Mormon,
we are able to learn precisely what kind of characters
were used in Central America by its ancient inhabitants,
* * in Copan and Palenque are found in abundance

the strange hieroglyphics, the written language of the people."

Consider this: "Egyptian writing is of THREE DISTINCT kinds, which are known respectively by the names of Hieroglyphic, Hieratic and Demotic or Enchorial. The hieroglyphic is that of almost all monuments, and is also occasionally found in manuscripts. The hieratic and demotic occur with extreme rarity upon monuments, but are employed far more commonly than the hieroglyphic in the papyrus rolls or books of the Egyptians."—Rawlinson's Egypt, vol. 1, p. 120.

In the Book of Mormon reformed Egyptian was used.

Consider this: "We find THREE species of hieroglyphics COMMON to Mexico AND Egypt."—Delafield's American Antiquities, p. 46.

The reader is also referred to Atlantis, page 219, where two distinct and then other forms of Maya alphabetic characters are given.

Mr. Lamb is down and out again, while Smith's claim remains undimmed.

Mr. Lamb, page 300, says: "Facts are stubborn things, and the simple testimony of past history already presented, buries the fabrications of the Book of Mormon beyond the possibility of resurrection." Then he proceeds to deny the existence and use of iron and steel in ancient times on this continent. See chapter 10, Book Unsealed. Mr. Lamb devotes pages 306 and 307 to a denial of horses, cattle, sheep and goats as having existed in America anciently. The reader is referred to chapter 6, Book Unsealed.

Extract from a letter of Augustus Le Plongeon, corresponding with S. F. Walker, of Lamoni, Iowa:

"204 Washington St., BROOKLYN, N. Y., 1, 8, '89.
"S. F. Walker Esq.,

"DEAR SIR:—Your favor of December 28th, came
to hand three days ago. * * This calls to my mind the
visit of a certain Rev. Mr. Lamb, who introduced himself to me by stating that he resided at Salt Lake City,
and was there combating the Mormon doctrine and
showing that their pretended revelations were all hum-
bug.   He presented me with a book published by him
in which he pretended to show many absurdities contained in the Book of Mormon.   He finished by telling
me that he had called upon me in order to OBTAIN MY
opinion on what is SAID in the BOOK relatively to the
ANIMALS such as the HORSE, the pig, the cattle and
sheep that lived anciently on the Western Continent,
which he contended proves that the whole book is an
absurd fabrication; and hoped that I would help him
with my knowledge in showing it to be such.   The man
evidently either had been misinformed concerning me,
or had not taken the trouble to enquire.   When he
ceased speaking, I asked him if he was a Christian, to
which he emphatically answered, 'Yes!' and I as emphatically replied no! because he did not follow the
doctrine of Jesus—'do not do to others what you do
not wish others to do to you.'   I informed him that I
did not care a straw if the Book of Mormon was a revelation or a fabrication.   That I considered every man
had an absolute right to worship Deity as best he
thought.   That on the other hand I could not join him
in disproving the Book of Mormon in the part in
which the animals mentioned are said to have lived on
the American Continent, because I was not in the habit
of making a fool of myself if I could help it.   Then I

informed him that seventeen species of fossil horses
had been discovered in America, that the buffaloes
were cattle, that the mountain sheep still lived in the
Rocky Mountains, and that peccaries or wild pigs
roamed yet in large numbers in the forests of Central
America. After that I gave him a piece of my mind
and bowed him out of the house. * *

"[Signed.]   AUGUSTUS LE PLONGEON, M. D."

The reader will now please refer back to opening
page of this examination of the Golden Bible and see
how Lamb uses Le Plongeon's name as an authority,
after he had set down squarely on him. Lamb had out
a previous smaller work, a copy of which he evidently
handed Le Plongeon.

Any one who is conversant with one or more works
on American antiquity will readily notice that the very
few quotations Lamb gives from such works are abundantly offset, in the same works by vastly more testimony
to the reverse in most instances. Those who are not
students of such works, will find an abundance of evidence in the Book Unsealed. Almost all writers on antiquity give the varied views of others as well as their own,
hence the different evidences, pro and con. The great
preponderance of which supports the Book of Mormon.

Mr. Lamb solemnly and benevolently closes the
preface to his work in a postscript thus: "It may be
proper to state in this connection, that this work has
been wholly a work of love, a benevolent and not a
mercenary enterprise. The author has given a year
without salary or compensation, to the work, and all
contributions made, aside from the bare support of his
family, will be sacredly used in distributing copies of
the book among the Mormons." Whoever saw so much

falsifying just for "LOVE!"   How could he expect
Mormons or other persons to believe such a mess of
stuff.   Is it not strangely significant that all who make
such herculean efforts to down the Book of Mormon
enshroud themselves in a mass of falsehood?

No change in Book of Mormon.   Mr. Lamb says
on page 116:   "I have seen two copies of the first
edition of the book, published in Palmyra, New York,
in 1830, and a brief comparison with the latest edition,
will satisfy any reasonable person that the church has
never ventured to change a sentence except the title page
as already mentioned."

A GLANCE AT E. A. ALLEN'S "PREHISTORIC WORLD, OR VANISHED RACES."

ISSUED BY CINCINNATI CENTRAL PUBLISHING HOUSE, 1885.

[This work is not directed against Mormonism specially, but
is put under examination and criticism, as the twelfth work
against Mormonism because of some of the statements found in it
which are at variance with the testimony of the Book of Mormon
and with demonstrated facts.   On the title page we announce
"Eleven Works Against Mormonism Reviewed," but have since
decided to add this and make twelve.]

This work contains eight hundred and twenty
pages, the most of which is devoted to prehistoric man
of the New Continent.

On the title page occurs: "Each of the following
well known scholars reviewed one or more chapters,
and made valuable suggestions."   Then follows these
distinguished names: C. C. Abbott, M. D., author of
"Primitive Industry;" Prof. F. W. Putnam, Curator of
Peabody Museum of Archæology and Ethnology, Harvard University; A. F. Bandelier, explorer for Archæological Institute of America, author of "Archæologi-

cal Tour in Mexico;" Prof. Charles Rau, Curator of Archæological department of Smithsonian Institution; Alexander Winchell, L. L. D., Professor of Geology and Paleontology, University of Michigan; Cyrus Thomas, Ph. D., of the Bureau of Ethnology; G. F. Wright, of the United States Geological Survey, Professor in Theological Seminary, Oberlin, Ohio.

Thus the book is given force. On pages 325, 331 and 377, the Mound Builders are declared to have been destitute of the use of metals for tools, also of domestic animals. The chapter on Mound Builders was reviewed by Prof. Putnam. On page 631, metalic tools are again denied, and on pages 640 and 675, both metalic tools and domestic animals are still denied. The chapter on Maya Tribes is not mentioned as reviewed by any one, so it will be seen that while Prof. Putnam is committed by statements on the three pages cited from the chapter on Mound Builders, no one but Mr. Allen is responsible for the other three in the chapter pertaining to the Mayas.

That Prof. Putnam should have so committed himself seems queer, as he must be a man of extensive reading. And that Mr. Allen, quoting Dana and Winchell as much as he does, is not better informed on the existence of domestic animals, to say nothing of what else he should have found in his reputed wide research, is equally strange; and more strange still that his own reports of works achieved by the ancient Americans, does not impel him to conclude that metalic tools of variety and high order, as well as domestic animals must have been had.

Mr. Allen's work being recently issued and having the support of these eminent men, will doubtless play a part yet in discussion.   As I do not remember that it has been quoted from, for the benefit of those to whose convenience it may be, I give a few extracts.

Of fossil remains of man, page 308 says: "On our Western Continent we have the mysterious remains in the gold-bearing gravels of the Pacific coast, the significance of which is yet in dispute.   We have the Paleolithic Age of Europe, represented by the remains found in the gravels of the Delaware at Trenton, New Jersey.   When deposited there, and by what people used, is, perhaps, still enshrouded in doubt.

Page 310:   "We must not forget that these are the antiquities of our own country, that the broken archæological fragments we pick up, will, when put together, give us a knowledge of tribes that lived here when civilization was struggling into being in the east. * * In a general way we have regarded the Indians as a late arrival from Asia, and cared but little for their early history.   It is only recently that we have become convinced of an extended past in the history of this country, and it is only of late that able writers have brought to our attention the wonders of an ancient culture, and shown us the footprints of a vanished people."

Page 311:   "Indeed, to judge from the difference of the remains, they must have been the work of different people or tribes, who were doubtless possessed of different degrees of culture."

Page 324 gives a cut of the Grave Creek Mound, twelve miles below Wheeling in West Virginia.   A description follows, then, on page 325, we read: "A moment's thought will show us what a great work such a mound must have been for a people destitute of metalic tools and domestic animals."

Page 330 presents a cut of Cahokia Mound which is opposite to St. Louis, Missouri.   The description ends with: "The areas of all the platforms are not far from six acres.   We require to dwell on these facts a moment before we realize what a stupendous piece of work this is.   The base is larger than that of the Great Pyramid, [Egypt.—R. E.] and we must not lose sight of the fact that the earth for its construction was scraped up and brought thither without the aid of metallic tools or beasts of burden, and yet the earth was obtained somewhere and piled up over an area of fifteen acres in one place to a height of one hundred feet, and even the lowest platform is fifty feet above the plain."

Page 376 gives a cut of Fort Ancient, forty miles east of Cincinnati, Ohio.   The description given closes thus on page 377:   "The total length of the embankment is about five miles, the area enclosed about one hundred acres.   For most of this distance the grading of the walls resembles the heavy grading of a railroad track.   Only one who has personally examined the walls, can realize the amount of labor they represent for a people destitute of metallic tools, beasts of burden, and other facilities to construct it."

Page 332, dealing with the magnitude of Cahokia Mound says: "If the result of religious zeal, we may be sure that a religion which exacted from its votaries the erection of such a stupendous piece of work was one of great power.

On page 361, Mr. Allen quotes Mr. Squier: "We have reason to believe that the religious system of the Mound Builders, like that of the Aztecs, exercised among them a great, if not a controlling, influence."

The foregoing extracts are from chapter 10 "The Mound Builders," and on page 413, the last of the chapter, occurs: "In fact there is no good reason for separating them from the Indian race as a whole."

This conclusion is no doubt, as well founded as, that there were no domestic animals or metallic tools had among them.

We now present extracts from chapter 14—"The Maya Tribes."

Page 568 presents a cut of the ruins of Copan, in the State of Honduras, Central America, and on page 569 occurs: "Though Mr. Stephens warns us that this terrace was not as large as the base of the Pyramid of Ghizeh, still it must have required an immense amount of work, since careful computations show that over twenty-six million cubic feet of stone were used in its construction. This stone was brought from the quarries two miles away. We must not forget that this work was performed by a people destitute of metallic tools." Just because, forsooth, Mr. Allen thought so!

Of fourteen statues, a cut of one being given on page 571, page 570 says: "The places where these statues are found is seen to the right of the main body of ruins. It will be seen that only one is within the terrace area of the temple. Three others are situated near it, but the majority are near the southern end of the enclosure. We are not given the dimensions of all, but the smallest one given is eleven feet, eight inches high, by three feet, four inches width and depth; the largest, thirteen feet high, four feet wide, and three feet deep. No inconsiderable part of the labor on the statues must have been that of quarrying the large blocks of stone out of which they were carved, and transporting them to the place where found. They came from the same quarry as the other stones used in building, and so were transported a distance of about two miles."

Mr. Allen would have us believe stone columns could be quarried and carved in the fine lines he illustrates in his cuts, and describes elaborately, with STONE MAULS, etc.

Of a palace at the city of Utatlan, Guatemala, page 582 says: "Mr. Stephens describes a large ruin which is called The Palace. It is said, in round numbers to have been eleven hundred by twenty-two hundred feet. As this area is more than fifty-five acres in extent, we can see it was not a palace in our sense of the word. The stones of which it was composed have been largely removed to build the modern town of Santa Cruz."

Pages 630 and 631 present three cuts of most intricate and elaborate carving, of a magnificent building at Uxmal Yucatan, and then says: "We must reflect that its builders were not possessed of metalic tools. It extends entirely around the building, though the end and rear walls are not as elaborately decorated as the front. A little calculation shows that it contains over ten thousand square feet of carved stone." What finger-nails those fellows must have had!

Page 640, reviewing the ruins of Uxmal in a general way, after the splendid cuts and explanation of intricate carving, says: "When we reflect on the patient labor that must have been expended on this pyramid and these buildings, we are filled with admiration for their perseverance and ingenuity. They had neither domestic animals or metalic tools. The buildings were massively built and richly ornamented. The sculptured portion covers over twenty-four thousand square feet."

Page 644 says: "We want to repeat that Yucatan, even to this day, is far from being thoroughly explored Almost our only source of information is the writings of Mr. Stephens. But he only describes a few places. In a trip of thirty-nine miles he took in a westerly direction from Uxmal he saw no less than seven different groups of ruins. * * As to the question of use to which these buildings were applied, we must either suppose they had an immense number of temples and palaces— one or the other every few miles—or else they were the residences of the people themselves. And, though it may seem very strange that an imperfectly developed people should ornament so profusely and delicately their ordinary places of abode, yet it is difficult to understand why they should rear such an abundance of temples and palaces."

Page 675, speaking of Mexico and Central America, says: "We must remember that throughout the entire territory we are considering the tribes had no domestic animals, their agriculture was in a rude state, and they were practically destitute of metals."

Pages 810 and 811 present cuts of large and magnificent stone structures and says: "Round holes were drilled in the bottom and top of each stone. There is reason to suppose that bronze pins fitted into these holes." But, Mr. Allen, bronze is a combination of metals and they were destitute of them!

Page 815 says of ruins at Cuzco, Peru: "Some of the stones must weigh several tons, and they are fitted together with marvelous precision, one stone having as many as twelve angles."

Since writing the above, I have found the following in the May number of "The Archæologist" of 1894,
published at Waterloo, Indiana, the editor of which is
Warren K. Moorehead; whose location is Orton Hall,
State University, Columbus, Ohio, and who had an
exhibit at the World's Fair: Quoting from Prof. Putnam on page 131:   "It is fully time that we acknowledge that our old peoples, particularly the people who
made the great earth works in the Ohio Valley, were
pretty far advanced in many of the arts, and certainly
had reached a high plane of achievement in the working of native copper, native silver, native (meteoric)
iron, and occasionally gold, all by hammering, pressure,
rubbing and cutting."

Right glad are we to record Prof. Putnam as a witness that iron was had and worked by prehistoric people of the Western Continent.   Mr. Allen's only witness who had passed upon what Allen had written is
thus found on the other side.   And in Prof. Putnam's
language we may conclude, "It is fully time that we
acknowledge * * iron."   The character of works
abounding impel the intelligent reasonable mind to this
conclusion.   And as for the domestic animals having
existed, their remains are found in such quantity and
variety that the existence of the moon may as well be
denied.

BRADEN'S MISTAKES.

1st. States on page 34 of Braden and Kelley Debate that the Book of Mormon speaks of "ore plates," when the language of the book is "I did make plates of ore."

2d. On page 43 he says he proved certain things by sixteen witnesses who from reading it, (Spaulding Romance), and hearing him read it, became more or less familiar with its contents; when he had produced testimony from only six who testify to having read or hearing it read.

3d. On page 43 he says he proved by these sixteen witnesses that Solomon Spaulding, "between the years 1809 and 1816," "spent much of his time in preparing manuscripts," &c. He had produced testimony from NONE giving these dates.

4th. He had produced testimony from only ONE who spoke of manuscripts in the plural.

5th. On page 43 he claims the sixteen give "an outline of the historic portion of the Nephite part of the Book of Mormon." He had produced testimony from only NINE who relate any incident related by the Book of Mormon.

6th. On page 43 he claims his sixteen witnesses give names "of the principal characters." Only SEVEN pretend to give names.

7th. Claims on page 43. that the sixteen give the "starting point of the history," when only SIX of them mention it.

8th. On page 43, "They (the sixteen) ALL declare there was no religious matter in his manuscript." In their testimony as presented by Braden but few had said so.

9th. He says on page 43, "Oliver Smith testifies that Spaulding told him, just before going to Pittsburg, that he would prepare the manuscript for press," &c. This is not in Oliver Smith's testimony as produced by Braden. See p. 35 of Debate.

10th. On page 43 he says that J. N. Miller testifies: "Spaulding told him that he landed the people at the Isthmus of Darien which he called Zarahemla." This is not in J. N. Miller's testimony, found on page 35.

11th. On page 52 he says: "The Book of Mormon declares in several places the Nephites were Manassehites," which is not true.

12th. On page 62 he represents Mr. Gilbert as saying the manuscript "abounded in mis-spelled words," when Gilbert says: "The spelling was good." See p. 382.

13th. On page 64 he claims Spaulding was guilty of "carricaturing the Bible;" but on page 67 he says: "Nearly all of our witnesses are careful to state that the religious portion of the Book of Mormon was not in the Manuscript Found."

14th. On page 65 he claims Spaulding was "the very man that would attract company, and of the highest character and intelligence;" yet on page 64 he makes him out a skeptic, a liar, and his motives "very questionable."

15th. On page 66 he claims Mrs. Solomon Spauld-
ing, Miss Martha Spaulding, John Spaulding, Mrs. John
Spaulding, Lake, J. N. Miller, Smith, Wright, Howard,
Cunningham, Jas. Miller, McKee, Dodd and Sidney
Rigdon, testify to Spaulding's Romance being a history
of the first settlers of America; when he had produced
no testimony to this effect from Miss Spaulding, Jas.
Miller, McKee, Dodd, or Rigdon

16th. On page 66 quotes Miss Martha Spaulding,
Mrs. J. Spaulding, Smith, Cunningham and Jackson, to
prove the leaders' names as represented by Spaulding,
were Nephi and Lehi, which is false, so far as Miss
Spaulding, Cunningham and Jackson are concerned.

17th. On page 66 he says: "The end of their
wars, in two instances, was the total annihilation in
battle, of all but one," for which he quotes Jackson.
Jackson does not say so. See p. 42.

18th. On page 66 he quotes J. Spaulding, Mrs J.
Spaulding, Miller and Smith as authority for the
"Romance," giving an "account of the civilization,
arts, sciences, laws and customs of the aborigines of
America." Mrs. J. Spaulding nor Miller speak of this
point.

19th. On page 66, as authority that the Romance
was "written in Scriptural Style," he quotes "Rigdon,
Winter, Spaulding, Mrs. S. Spaulding, Mrs. J. Spaulding, Lake, Jas. Miller, Smith, Cunningham and Jackson. By examination it will be seen he had produced
no evidence upon this point from either Rigdon, Mrs.
J. Spaulding, Lake, Miller, or Smith.

20th. On page 66, as authority that the Romance
contained the phrases, "And it came to pass," "And
now it came to pass," he names Mrs. S. Spaulding, J.

Spaulding, Mrs. J. Spaulding, Lake, Cunningham and Jas. Miller.   Consult their testimony as produced by Braden, and you will find this false so far as Mrs. S. Spaulding, Mrs. J. Spaulding, Cunningham and Miller are concerned.

21st. On page 66 he says: "One party of emigrants landed near the Isthmus of Darien, which they called Zarahemla, and migrated across the continent in a northeast direction," and quotes J. N. Miller.   See Miller's testimony on page 35.

22d. On page 73 he says: "He spent five years on it,,' (The Romance), but on page 43, he says "seven years."

23d. On page 73 he says that Mrs. Spaulding, Miss Spaulding and Miller "declare that he had many manuscripts." He produced this testimony from none of them.

24th, On page 73 he says: "That he (Rigdon) had it (Spaulding Romance) in 1826, and declared it would be a great thing some day, to his neice Mrs. Dunlap."   Mrs. Spaulding does not say he had the Spaulding Romance.   See p. 45.

25th. On page 73 he says: "We have proved that he (Rigdon) knew of the publication of the Book of Mormon long before it appeared, by D. Atwater, A. Bently, Alexander Campbell, Green and Dille."   This is false, especially as regards Green and Dille.   See p. 46.

26th. Read what he says he proved by Campbell, Atwater and Bently, as found on pages 74 and 75, and then read their testimonies as found on page 45, and the reader will see a great mistake indeed.

27th. On page 95 he says that Mrs. Davidson said she "only gave him (Hurlbut) an order to examine a trunk hundreds of miles away, in Hartwich, New York, to see if it (the manuscript) was in the trunk." If the reader will refer to Mrs. Davidson's testimony he will discover this to be a false statement.

28th. On page 96, in regard to the charge that Hurlbut sold the manuscript to the Mormons, he says: "These charges, Hurlbut never met but laid under them until his death." On page 91, in a letter Hurlbut wrote to Mr. Patterson of Pittsburg, dated August 19th, 1879, he says: "I did not destroy the manuscript nor dispose of it to Joe Smith or to any other person."

29th. Will Mr. Braden tell us where he finds his authority for saying that Joseph Smith claimed to have "examined all religious parties?" See p. 98.

30th. Will he also tell us why he says Joseph Smith claimed to "found a purer system than the world had ever seen?" See p. 98.

31st. On page 107 he garbles the testimony of the Three Witnesses. See p. 5.

32d. On page 108 he states, in speaking of what the Book of Mormon teaches, that Nephi "makes Laban drunk." This is false. See Book of Mormon, p. 8.

33d. On page 109 he says Lehi prophesied "that these plates of Laban shall go forth to all nations;" but the book adds, "who were of his seed." See Book of Mormon, p. 11.

34th. On page 111 he represents that the Book of Mormon claims that Nephi and his company left only Laman and Lemuel and their families when departing into the wilderness, which is absolutely false. See Book of Mormon, p. 62.

35th. On page 119 he represents Mrs. Salisbury as saying the plates were translated "at their father's," which she does not say. See p. 100.

36th. On page 120 he says: King Jacob tells us that "a hundredth part of the wars, contentions and exploits of the Nephites could not be engraven on his plates." A quotation not to be found.

37th. On page 120, in speaking of events recorded on page 118 of Book of Mormon, he says: "About forty years before this, six women left Jerusalem," when, according to the book, at least fifty-five years had passed. See Book of Mormon, p. 112.

38th. The number of women as stated above is wrong. There were Lehi's wife, (see page 4,) Ishmael's wife and five daughters, (see page 12,) besides Nephi speaks of his sisters, how many we do not know. See p. 64.

39th. Braden adds, "but one (of these women) was then married." Doubtless the wives of Lehi and Ishmael were both married.

40th. On page 120 he garbles a quotation from page 120 of the Book of Mormon as follows: The book says: "It began to put forth somewhat a little, young and tender branches." Braden quotes it: "It began to put forth somewhat a tender little branches."

(Note.—Nearly every passage I have examined purporting to be from Book of Mormon is more or less garbled. Space will not allow me to notice all.)

41st. He says on page 130: "Moroni takes up Mormon's work, and he informs us that masonry shall be prevalent when the Book of Mormon appears," when the word mason or masonry does not appear in the book.

42d. On page 132 he says: "Moroni prophesies the one who finds these plates shall show them to three persons. Joe showed them to eleven." The language of the book is: "And behold ye may be privileged that ye may show the plates unto those who shall assist to bring forth this work; and unto three shall they be shown by the power of God."

43d. He says on page 34: "It is our purpose to prove that the Book of Mormon originated with Solomon Spaulding," but on page 139 he calls "Rigdon the author of the book."

44th. On page 141 he says: "Amulek declares that Nephi, and all who went with Lehi were Mannassehites, and not Jews at all. Amulek only says, "Lehi was a descendant of Mannasseh." See Book of Mormon, p. 231.

45th. On page 141 he says: "On page 375 we are told the devil led Jared and his people." It is not there.

46th. On page 148, after many falsehoods in regard to the Jaredites, he says: "Sidney did not stop and figure that story out when he wrote it;" but on page 43 he says: Spaulding "added the Jaredite emigration."

47th. On page 150 he claims that events recorded on page 136 of the Book of Mormon transpired two hundred and fifty years B. C.; but on page 151 he says this page relates to things happening four hundred years B. C.

48th. On page 151 in trying to make the Book of Mormon to agree with Shakespeare he misquotes the former.

49th. On page 159 he says, speaking of the Book of Mormon: "It had not a mark of punctuation in it;" but on page 160 he says: "The fabrications of the Book of Mormon copied * * the punctuation of King James' version."

50th. On page 159 he says it was "badly spelled;" but Gilbert says, (see p. 382), "The spelling was good."

51st. On page 161 he tries to make Spaulding out an ignorant man, but on page 75 he says, "he received the degree of A. M. from Dartmouth College."

52d. On page 161 he says: "It was like Josh Billings' spelling." Gilbert says: "The spelling was good."

53d. On page 161 he says: "We have proved by historic evidence that Rigdon remodeled Spaulding's manuscript;" but on page 171 he says: "We can trace it no farther back than Joe Smith in 1830."

54th. On page 33 he tells us he expects to prove the Book of Mormon had its origin "about seventy years ago," (1814), then admits his failure on page 171 by saying: "From the Tower of Babel to 1830, not a human being knew of the book, or knew a single particle of its pretended history."

55th. On page 173 he says a certain document was signed by "Sidney Rigdon and eighty-four other leading Mormons," and on same page says, "Rigdon and eighty-three other leading Mormons."

56th. On page 173 he accuses O. Cowdery of living in adultery at Nauvoo, when he did not reside there at all.

57th. On page 180 he says: "The eight witnesses tell us that the leaves Joe had translated were loose, separated from what he had not translated." This is false, as will be seen by reference to their testimony found on page 5.

58th. On page 180 he tells us that the eight witnesses testify that they did not see the plates which were not translated. False again. See p. 5.

59th. On page 202 he relates what a "Mr. More-ton, one of the first apostles, told his daughter." There was no man of that name among the first apostles.

60th. On page 206 he falsely states: "The Jose-phites publish, and use as their standards, the works of the Pratts and other Utah Mormons."

61st. On page 206 he misquotes the Book of Mormon on the subject of polygamy.

62d. On page 214 he falsely states that William Marks was once the editor of "their (the Josephite) official organ."

63d. On same page he makes the same false assertion in regard to Zenas H. Gurley.

64th. On page 216 he claims to have produced testimony from Rigdon to the effect "that Solomon Spaulding wrote a romance," which can not be found in the book.

65th. He claims on page 218 to have proved that Cowdery "died a drunken sot, with delirum tremens." This he has not attempted to prove.

66th. He almost invariably misquotes the Bible. I will ask the reader to read the two passages found on page 222 as samples of his garbling.

I have not written this to refute the position taken by Mr. Braden; this was neatly and thoroughly done by his opponent. But as Mr. Braden was introduced as a witness in my late debate, and may be so introduced again, I write it to show his utter unreliability. I thought first to speak of all his mistakes, but they multiplied so rapidly, I concluded to pass by misrepresentation of other books, and confine myself to the book under consideration, and the standard of evidence. I soon found however that this would have to be

abridged.   Then when I had passed through one proposition, noting perhaps half of his mistakes, I concluded
if I examined the other two, it would be too voluminous
to publish, and so conclude.   Surely here is enough to
accomplish my object.   HEMAN C. SMITH.

FOUR PROMINENT MEN, VOUCHED FOR BY OTHERS. TELL WHAT THEY SAW.

WISE REVERENDS DIFFER—JOSEPH SMITH A VERY REMARKABLE YOUTH.

The Christian Cynosure published by Ezra A. Cook, at Chicago, Illinois, contained in its issue of December 20th, 1877, an article entitled, "Joseph Smith the Mormon," by the Rev. Samuel D. Green, who says of Smith: "He saw money deposited by an early settler, who sat down by this river and deposited his money in the earth just where the miller was erecting his abutments, some of Smith's believers went and dug for the money and one of the walls fell.   The diggers were disappointed, and helped rebuild it.   This is the only act of mischief I ever heard of him, and of this I never searched the truth, it was a report, and whether true or not, I have no knowledge.

"There was living in Bethany, a Rev. M. Spaulding. * * He had written some chronicles on the ruins of Central America and some Bible truths mixed up together.   Some early history of the character of the inhabitants, connected with bigamy, etc.   Joe Smith and Cochran got some knowledge and borrowed it, and from the help of Spaulding's manuscript they made the Mormon Bible.   Rev. Mr. Spaulding called and sent for it a great many times, and his wife came for it, but

Smith would not let them have it.   Smith told Spaulding, and I heard him, that he had made a Mormon
Bible of it, and the Lord had taken it into the wilderness.   And he, Joe Smith, prophesied where it was
deposited in Palmyra woods about twelve miles east of
Rochester, New York.   James Harris was appointed
to go and get it.   He went and pretended he found it
beside a log just where Smith said it was.   This is the
true history of Joe Smith and the beginning of Mormonism, and the people who settled at Salt Lake.
After Mr. Spaulding died, his wife came east to Mun-
son, Massachusetts, while I lived there, to visit her
friends or relatives, Dr. McKingsbury's family, my near
neighbor."

SUMMARY OF THE ABOVE.

1st, As Mr. Green wrote in 1877 and knew Smith
was only guilty of one act of mischief, which was but
a report; so Smith is clear of all else at least.

2d, As Mr. Spaulding died in 1816 as repeatedly
published in his wife's letter.   Mr. Smith told in
Green's presence the name of the Book of Mormon
when but eleven years old, as he was born in 1805, and
as the plates were not had till 1827, Mr. Smith is made
a prophet at eleven years of age.

3d, Mr. Green being totally ignorant of what he
writes, gives the name Cochrane for Cowdery, James
Harris for Martin Harris, and McKinsbury for McKin-
stry.

Elder M. T. Short of Millersburg, Illinois, reviewed the letter of Mr. Green in the issue of the Cynosure of July 25th, 1878, of which the editor in an appended statement said: "The above is the history of
the Spaulding book from a Mormon standpoint, most

of our readers will recollect the letter from Samuel D. Green in the issue of December 20th, 1877, giving a history of Joe Smith, while stopping at his hotel in Batavia, New York, and the origin of the Book of Mormon. Mr. Green saw this Mr. Spaulding as late as 1827, knew that he lent his manuscript to Smith and called for its return several times in vain, and heard Smith tell him it was disposed of. The writer of the above would do well to study Mr. Green's letter as it is altogether reliable and its author is yet living in Chelsea, Massachusetts."

"CHELSEA, Mass., May 12th, 1879.
"Mr. I. N. WHITE.

"DEAR SIR:—I send you the Christian Cynosure of the 20th of December, 1877. If you had taken the Cynosure, one of the best, open, candid, Christian papers published, you would long ago know all the questions you asked me. * * I saw Mr. Spaulding as late as 1827 and I have a letter from Wm. Jenkins (now dead) that he saw Spaulding in Attica in 1829, and he wanted to preach there. Another needful you will get from the Cynosure. * *
"Yours truly,
"SAMUEL D. GREEN.

"P. S.—Send for the 'Broken Seal' to Ezra H. Cook & Co., Chicago, Illinois."

QUOTATIONS FROM THE BROKEN SEAL.

"Samuel D. Green, of Chelsea, Massachusetts, a Master Mason, who was a member of Batavia Lodge, to which Morgan belonged, and an intimate friend of Morgan's, and was, at the time of this abduction, mayor or president of Batavia, and a member of the Presbyterian church.

"A Masonic Revelation.—Mr. Samuel D. Green is a venerable gentleman of the highest respectability, whose statements seem to be worthy of full credence. The Broken Seal, or, Personal Reminiscences of the Morgan Abduction and Murder, is the title of a book of some three hundred pages just issued by him, purporting to give a full and accurate account, from personal knowledge, of the Morgan 'abduction,' and other Masonic matters which made such an excitement in this country, now almost half a century ago."—Congregationalist and Recorder, Boston.

"A Book for the Times.—We have received from the publisher a book of thrilling interest, entitled 'The Broken Seal, or, Personal Reminiscences of Samuel D. Green, on the abduction of William Morgan by Freemasons, in 1826.'

"Mr. Green is an acquaintance of ours. He is a venerable gentleman, of high respectability and intelligence, upwards of eighty-two years of age, a member of the Congregational church, and we esteem him as a Christian man."—World's Crisis.

In the Congregationalist of October 24th, 1877, the Rev. Tryon Edwards, D. D., of Philadelphia, tells what he knows about Mormonism; he says: "The Book of Mormon was in substance written by Rev. Solomon Spaulding, who was a graduate of Dartmouth college and a Presbyterian minister, once settled in Cherry Valley, New York, and afterward living in New Salem, (also called Conneaut), Ohio. Beginning in 1809, and writing at intervals as he did, he often read parts of the work to his neighbors, and among the listeners was Joseph Smith, who not only attended the readings, but borrowed the manuscripts, as he said, to read to his family at home.   In 1812 the completed manuscript was placed in the hands of a printer in Pittsburg, Pennsylvania, by the name of Patterson, with a view to its publication.   While the printing was delayed, Mr. Spaulding left Pittsburg, for Washington county, Pennsylvania, where he died in 1816.   While the manuscript was in the hands of Patterson, Sidney Rigdon was working for him as a journeyman printer, and it is supposed that he, having copied the manuscript, with Smith concoted the idea of the new religion!!!"

MEDITATIVE OBSERVATIONS.

Mr. Smith who was born December 23d, 1805, must have been a very interested listener to the reading of the manuscript, which was completed "in 1812," and "placed in the hands of a printer."   And with what elegance he must have read it to "his family!" Not many boys of seven have a family.   The vilifiers of Joseph Smith often make him more remarkable than his friends do.

But Mr. Edwards places Mr. Green in a bad fix, as Spaulding died in 1816 he says, while Green saw Spaulding in 1827, Mr. Green having heard Smith tell Spaulding he "made a Mormon Bible out of it," (manuscript) and as Spaulding died in 1816, Smith was a literary wonder at eleven years of age.

In the Detroit Tribune of February 1st, 1872, appeared an article entitled, "The Mormon Church." The writer, J. F. D., mentions a celebrated discussion held in New York City, in 1836 or 1837, at which he was present, and of which he says: "It was shown that Mr. Spaulding, from reading the discoveries made by Mr. Stephens and others in Central America, was led to select the subject of his novel." Mr. Stephens says: "Being entrusted with a special confidential mission to Central America, on Wednesday, October 3d, 1839, I embarked on board the British Brig, Mary Ann, for the bay of Honduras." See Stephen's work, Vol. 1, chap. 1, p. 9.

EXTRACT FROM "LIFE OF KIT CARSON," BY JOHN S. C. ABBOTT.

Mr. Abbott introduces one Wm. E. Goodyear, and vouches for his intelligence and veracity; inserts a letter from him in which he says: "In the year 1852, I, then a young man, in all the vigor of early youth, and of unusual health and strength, when the wildest adventures were pleasure, was led by peculiar circumstances to undertake a trip across the continent. * * We reached the Great Salt Lake, the home of the Mormons, in safety. Here we remained for nearly a month. I called on Brigham Young and also on the old patriarch Joe Smith; from the latter, I received a commission, or power of attorney, for the consideration two dollars, authorizing me to heal the sick, to raise the dead, and to speak all languages. Perhaps my want of faith left me as powerless as other men, notwithstanding my commission."—pp. 286–292.

The old patriarch, Joe Smith, as he is here vulgarly called, died at Nauvoo, Illinois, September 4th, 1840, and Hyrum had succeeded him, he being killed in 1844, and beside there has been no man of that name among the Brighamites as patriarch to this day. Seeing a man who had been dead twelve years is but a small item in lying on the Mormons.

JOHN L. HILDRETH DEAD.—ONE OF THE BEST KNOWN
MEN IN THE WEST DIES IN PUEBLO—LIFE OF THE
MAN WHO LOST THREE FORTUNES—
CAUSE OF HIS DEATH.

Special to The News

PUEBLO, Colo., Feb. 18th, 1894.—John L. Hildreth died this evening, aged seventy years. Deceased had a very adventurous life in California, Colorado, and the west generally, until about twenty years ago. In 1849, with his parents and the family, he went to California, from Hannibal, Missouri, and from Salt Lake his party were guided by Joseph Smith, afterwards chief prophet of the Mormon church. They suspicioned treachery on the part of Smith, however, and sent him back. In their party were the Oatman family, who got tired of the slow progress of the train one day, and pushed ahead, They were killed in the Mountain Meadow massacre and their wagons were burning when the Hildreth party came on the scene.— Rocky Mountain News, February 18th, 1894.

Joseph Smith, the chief prophet of the Mormon church, never was west farther than Missouri, and had been dead over four years when this well known man saw him. The Mountain Meadow Massacre was in 1857, think of these poor people eight years in transit, how tired they must have been!

EXTRACT FROM THE "WILD WEST," PUBLISHED
BY R. S. PEALE, 1888.

This purports to be an account of a dialogue between one Simpson, leader of U. S. Army train, and Joseph Smith, in 1857. Simpson asks: " 'But who are you?' 'I am Joe Smith,' was the reply. 'What!

the leader of the Danites?' asked Simpson. 'You are correct,' said Smith. * * 'What do you propose to do with us now?' 'I intend to burn your train. * * I have no way to convey the stuff to MY PEOPLE, I'll see that it does not reach the U. S. troops.' "—pp. 436–9.

The name "Joe Smith," as well as the phrase "my people," shows it was the man who was killed in 1844, thirteen years before. Beside there has been no Joe Smith at the head of the Utah church or its Danite band!

JOSEPH SMITH'S WIVES—WRITERS VARY.

Ann Eliza says Smith lived with eleven girls as adopted daughters.

"Joseph Smith had a dozen spiritual wives; but three sons survived him—all of his legal wife."—Beadle p. 375.

"Joe Smith had over forty wives at Nauvoo, and yet the number of his offspring fell far short of even that of Young."—Smucker p. 416.

F. D. Richards, apostle and assistant historian in behalf of the Utah Mormon church, whose all depends upon the matter, says: "In a chapter furnished a book, entitled "What the World Believes," page 600, "It is well understood among the Latter Day Saints that Joseph Smith and many other prominent members of the church married or had sealed to them several wives. Joseph Smith's first wife was Emma Hale, who was married to him January 18th, 1827. Of the names or number of his other wives, as also dates of their marriage to him, we are not informed." Richards has seen the fixing of names and dates go to the wall too often to do so.

EXTRACTS FROM SIX U. S. HISTORIES, COMPARED WITH EACH OTHER AND WITH FACTS.

"The Mormons or Latter Day Saints, are a religious sect, founded in New York State in 1830, * * afterward moved to Utah. The founder of this sect was Joseph Smith, who pretended to preach a new gospel. He published 'his revelation' as the 'Book of Mormon,' which he induced a small number of fanatics to accept as a New Bible. The sect located first in Ohio, in 1831, and next at Independence, Missouri, where their religious law brought them into conflict with the civil authorities. In consequence of this, they moved, in 1838, to Illinois, where the legislature gave them a charter for a city, Nauvoo. Here Smith set the example of polygamous marriages, and polygamy became the practice of the leaders, though not adopted by the Mormon church as a part of their creed until later. This custom and numerous depredations upon property, brought the Mormons into trouble with the authorities of Illinois. Joseph Smith was shot in a riot, (1844). Brigham Young took Smith's place at the head of the church, and under Young's leadership most of the Mormons emigrated to the vicinity of Great Salt Lake, in Utah, (1847–8)." Extract from California State Series History of the U. S., pp. 262–3.

The errors in the above are, first, Joseph Smith did not pretend to preach a new gospel, but that of the New Testament which is old; second, about two hundred thousand accepted the Book of Mormon as true and divine, instead of a "few fanatics;" third, the Book of Mormon was never presented as a Bible, either new or old, but as distinct from the Bible as are the continents from each other; fourth, their religious views did not bring them into conflict with the Missourians. President Van Buren said, "Your cause is just."—Beadle, p. 60; fifth, Joseph Smith did not establish polygamy; all his life's labors were opposed to it, as shown in the recent decision by Judge Philips in the Temple Lot case; sixth, Joseph Smith was not shot in a riot, but in jail. Jail and riot are hardly synonymous.

"The trouble in Utah was with the Mormons. This sect, known as Mormons or Latter Day Saints, tolerating a plurality of wives, arose some time before. Joseph Smith was the founder. He was born in 1805, in Vermont, of humble origin. He removed with his father when quite a boy to the neighborhood of Palmyra, New York. The family was of that thriftless class who made a livelihood by hunting, trapping, well-digging and peddling cakes and beer. He pretended to have received his call as a 'prophet' in 1823, by a divine revelation. The revelation was made to Mormon, a former prophet, and it was called the Book of Mormon, and hence the name of the sect. But it was not till 1830 that Mormonism began to take shape as a distinct sect; a considerable number of accesions was soon made to its ranks. At Kirtland, Ohio, and Independence, Missouri, settlements were established. But

public opinion soon drove them from Missouri and
Ohio. They migrated to Illinois in 1839, and built the
city of Nauvoo. * * Within the space of two years,
two thousand houses were constructed. After a short
while, ill feeling was engendered betwixt them and the
people of the neighborhood, which threatened to result
in a conflict of arms. On this perturbed state of things
Smith himself was apprehended, lodged in jail, and
while there killed by a mob in June, 1844."—Alex. H.
Stephens, Pictorial History of the U. S., 1882 edition
published by National Publishing Co., Chicago. Ill.

First, this account is short the usual tale, of water
witching, digging for treasures, sheep stealing, etc., but the
"peddling of beer and cakes" makes up the deficiency!
Second, "A considerable number of accessions was soon
made to its ranks," while the previous one had it "a few
fanatics." They disagree! Third, "Ill feeling was
engendered, * * Smith himself was apprehended,
lodged in jail and while there killed by a mob in June,
1844." That is a very general statement which prejudice decides against Smith. Eighteen hundred years
ago, ill feeling was engendered. Christ was apprehended, lodged in several places, and killed by a mob.
Fourth, By comparison of these two extracts and the
following, by Bryant, it is clearly seen that history on
the matter has been very carelessly written.

"In the autumn of 1857 the defiant resolution of
the Mormons in Utah compelled the president to remove the governor, Brigham Young, and appoint
Alfred Cumming, an officer of the army his successor.
* * Driven first from Missouri to Illinois in 1838, and
thence, ten years afterwards into the wilderness, they
sought a resting place and refuge in what was then

called 'The Great American Desert.' * * In after years the treacherous temper of their chief saints had imposed the system of polygamy as a latter revelation to Smith." —pp. 427-8, Bryant's Popular History U. S., published 1881, by Chas. Scribner, N. Y.

"The immorality of the Mormon doctrines, among which, that of polygamy, or the allowing of a plurality of wives, was prominent, recommended them to some, and in 1833, Smith found himself at the head of twelve hundred followers. Jackson county, Missouri, became their headquarters. * * They crossed to Illinois, * * founded the city of Nauvoo. * * At last, Joseph Smith, still the leading spirit among the Mormons, was arrested, and with his brother, lodged in jail at Carthage. Here on the 7th of July, 1844, they were killed by a mob which broke into the prison."—Quackenbos, History U. S., published by D. Appleton & Co., N. Y.. 1875.

This reckless writer charges polygamy as leading to the success attained in 1833. Bitter enemies as well as conclusive evidence to the contrary notwithstanding. The killing of the Smiths he gives as July 7th, whereas it was June 27th. This could hardly be a typographical error, and shows extreme recklessness.

"Being expelled from Ohio, in 1838, and from Missouri in 1839, Smith attempted to introduce polygamy in the Mormon belief when they settled at Nauvoo, Illinois, but was strongly opposed by certain of the community, who established a press and published opposition articles. Smith headed a mob which demolished this press, but this act cost the prophet his life." —Eclectic History U. S., by M. E. Thalheimer, published by Antwerp, Bragg & Co., Cincinnati and New York. Article on the Mormons and Joseph Smith.

While Quackenbos, the last examined, set forth polygamy as existing before 1833, this one places its introduction after 1839. Smith did not introduce polygamy, neither did he head the mob that demolished the press.

"Mormonism gives its followers license to commit every crime that may be sanctioned by the leading prophet, especially does it, by allowing polygamy, degrade and demoralize women. * * But murders, robberies and other secret crimes became frequent in their neighborhood. The surrounding people were enraged; the Mormon prophet and his brother were seized by the state officers, and confined in jail at Carthage. A hundred armed men in disguise broke in and murdered them. * * The Rev. Mr. Spaulding wrote the Book of Mormon as a work of imagination."—History of the U. S., by Emma Willard, published by A. S. Barnes & Co., 1870.

In the above no distinction is made at all between the career of Smith and Young. It is now a matter of United States Court decision in Temple Lot case that Joseph Smith and Brigham Young were widely different. None of the above allegations were true as occurring under Smith's presidency and sanction. See part 3, chapters 6 and 7, and on last clause chapter 4 of same. These six examined show a queer medley of history for the proud nation of United States.

ENCYCLOPEDIAS EXAMINED.

Extracts from, and Brief Comment on, American Encyclopedia of 1863 and 1875. Britannica of 1863, (Scribner's) 1844, (Stoddart's) and that of 1890, (Peale's). Johnson's of 1888 and 1891. Columbia of 1891. Constituting Four Leading Encyclopedias and Eight Editions.

The comments or references to evidences, showing their errors, are notes numbered 1, 2, 3, 4, 5, 6, 7, 8 and 9; to avoid needless repetition they appear consecutively and reference is made to them farther on as occasion requires.

Chambers' edition of 1881 has the only fair account of the origin, rise and development of the Latter Day Saints. Subsequent editions not now at hand for comparison evidently are identical. It is a credit to Chambers, that an attempt to give facts was made, whereas the others have been made up from trashy stories on Mormonism, and from each other.

American Encyclopedia, by D. Appleton & Co., 1863, Vol. 11, p. 733: "From the testimony of their neighbors in Palmyra, the reputation of the Smiths was bad. They avoided honest labor, and occupied themselves chiefly in digging for hidden treasures, and in similar visionary pursuits. They were intemperate and untruthful, and were commonly suspected of sheep stealing and other offences. Upward of sixty of the most respectable citizens of Wayne county, testified, in 1833, under oath, that the Smith family, were of immoral, false, and fraudulent character, and that Joseph was the worst of them. These statements are not in general, contradicted by the Mormons." (See note 1 at close of quotation).

Referring to the testimony of the three witnesses, Harris, Cowdery and Whitmer, to the Book of Mormon, says: "Several years afterward, however, all three of the witnesses quarreled with Smith, renounced Mormonism, and avowed the falsity of their testimony." (See note 2).

Pages 735–740: "According to the opponents of Mormonism, from investigations soon after the appearance of the 'Book of Mormon, the fact is fully established that the real author of the work was Solomon Spaulding, who was born in Ashford, Connecticut, in 1761, was graduated at Dartmouth College, and afterward ordained." * * (See note 3). "As early as 1813 this work was announced in the newspapers as forthcoming, and as containing a translation of the Book of Mormon. (See note 4). Spaulding entitled his book 'Manuscript Found,' and intended to publish with it by way of preface or advertisement, a fictitious account of its discovery in a cave in Ohio. * * John Spaulding, a brother of Solomon, says in a deposition: 'I made him (Solomon Spaulding) a visit about three years after and found that he had failed, and was considerably involved in debt. He then told me he had been writing a book, which he intended to have printed, the avails of which he thought would enable him to pay all his debts. The book was entitled "Manuscript Found," of which he read to me many passages. * * By what means it has fallen into the hands of Joseph Smith, I am unable to determine.' Martha Spaulding, the wife of John Spaulding, Henry Lake, the partner in business of Solomon Spaulding, and many others corroborated these statements in the fullest manner. John N. Miller of Springfield, Pennsylvania, testified in September, 1833, that in 1811 he was in the employ of Spaulding, and lodged and boarded in his house, and frequently perused portions of the 'Manuscript Found,' which the author also sometimes read to him. Miller says: 'I have recently examined the Book of Mormon and find in it the writings of Solomon Spaulding from beginning to end, but mixed up with Scripture and other religious matter, which I did not meet in the "Manuscript Found." Many of the passages in the Book of Mormon are verbatim from Spaulding and others in part.' (See note 5). The names of Nephi, Lehi, Moroni, and in fact all the principal names are brought fresh to my recollection by the gold bible.' " (See note 6).

Encyclopedia Britannica, ninth edition, J. M. Stoddart & Co., Philadelphia, Pennsylvania, 1884, Vol. 16, p. 852: "Smith was born December 23d, 1805, at Sharon, Windsor county, Vermont, from which place ten years later, his parents, a poor, ignorant, thriftless, and not too honest couple, removed to New York, where they settled on a farm near Palmyra, Wayne county, (then Ontario)." (See note 1). Speaking of Harris, Cowdery and Whitmer, as witnesses and their testimony found in Book of Mormon, says: "This testimony, all three on renouncing Mormonism some

years later, denounced as false; (see note 2), but mean-
while it helped Smith to impose on the credulous, particularly in the absence of the gold plates themselves
which suddenly and mysteriously disappeared." "This
is Smith's account of the book, but in reality it was
written in 1812 as an historical romance by one Solomon Spaulding, a cracked brained preacher, and the
manuscript falling into the hands of an unscrupulous
compositor, Sidney Rigdon, was copied by him and
subsequently given to Smith." (See note 7 at close of
this).

The ninth edition, by Scribner, of 1883 and that of
R. S. Peale & Co. of 1890 are identical.

Johnson's Encyclopedia, issued 1888, Vol. 7, p.
304: "Joseph Smith was born at Sharon, Vermont,
December 23d, 1805, removed while a child, with his
parents, to Palmyra, New York, where he grew up
almost without education, leading an idle and rather
disreputable life, (see note 1), and about 1828 began
to put forth vague claims as the founder of a new religion, or rather as the restorer of the original true faith."
Of the three witnesses to the Book of Mormon, says:
"Subsequently all three of the witnesses fell out with
Smith and declared the whole matter to be a hoax."
(See note 2). "There can be no doubt that the Book of
Mormon was a kind of historical romance, written
nearly twenty years before by Samuel Spaulding, at
one time a clergyman." (See note 5).

Vol. 5, page 540: "It was soon proved beyond
doubt that the Book of Mormon was simply a sort of
historical romance written in 1812, by one Solomon
Spaulding * * and that the manuscript became lost in
a printing office in Pittsburg, under the hands of an

apprentice, Sidney Rigdon, who in 1829 became an associate of Joseph Smith." (See note 7). Describing Brigham Young, it says: "The whole success of the sect and all the elements of respectability are due to him, while all its miseries and all its excesses had their roots in Joseph Smith's character."

Mr. Johnson, appreciating Brigham's career as respectable, would of course set forth Joseph Smith's the reverse as they were opposites. No one will deny Mr. Johnson the right of choice. What of the Reorganization that Mr. Johnson entirely ignores? Johnson's reissue of 1891 is identical with the above.

The Columbian Encyclopedia by Garretson, Cox & Co., New York, 1891, Vol. 20, article Mormon: "Joseph Smith was born in 1805, at Sharon, Windsor county, Vermont, son of a farmer. His parents were ignorant and of low repute. * * The reputation of the family is said to have been of the worst kind; we are told that they avoided honest labor, were intemperate, untruthful, and suspected of sheep stealing and other offenses." (See note 1). "There is the most satisfactory evidence—that of his enemies—to show that from an early period he was regarded as a visionary and a fanatic." (Note 8). "The Book of Mormon finally appeared before the world in 1830 with the names of Cowdery, Harris and Whitmer appended to a statement that an angel from God came down from heaven and showed them the original plates, a statement which, a few years later, was declared false by all three witnesses." (Note 2). "The so called Book of Mormon was really borrowed or stolen nearly verbatim from a manuscript historical romance written in 1812, by a quondam clergyman, Solomon Spaulding, a man of some gifts but of unbalanced mind, who died in 1816. The Mormons of course declare the whole story of Spaulding's manuscript romance a scandalous fabrication. While the death of those who could have testified to the facts prevents the evidence of Spaulding's authorship from being absolutely conclusive, nothing has ever been shown disproving it." (See note 5 again). Of settlement in Missouri in 1831, says: "Land was largely bought, preaching was vigorously carried on, a printing press was established, * * everywhere was visible a spirit of industry, sobriety, order, and cleanliness. It is only fair to the Mormons to state these things. Account for it as we may, they were in many important respects, morally, socially and industrially, far in advance of their neighbors." (Note 9). "1832, March 22d, a mob of Methodists, Baptists, Disciples, and miscellaneous zealots broke into the prophet's house, tore him from his wife's arms, * * and tarred and feathered him."

This last item shows clearly why Smith and his co-workers were held to be such bad fellows; having exhausted all else to down them and their cause, TAR and FEATHERS was resorted to by this religious mob. Several extracts from Bancroft in part 3, chapter 6, set forth the same facts. Those who would descend to tar and feathers, would also malign and vilify. Lies go swiftly but truth wins in the end.

NOTE 1.—The statements referred to have been denied all along the line for sixty years by Mormons, and proved untrue from various sources and at divers times and places. See Facts from Painsville, Murdock's protest, and interview of citizens of Palmyra, New York. Part 3, chapter 3 of this work.

NOTE 2. - Never, in a single instance, did either of the three deny their testimony; even after they stood aloof from the church, and at death all reaffirmed their testimony. See chapter 14, Book Unsealed.

NOTE 3.—Mrs. Spaulding in 1834 delivered to Hurlbut the manuscript so it could be published. See part 3, chapter 4 of this work. "The Spaulding Manuscript Story in Brief."

NOTE 4.—Spaulding according to this was to translate the Book of Mormon fourteen years before Joseph Smith procured the plates, and seven years before he first saw them, and when Smith was but eight years of age. Lying may yet be found a good thing, but it certainly was overdone in this case.

NOTE 5.—What a miserable, reckless liar this Miller must have been. Howe did not publish the manuscript because "it did not read like we expected, and we did not use it." See part 3, chapter 4 again, especially the comparison made by Fairchild and Rice, also, that John N. Miller's name is in the postscript as witness to the verity of manuscript as Spaulding's.

NOTE 6.—Reference same as in notes 3 and 5, the reader will notice that Rice and Fairchild say: "There seems to be no name or incident common to the two." "There is no identity of names, of persons or places, and there is no similarity of style between them."

NOTE 7.—This date, 1829, is unfortunately late, as the manuscript of Book of Mormon was delivered to the printer in August, 1829. Mr. Braden in his vast research attending the labor of four debates with Elder E. L. Kelley, takes the position that 1827 was the best time to bring Smith and Rigdon together. Smith's home was Palmyra, New York; Rigdon in Ohio, several hundreds of miles apart and no railroads or even stage lines direct. Rigdon's whereabouts for 1827 as given by Kelley in the Lamoni, Iowa, debate: "My first date is January, 1827, Rigdon is at Mantua, O., Hayden's History, p. 237; February 27th, at Chester, O.; March and April, protracted meeting at Mentor, O.; June 5-7, Painsville, O., probate records; July 3-12, Mentor, O., probate records; July 19, Mentor, O.; August 23. New Lisbon, O.; Hayden pp. 55-57; September, returns home to Mentor, O.; October 9, Mentor, O.; October last part, Warren, O.; Hayden, p. 59; November, New Lisbon, Hayden, pp. 72-76; December 6, Kirtland, O., probate records; December 13, Concord, O., probate records." See also part 3, chapter 5 of this work.

NOTE 8.—"There is the most satisfactory evidence, that of his enemies." Is not that a brilliant view of evidence? No juror is admitted who has formed an opinion on a case! Whose reputation or character on earth, or the angels of heaven either, would be safe from this point of view? Shame on such work.

NOTE 9.—The date given is 1831, remember. This strong statement from an opposing witness, showing the virtues of this people in advance of those surrounding them, nicely offsets much of the villainous lying that has been done. Joseph Smith being an honorable, honest, conscientious, God-fearing man, gathered such around him. See also extract from Bancroft's New History of Utah, p. 164, as found in part 3, chapter 6 of this work.

Let those who fight Joseph Smith so hard and prove nothing against him, consider Moses who slew the Egyptian, and David who placed Uriah in front of battle, and this also: "The smoke ascending from the funeral pile of Servetus was a witness of the stain upon the character of John Calvin that all the special pleading of men can not remove.   The followers of Calvin or Knox forget to tell the world that the former burned Servetus.   The Presbyterian of today would quickly resent the insult offered his faith, were we to tell him that Presbyterianism sanctioned murder.   He would suddenly discover that individual unholy acts did not condemn the doctrines held by the transgressor, unless they were the legitimate consequence of them."   Even of our good Mr. Wesley it is related that: "He was accused of diverting the people from labor, (while laboring as a missionary at Savannah, Georgia,), of fomenting divisions, of claiming high and unwarranted ecclesiastical authority.   His conduct towards a neice of one of the principal settlers, (a Miss Williams), was highly resented by her friends.   Thirteen indictments for alleged offences, were found against him, but before the time of trial he returned to England, (left under cover of his friends at night,) and there for many years pursued a successful and distinguished career of piety and usefulness."—History of the United States, by Wiley, published in 1830, in New York.

REFERENCES RELATIVE TO THE REORGAN-
IZED CHURCH OF JESUS CHRIST
OF LATTER DAY SAINTS.

———

Encyclopedia Britannica, Vol. 16, p. 828: "Already there are not wanting signs of approaching disso-
lution, of which, perhaps, the most significant is the
conference of the 'Reorganized Church of Jesus Christ
of Latter Day Saints,' held on the 6th of April, 1883,
at Kirtland, Lake county, Ohio. This sect originated
in 1851, seven years after the death of Joseph Smith,
when several officers of the church met and claimed to
have received a revelation from God, directing them to
repudiate Brigham Young as not being the divinely
appointed and legitimate successor of Joseph Smith,
and as being the promulgator of such false doctrines as
polygamy, Adam God worship and the right to shed
the blood of apostates.

"Nothing of special importance occurred, however, until 1860, when Joseph Smith, jr., the eldest son
of the founder of the faith, became identified with the
Reorganized Church as its president.   Since then the
seceders have prosecuted misssionary work throughout
the United States, Great Britain, Canada, Scandinavia,
Switzerland, Australia and the Society Islands, until
their communicants are said to number over twenty-
seven thousand.   Their headquarters are at Lamoni,

Iowa, to which place they removed from Plano, Illinois, 1881.

"The Reorganized Church holds that the legitimate successor to Joseph Smith was his eldest son; that the allegation that Smith introduced polygamy on the strength of divine revelation was an invention of Brigham Young; that the Utah Church has departed grievously from the faith and practices laid down in the Book of Mormon and subsequent revelations of Joseph Smith, and that the Reorganized Church is the only true and lawful continuation of and successor to the the original church and as such is legally entitled to all that church's property and rights; and it was to celebrate the decision of the United States' Court of Ohio, confirming this last claim, and vesting in them the right to the temple consecrated in Kirtland, Ohio, in 1836, and for nearly forty years disused, owing to litigation, that the Reorganized church met in that temple on the 6th of April, 1883."

The above is from edition of 1883, that of 1890, by Peale, being identical.

"A portion of the Mormons reject polygamy, and do not approve of Brigham Young or of the church in Utah. Joseph Smith, the son of the prophet, is regarded by them as the true living head of the church, and under his direction they have established themselves at Nauvoo."— American Encyclopedia, issues of 1863 and 1875. The supplement for 1894 has the first article as furnished by the Reorganization, all hitherto being refused though different encyclopedias were furnished copy.

"The great social peculiarity of the sect is their practice of polygamy. It was not so, however, at first.

Rigdon, Kimball, Pratt, Hyde and Young, are its true originators.   Emma, wife and widow of the prophet Smith, stoutly denied that her husband ever had any wife but herself: Young's 'revelation' she declared to be a fraud, and in consequence she withdrew to Nauvoo. Her four sons followed her, and have now founded a monogamic Mormon community, called the Josephites, but naming themselves the Reorganized Church of Jesus Christ of Latter Day Saints."

The above is from the Columbia Encyclopedia of 1891.   Chambers of 1891 being identical as to facts and almost verbatim in word.

THE DIFFERENCE STATED OFFICIALLY.

"DEPARTMENT OF STATE,   }
"WASHINGTON, April 4, 1883. }

"Messrs. Joseph Smith and Z. H. Gurley,
    Committe, etc., Lamoni, Iowa,

"GENTLEMEN:—I have to acknowledge your communication of the 23d of February last in regard to a circular letter issued by the Hon. W. M. Evarts, when Secretary of State, to the diplomatic agents of this country abroad, requesting foreign Governments to discriminate against the emigration of Mormon converts to the United States, and you ask that a distinction be made between the polygamous Mormons of Utah, and the non-polygamous Mormons of the Reformed Church to which you belong.   In reply, I have to say that Mr. Evarts' circular was directed against polygamy, and intended to warn those persons abroad who emigrated to this country for the purpose of joining polygamous communities that they would thereby expose themselves to the operation of the penal laws of the United States.

It is contrary to the practice of this government to give by circular, as is proposed, any sanction or indorsement of a specific form of belief.

"It is for the agents of any religion to make known its character.   Law-abiding emigrants are secure against interference.   I am, gentlemen,

"Your obliging servant,

"FREDERICK T. FRELINGHUYSEN."

Governor Murray says in The North American Review for January, 1884:   "The Mormons known as the 'Reorganized Church,' are entitled to the respect of all, and that Church recognizes and receives in common with all others, every protection under the constitutional guarantee.   But polygamous Mormonism, which has overridden the Constitution, nullified Federal legislation, and defied the Government, has made of Utah a deformed child."

KNOWN FAVORABLY THROUGH THE PRESS.

Of very many collected, the author of this work has had difficulty in confining himself to the few notices of the press given.   The first thought was to present one from each paper; that being precluded the next was one from each locality, but finally they are passed by from east, west, north and south, and only the few that follow selected.

History Decatur county, Iowa, pp. 513, 514, says of President Joseph Smith of the Reorganized Church: "His youth was passed amid trials, sorrows and afflictions that would have embittered one of less noble character against the world.   His life has been saddened by the events of those years, but his manhood has not deteriorated, and it may be that the persecution of his family, which did not end with the death of his father, has had much to do with forming his character.   No semblance of intolerance has place there.   The same liberty of action and thought he exercises himself, he freely accords to all. * * In religion, loyal to the faith of his father, he recognizes in every worker of good, a brother.   As a citizen, no man outranks him in fealty to the government.   As a man, his character of honor and integrity stands unquestioned. * * He has with others labored diligently, * * has seen the church over which he presides grow from a handful, obscure and unpopular, into a body of persistent workers of many thousands of honest, honorable men, known and loved of their neighbors, and loyal to their country."

The Kendall County Record said of President Joseph Smith's departure, when removing to Lamoni, Iowa, in October, 1881: "Mr. Smith leaves Plano, but carries the good will of Plano's citizens with him. He has lived here for the past fifteen years, and has always borne the reputation of a good citizen.   Always to be found on the side of right, he maintained his position to the end, and goes to his future home with sad farewells and good wishes of his many friends."

Iowa contains more of the members of the Reorganized Latter Day Saint Church than any other state. The leading paper of the state says editorially: "The Reorganized Mormon church under President Smith not only refrains from endorsing polygamy, but is perhaps the most alert and active enemy that the abomination has.   As a church under this president, it is as much entitled to recognition and public favor as any of the many churches of the day, so far as honesty of purpose and action are concerned."—Register, March 20, 1887.

The Cleveland Herald says of the Reorganized Church in conference, April 1883, under date of April 6th: "The flood-gates were lifted this morning, and the deluge of praise and thanksgiving, of reminiscence and story, that for ten days is to envelop Kirtland, came down in full force. All day yesterday and all through today the crowds have poured in until this little village is full. * * Although many more are expected, enough are already present to comfortably fill the spacious audience room. As a class, the Mormons gathered within the old temple this afternoon were as fine a looking religious body of men and women as ever gathered together. Many of them saw the interior of the old temple for the first time in over forty years. To others it was the first realization to them of the familiar story of the early struggles of their fathers in the faith, when the Church was in its infancy."

Under date of the 7th it says: "To say the opening [of conference] was a magnificent success, is not putting it too strong."

The Herald of the 9th contained the following: "The affair is certainly a success. Nearly six hundred votes are cast at the business meetings. * * It is the anniversary of the founding of a church that has attracted the attention of people in all parts of the world. * * A more devoted or conscientious body of delegates never assembled for a like purpose. * * Nothing can exceed the persistency with which the Mormons gathered here denounce the evils of their brethren of the Utah Church. The consciousness that they are continually reproached on that account evidently aggravates them greatly.

"Said President Smith to your representative this

morning, 'We differ from them in almost everything.
They are a theocracy.   What they are told to do must
be done.   There can be no excuse.   With us there is
freedom of thought.'   The Hon. R. P. Harmon, in
speaking of the ministers present says: 'In intellectual
acumen I think they stand above the average clerical
assemblies.' "

INVITED BACK TO KIRTLAND, OHIO.

"EDITOR WILLOUGHBY INDEPENDENT:—Saturday
evening last will be long remembered as one of the largest
and most enthusiastic gatherings in the history of Kirtland.   The event that called forth this company was the
work of the late discussion between the Rev. Clark
Braden, of Illinois, of the Disciple Church, and E. L.
Kelley, now of Kirtland, formerly of Glenwood, Iowa, of
the Reorganized Church of Christ of L. D. S.   The gathering was in recognition of the work of Mr. Kelley during the discussion, and made a surprise to him and his
family—and also a further honor to Elder Wm. H.
Kelley, of Coldwater, Michigan, who has for the past
year rendered at times ministerial labor in Kirtland.
The company consisted of seventy-five citizens of Kirtland, nearly all of whom had attended upon the eighteen sessions of the discussion just closed, and none of
whom are connected with the church of which Mr.
Kelley is a member; and a number of other citizens who
had attended upon the discussion sent their regrets at
not being able to be present from various causes of
hindrance. * * Speech by L. V. Sanborn, Esq., of
Kirtland, as follows:

" 'MR. E. L. KELLEY:—A few of your friends and
neighbors have met at your house this evening for the

purpose of expressing, by word and by deed, our appreciation of you as a citizen, as a neighbor, and as a
christian. We come in unity of sentiment with regard
to our views as to the sincerity of your belief. During
the late discussion in which you have been engaged, we
have had strong evidences of your faith by the charity
of your language, in return for the abuses of your opponent. But in strict keeping with the agreement for the
discussion. You have met the enemy on every issue
and he is vanquished; and now we have come to crown
the success of your efforts, and to encourage you, if
possible, by our visit and our sentiments, in the main-
tenance of that manly bearing and christian spirit which
has so characterized your conduct and your language
through the entire discussion. We admire the honest
and able manner in which you discussed the questions
at issue, and especially denounce the dishonest, unqualified language of your opponent, whose part of the
debate was not argument, but mere slander and vilifi-
cation, which pleased and satisfied only the bigoted,
the prejudiced, or the weak minded. And we believe
it would be a serious mistake for members of this community to support or favor such an act, knowing the
dishonorable reputation of the man, whose manner and
language does not belie that reputation—just because
he opposes the religion of the Reorganized Church of
Latter Day Saints, whose only sin (if it may be called
a sin) is in believing the whole of the Bible, and a little
more.' "

At a later social occasion the following was said:
"'To Mr. and Mrs. Kelley and Elder Columbus Scott:
The citizens of Kirtland who have met at this social
gathering, welcome you back to the place of worship,

and home of your fathers; and may your every effort
be blessed in doing good, and to this end do we extend
our sincere sympathy and warmest congratulations."

INDEPENDENCE, MISSOURI.

"The Reorganized Church of Latter Day Saints is
holding an annual conference of the world here at the
present time. The leading men of the church are here
and it is fully represented in all its parts.

"The conference is composed of a greater number
of delegates than ever assembled at Independence prior
to this time, and of a representation from a greater territory than has gathered together for similar purposes in
many years.

"The people who have come here have the appearance of honest, zealous, faithful men, engaged in what
they conceive to be the propagation of great truths that
have been confided their care and been made their
especial responsibilities. They teach the cardinal virtues
of the christian religion and such the orthodox churches
hold and believe. They claim a new revelation and
that the day of special revelation has not passed. They
invite investigation, and are open and candid in their
lives and conduct.

"It is not longer excusable to charge upon the Reorganized Church sympathy with the polygamists. They
regret the Salt Lake dogma with loathing and disgust,
and teach and keep the marriage relation as sacredly as
other Protestant people.

"The sobriety of the Mormon people of this community and their testimony against all forms of dissipa-
tion does them great honor and ought to silence the
tongue of ignorant criticism.   Men are entitled to

credit for lives of usefulness and morality ·and there should be no disposition to withhold it from them.　It can not be an unprofitable thing for other than the Mormon citizens of Independence to make this confer· ence the means of learning more about the sect or denomination that has become so numerous in and about the city and which is destined, it seems, to take so prominent a part in moulding the minds of so many people."—Editorial, Independence (Mo.) Daily Sen- tinel, April 7, 1888.

Of the conference of 1882, the Stewartsville, Mis- souri, Independent said:　"The conference of the Church of Christ (Latter Day Saints) is in session in this city, and is attended by large numbers of members from all parts of the union.　Every train has brought new additions to the already large number, until the city presents a very lively appearance.　It is thought that the visit of many of them will result in the pur- chase of property and becoming residents.　They are a good class of citizens and should be given every facility to become residents if they wish."

INVITED TO NAUVOO.

Herald, January 1, 1878, contained this:　"On the 18th of December, 1877, we received by express, a petition of which the following is a copy, addressed to the Church of Jesus Christ of Latter Day Saints:

" 'We, the undersigned citizens of Nauvoo, and surrounding country, most cordially invite the head or leaders of the Reorganized Church of Jesus Christ of Latter Day Saints, to establish the headquarters of their church in said city of Nauvoo.

" 'We believe that the odium rightfully attached

to the Brighamite Mormons in the infamous practice of polygamy is detached from the Reorganized Church of Latter Day Saints; we believe you will receive a cordial welcome and reception from all philanthropic people of our county, and we further believe by establishing the headquarters of your church in the aforesaid City of Nauvoo, with our united efforts we can build, or make it one of the most popular cities in the military district.'   (Signed).

"This petition is followed by a list of signers three and a half yards long, some portion of its length signed in double columns, comprising the names of nearly all the leading business, professional and laboring men of the city and its immediate vicinity.   We are pleased to note the names of many citizens whom we knew while residing at Nauvoo, whom we respected, and with whom we labored for the good and quiet of the town. * * Nor was our joy made less upon seeing in the Carthage Gazette, a paper published at the county seat of Hancock county, by Mr. Thomas C. Sharp, whom all Saints have reason to remember, the following editorial:

" 'The Nauvoo Independent says that a petition, signed by some four hundred persons, has been forwarded to Joseph Smith, Jr., requesting him to make Nauvoo the Head Quarters of his reformed church of Latter Day Saints.   Some of the old anti-Mormon citizens are a little nervous over this matter—we are not. * * '—Carthage Gazette, Dec. 26th, 1877."

REUNION AT LOGAN, IOWA.

"The Globe, of Council Bluffs, Iowa, in its issue for October 13th, 1892, gave the Latter Day Saints the following flattering notice:

" 'COME TO COUNCIL BLUFFS.

" 'At Logan tomorrow the Latter Day Saints will decide upon the next place of meeting for next year. About fifteen thousand people attended the meeting at Logan, and it will be seen that the city that secures the meeting captures a big prize. Council Bluffs will make an effort to have the next meeting held here. The Chautauqua grounds are especially fitted for such and the city could easily care for this large assemblage. The people of Council Bluffs will gladly welcome them and the Globe bespeaks for them a generous and kind treatment in the event of their coming. The Latter Day Saints can rest assured that if they honor Council Bluffs by holding their next annual reunion here, and it is an honor to the city to be the scene of the meeting of such a body of respectable citizens, they will be given the best of treatment.' "—Herald.

"Many are the agencies that together are shaping the future of the great civilization now centering in this Garden Valley of the world. Silent and unnoticed are the forces moving into position for the final fulfillment of our destiny as a nation. * *

"By disintegration the Latter Day Saints found themselves separated from the polygamous Mormons and left to develop into a moral civilizing force in the fertile valleys where Mormonism first found foothold, while the evil portion went on to its rapid rise to power and even more rapid fall to pieces. * * These Latter Day Saints in camp in our country for their annual harvest of souls, point with pride to their open creed as evidence of their true Christian spirit and the world cannot but say: 'Ye have done well, abide with us.' Their devotions are genuine. Their moral lives of the

best.   Their presses are messengers bearing good tidings.   Their loyalty leads them to place the national
colors over their holy altars.   It is well. * * Tried by
these signs the Latter Day Saints are worthy of a welcome as one of the forces that will at all times hold
high the starry banner, honor the powers that in creat-
ing it gave them a home where freedom of conscience
is the keystone of all liberty, of all Christianity, and of
all civilization."—Editorial, Missouri Valley News.

"The Reunion of the Latter Day Saint Church ended
yesterday.   This has been the largest ever held here
and has been very successful, a large number being
received into the church by baptism.   It was decided
to hold it here next year, which will be the fourth
reunion at this place.   The fact that the vote locating
it here for 1893 was almost unanimous, speaks well for
Logan, and that Logan people wished to have them
come for the fourth successive meeting, speaks well for
the people who attend the reunions.   The fact is, it
would be impossible to have a more quiet, devout
assemblage than has occupied the grove on the hill for
the last sixteen days."—Iowa State Register, Oct. 17,
1892.

"The World Reunion of the Latter Day Saints
closed Sunday night [16], taking their departure for
their homes on Monday.   This has been an exceedingly
pleasant gathering to them.   Their leaders have been
with them, their most eloquent preachers have addressed
them, and the meeting has been the longest and largest
ever held.   The remembrance of the reunion of 1892
will be long cherished.   No better meeting will ever be
held.   For sixteen days the interest was kept up and
the last Sunday found the tent well filled, every space

occupied.   The attendance was about as large as at
any time during the meeting.   Eighty four joined the
church by baptism.   On Friday last the vote was taken
by the church members on the question of locating the
reunion for 1893.   By nearly a unanimous vote it was
decided to hold it at Logan.   Council Bluffs, Iowa,
Warrensburg and Clinton, Missouri, and Plano, Illinois,
were Logan's competitors, but when Logan's proposition to do just the same in 1893 as was done this year,
was presented, the other places were not in it.   Logan
has carried out every agreement with strict fidelity and
it is a well recognized fact that even more than the contract called for has been done."— Logan Observer.

PART III.

COMPENDIUM OF EVIDENCE.

Joseph Smith Exonerated.

CHAPTER I.

CHICAGO TIMES EDITORIAL.—JOSIAH QUIN-CY AND DR. FOSTER SPEAK.—DANITES DENOUNCED BY JOSEPH SMITH.

JOSEPH SMITH, FOUNDER OF THE LATTER DAY SAINTS.

The Chicago Times of February 20th, 1889, said editorially: "Do people in general want to know the truth about Joseph Smith, the founder of the sect which styles itself the 'Latter Day Saints,' and the origin of the book which they claim supplements the Old and New Testaments? Apparently they do not. * * It is fair to presume that few of these persons ever read any of the publications of the 'Saints,' or ever attended any of their meetings."

Time on its eternal march must yet exonorate Joseph Smith as it did Wesley who was also calumniated in his day by all classes.

HOW WESLEY WAS USED IN HIS DAY!

"March 2, 1891, is the centenary of the death of John Wesley. Many biographies of him have been written, and the minutest incidents of his life are familiar to the members of the religious community who are called by his name. Others are far less acquainted with his personality, and may not be sorry to be reminded what manner of man he was. * *

"We might think it strange that the desire to preach the gospel of Christ should invoke such deadly opposition, alike of the so-called respectable and religious classes, and of the rude and ignorant multitude. Yet so it was. * * Every form of opposition, we are told, was tried against him. 'Mill dams were let out; church bells were jangled; drunken fiddlers and ballad singers were hired; organs pealed forth; drums were beaten;' street-vendors, clowns, drunken fops, and Papists were hired, and incited to brawl or blow horns, so as to drown his voice. He was struck in the face with sticks, he was cursed and groaned at, pelted with stones, beaten to the ground, threatened with murder, dragged and hustled hither and thither by drinking, cursing, swearing, riotous mobs, who acted the part of judge, jury and executioner. 'Knock him down and kill him at once,' was the shout of the brutal roughs who assaulted him at Wednesbury. On more than one occasion, a mad or a baited bull was driven into the midst of his assemblies; the windows of the houses in which he stayed were broken, and rioters burst their

way even into his private rooms. 'The men,' says Dr.
Taylor, 'who commenced and continued this arduous
service—and they were scholars and gentleman—displayed a courage far surpassing that which carries the
soldier through the hailstorm of the battle-field. Ten
thousand might more easily be found who would con-
front a battery than two, who, with the sensitiveness of
education about them, could (in that day) mount a
table by the roadside, give out a Psalm, and gather a
mob.'

"III. To face all this, and to face it day after day,
and year by year, in England, in Scotland, in Wales,
in Cornwall, in Ireland, required a supreme bravery,
and persistence. Yet it needed even greater courage
to meet hurricanes of abuse, and tornadoes of slander.
Wesley had to face this also on all sides. The most
popular actors of the day held him up to odium and
ridicule in lewd comedies. Reams of calumny were
written against him; shoals of pamphlets, full of viru-
lence and falsehood, were poured forth from the press.
The most simple, the most innocent, the most generous
of men, he was called a smuggler, a liar, an immoral and
designing intriguer, a Pope, a Jesuit, a swindler, the
most notorious hypocrite living. The clergy, I grieve
to say, led the way. Rowland Hill called Wesley 'a
lying apostle, a designing wolf, a dealer in stolen wares,'
and said that he was 'as unprincipled as a rook, and as
silly as a jackdaw, first pilfering his neighbor's plumage,
and then going proudly forth to display it to a laugh-
ing world.' Augustus Toplady said, among floods of
other and worse abuse, that 'for thirty years he had
been endeavoring to palm on his credulous followers
his pernicious doctrines, with all the sophistry of a

Jesuit, and the dictatorial authority of a Pope;' and described him as 'the most rancorous hater of the gospel system that ever appeared in England.' Bishop Lavington, of Exeter, denounced the Methodists as a dangerous and presumptuous sect, animated with an enthusiastical and fanatical spirit, and said that they were 'either innocent madmen or infamous cheats.' "— Archdeacon Farrar, D. D , in The Contemporary Review.

JOSEPH SMITH AT NAUVOO.

From figures of the past.   From the leaves of old journals, page 376, by Josiah Quincy, Class of Harvard College, 1821, published at Boston, Massachusetts, by Messrs. Roberts Brothers, 1883.

"It is by no means improbable that some future text book, for the use of generations yet unborn, will contain a question something like this: What historical American of the nineteenth century has exerted the most powerful influence upon the destinies of his countrymen!   And it is by no means impossible that the answer to that interrogatory may be thus written: Joseph Smith the Mormon Prophet.   And the reply, absurd as it will doubtless seem to most men now living, may be an obvious commonplace to their descendants.   History deals in surprises and paradoxes quite as startling as this.   The man who established a religion in this age of free debate, and who was and is today, accepted by hundreds of thousands as a direct emissary from the Most High, such a rare human being is not to be disposed of by pelting his memory with unsavory epithets.   Fanatic, imposter, charlatan, he may have been, but these hard names furnish no solution to the problem he presents to us.   Fanatics and imposters are living and dying every day, and their memory is buried with them. But the wonderful influence which this founder of religion exerted and still exerts, throws him into relief before us, not as a rogue to be criminated, but as a phenomenen to be explained. * * Joseph Smith claiming to be an inspired teacher, faced adversity such as few men have been called to meet, enjoyed a brief season of prosperity such as few men ever attained, and finally, forty-three days after I visited and saw him, went cheerfully to a martyr's death. A fine looking man, is what the passer-by would instinctively have murmured upon meeting the remarkable individual who had fashioned the mold upon which was to be shaped the feelings of so many thousands of his fellow mortals. But Smith was more than this, and one could not resist the impression that capacity and resource were natural to his stalwart person. I have already mentioned the resemblance he bore to Elisha R. Potter, of Rhode Island, whom I met in Washington in 1826. The likeness was not such as would be recognized in a picture, but rather one that would be felt in a grave emergency. Of all men I have met, these two seemed the best endowed with that kingly faculty which directs, as by intrinsic right, the feeble or confused souls who are looking for guidance. * *

"On the right hand, as we entered the house, was a small and very comfortable, or comfortless looking bar room, all the more comfortless, perchance, for its being a dry bar room, as no spirituous liquors of any kind were permitted at Nauvoo. * *

"Polygamy, it must be remembered, formed no part of the alleged revelations upon which the social life at Nauvoo was based."

R. D. FOSTER'S TESTIMONY.

"LODA, Ill., Feb. 14th, 1874.

"Joseph Smith, President of the Church of Jesus
Christ of Latter Day Saints, Plano, Illinois.

"DEAR SIR:—Accept my sincere thanks for the
favors that came to hand this day, by mail, namely, a
copy of the Book of Mormon and a copy of Parley P.
Pratt's Voice of Warning, as well as your very welcome
letter with your photograph enclosed; the same now occu-
pies a page in my daughter's album and is very highly
appreciated.   Next in order comes many familiar
names that you enumerate as co-workers in advancing
the cause of gospel truth.   While reading them over I
was carried back some thirty odd years, and many
incidents of, or about that period were made vivid in
my memory; scenes that occurred when you was quite
a little boy and I was in the prime of manhood.   One
particular circumstance I will mention, as it appears to
me to be incontrovertible evidence of the fact that your
father was no false pretender, but that he was a true
prophet of the living God.   I was practicing my profession in Kingston, Illinois, in the year 1837, and
boarding with a Benjamin S. Wilber, a member of the
Latter Day Saints' Church; his wife was also a member,
and a most excellent little lady and very intelligent.
In the fall of this year President Joseph Smith, Sidney
Rigdon, Judge Elias Higbee and Porter Rockwell, came
to this house on their way to the city of Washington, in
accordance with a revelation given to the church at
Commerce, (afterwards Nauvoo), through Joseph
Smith, the prophet, to lay their grievances before the
President of the United States, (Martin Van Buren),
for the sufferings they underwent in Missouri, from

which state the church had been driven by mob law, after many of them had been inhumanly murdered, and others driven from the lands they had purchased of the United States government in that state. On the arrival of this company at Mr. Wilber's I was told by Joseph Smith, the prophet, that if I was willing to obey the will of God, and be obedient to his commandments, I must quit my practice and start the next day with them to the city of Washington. * *

"I have many incidents, dottings and jottings, taken during our journey, one of which I will mention. After we got to Dayton, Ohio, we left our horses in care of a brother in the church, and proceeded by stage, part of us; and the same coach that conveyed us over the Allegheny Mountains also had on board, as passengers, Senator Aaron of Missouri, and a Mr. Ingersol, a member of Congress, either from New Jersey or Pennsylvania, I forget which, an1 at the top of the mountain called Cumberland Ridge, the driver left the stage and his four horses drinking at the trough in the road, while he went into the tavern to take what is very common to stage drivers, a glass of spirits. While he was gone the horses took fright and ran away with the coach and passengers. There was also in the coach a lady with a small child, who was terribly frightened. Some of the passengers leaped from the coach, but in doing so none escaped more or less injury, as the horses were running at a fearful speed, and it was down the side of a very steep mountain. The woman was about to throw out the child, and said she intended to jump out herself, as she felt sure all would be dashed to pieces that remained, as there was quite a curve in the road, and on one side the mountain loomed up hundreds of feet above the horses, and the other side was a deep chasm or ravine, and the road only a very narrow cut on the side of the mountain, about midway between the highest and lowest parts. At the time the lady was going to throw out the child, Joseph Smith, your father, caught the woman and very imperiously told her to sit down, and that not a hair of her head or any one on the coach should be hurt. He did this in such confident manner that all on board seemed spell-bound; and after admonishing and encouraging the passengers he pushed open one of the doors, caught by the railing around the driver's seat with one hand, and with a spring and a bound he was in the seat of the driver. The lines were all coiled around the rail above, to hold them from falling while the driver was away; he loosed them, took them in his hands, and although those horses were running at their utmost speed, he, with more than herculean strength, brought them down to a moderate canter, a trot, a walk, and at the foot of Cumberland Ridge, to a halt, without the least accident or injury to passenger, horse or coach, and the horses appeared as quiet and easy afterward as though they never run away. One by one the passengers came along, some of them limping badly, others bruised, and some of them swearing about the driver and threatening to have him arrested, etc.

"At last the driver took his place and we were all going along nicely, when one of these members of Congress, after hearing the history of our ride and escape, from the lady on board, said it was a miracle, and if Joe Smith could perform such a miracle, he would then believe he was a prophet sent from God. This was Mr. Ingersol. Mr. Smith and Sidney Rigdon were both traveling incog., as, if their real names had been made public on the way, especially that of Mr. Smith, we should have been very much annoyed by the inquisitive. Little did those gentlemen think that Joseph Smith was the identical man that was instrumental in the hands of God in saving that coach load of human beings from a terrible death.

"We made our first stop at Gadsby's hotel, in Washington City. * *

"We staid there during the winter of 1839 and 1840 to testify before committees and attend to all we could in the premises and in the meantime to preach and talk to the heads of the nation upon the mission and calling of Mr. Smith in this latter day. Curiosity was on tip-toe, until many believed, and some were baptized and went back to Nauvoo, or Commerce, as it was then called.

"Benjamin Winchester and Elder Barnes were preaching at that time in Philadelphia, and Mr. Smith and Mr. Higbee went there and did some preaching, leaving myself in the city of Washington to take care of Mr. Rigdon, and also to wait upon every preacher in the city, irrespective of his church organization, and particularly to declare unto them the tidings of the Latter Day Saints, committed to this generation through Joseph Smith, Jr., and to warn them against the danger consequent upon its rejection. I commenced my duties as soon as I had any time, and called upon all the leaders of the different organizations of religion in the city. As a general thing I was pretty well received and very kindly treated. * * I thought that my report would be uniformly favorable, but I had one more visit to make; that was to Geo. C. Cookman, the chief preacher and elder of the other branch of the Methodist

Church; and he was then chaplain of the United States Senate. On my introduction he was rigid as marble and cold as an icicle. He was proud, tonguey and arrogant in the extreme. * * I begged him to take time and consider the matter; not to decide hastily; that it was unwise to give a decision until both sides were fairly and fully before him. I asked him for his church, and told him that either Mr. Smith or Mr. Rigdon would be glad to illustrate the subject any time before him and his congregation. He said that my impudence could only be attributed to one of two causes, and he was constrained to believe it was not from ignorance, but was intended as an insult; that he would neither let me have his church nor hear anything further on the subject, and should take good care to warn his brethren and sisters against listening to any such blasphemy. With this he opened his library door, conducted me to the outer hall door, and refused to give me his hand. I reported this to Mr. Rigdon, and wrote to Philadelphia to Mr. Smith the result of my labors. On the following Sunday this same George C. Cookman preached in his church, and told some strange tales; that he had had an interview with Jo Smith, that arch imposter, and that the doctrines he taught were very irreligious and inconsistent with Bible truth; that he, Smith, did not believe in the Bible, but had got a new one, dug up in Palmyra, New York; and that it was nothing but an irreligious romance, and that Smith had obtained it from the widow of one Spaulding, who wrote it for his own amusement. I wrote this to Mr. Smith, and he said there must be some preaching in Washington to counteract these statements, as he was sure God had some people in that city. We first got an upper room of an engine house to speak in, but half, no, not a quarter, of the people could get in. We had speaking then in the open air, on Pennsylvania Avenue, near that place, and gave out that there would be further services as soon as a room could be obtained. Before night some people secured the use of Carusi's saloon, one of the largest and most suitable rooms in the city, outside the capitol building, and at night there was held service. A great many of the members of Congress and heads of departments were present, as well as Martin Van Buren. We, of the committee from Illinois, all took the speaker's desk. And when near the close, who should come into the hall but Joseph Smith himself. We speedily got him up on the stand, and I had the honor of introducing him to that vast audience. He had just come in on the train from Philadelphia, and was tired, but he arose by the invitation of many who called for him, and on that occasion he uttered a prophecy, one of the most wonderful predictions of his life. He adverted to the statements made by this George C. Cookman, declaring them to be wilfully and wickedly false, and that if he, Cookman, did not take it back and acknowledge that he had dealt falsely of him, his people, and his own congregation, also that he must turn and preach the truth and quit deceiving the people with fables, he should be cut off from the face of the earth, both he and his posterity. And he said that this should be so plainly manifest that all should know it. At this, many gentlemen took out of their pockets their tablets and began to take notes of the prophecy; and Mr. Smith noticing them, 'Yes,' said he, 'write it on your tablets; write it in a book; write it in your memory; for as sure as God ever spoke by my mouth, all these things shall come to pass.'

"Henry Clay, Felix Grundy, Tom Benton, John Q. Adams and many other celebrated characters were present at this time. Now, instead of Cookman doing according to justice and truth, he became more virulent than ever, and laid all the obstacles in our way that he could during our stay in the city. The matter appeared to be forgotten by many, and I thought often upon the subject, having taken notes also. Soon after this there was an extraordinary excitement in the religious world, and they appointed a conference of all orthodox religions to assemble in England, at a certain time, to adopt measures of harmony between all the sects; the United States were invited and accepted a part in these proceedings to break down the partition wall that separated the various churches. George C. Cookman was elected or appointed as a delegate for the District of Columbia to represent his views on the subject, standing, as he did, at the very head of the church, and Chaplain of the United States Senate. Now he, being an Englishman by birth, and his family in suitable circumstances for a pleasure trip, at the appointed time he (Cookman) thought it would be very pleasant to take his whole family with him, and this he did. Both he, his wife, and all his children went on board the steamship 'President,' and neither the ship nor a soul is left to tell what was their sad end. But the prophecy is fulfilled to the letter, and the words uttered on that occasion have never been forgotten by me, nor I presume by hundreds of others. Had Cookman gone alone, it might be charged to chance, but why was it that his whole family were so suddenly cut off, both root and branch!

"This, sir, is one of many wonderful evidences that Joseph Smith was as much a prophet as Jonah, who foretold the destruction of Nineveh; or Nahum, who prophesied concerning the present locomotion for traveling; both of them took centuries and one of them thousands of years for their fulfillment; but the prophecy by Joseph Smith on George C. Cookman has been literally fulfilled in the shortest possible period; and that too in its fullness, beyond the possibility of question from any source. * *

"I will tell you also another prophecy that Joseph Smith uttered in my presence, that has been proved true. This was in relation to Stephen A. Douglas. He said he was a giant in intellect, but a dwarf in stature, that he would yet run for President of the United States, but that he would never reach that station; that he would occupy a conspicuous place in the counsels of the nation, and have multitudes of admiring friends; and that in his place he would introduce and carry out some of the most gigantic measures in the history of the nation. This was said when Douglas was Judge in that district of Illinois, and before he ever went to Congress. Has it not been fulfilled? Did he not get Andrew Jackson's fine remitted by law, a thing that was by all considered impossible? Did he not introduce the bills for the covering of Illinois with railroads, without one cent's expense to the general government? Under his management, were not the Illinois bonds raised from a condition nearly worthless to a value nearly par with currency? Did he not rule in and through the State of Illinois, work and carry out its destiny for twenty consecutive years, more than any and all other men together? Was he not always one of the greatest men in the Senate? Did he not do more for the line of compromise on slavery than any other one man? Did he not say, 'and cursed be the ruthless hand that attempts to remove it?' Did he not run for President and get defeated? Did he not take the most active part in removing or breaking down that line of compromise? Let the history of Kansas and Nebraska tell the story! Did he not fulfill his destiny, and at last, on his dying bed, bequeath his children to his country, and counsel them to obey the laws and the constitution? Did he not utter these memorable words at the commencement of the rebellion, 'That there were only two parties in all the land; the one he called Patriots, the other Traitors?' Was it not true? Did he not throw his adhesion to A. Lincoln at the time of deep trouble? And does he not now occupy an honored spot in the memory of his many friends, and a sacred spot in his own loved city of Chicago? Yes, this prophecy has been literally ful filled in my day, and I bear testimony to its truth, when compared with history. * *

"I know something about some of the leaders at Salt Lake City, and to my sorrow too, as many of them forgot to settle claims that I still hold against them. I and my whole family were driven from the city, [of Nauvoo, Author.] my property confiscated, and thousands, yes, tens of thousands of dollars worth of my property was taken and sold, and I was defrauded out of the whole by wicked and corrupt men, aided by the head men that now live in Salt Lake City. The records of my property were carried away, and never could be obtained, and I was reduced from affluence and wealth to poverty by their means. And they claim to have done all these things in obedience to the commands and will of God.

"With considerations of very kind regards, I am, sir, yours for the truth.

"ROBERT D. FOSTER."

From Saints' Herald, April 15th, 1875.

Joseph Smith, speaking of his angel visitor at the time of his early experience, said: "He called me by name and said unto me that he was a messenger sent from the presence of God to me, and that his name was Moroni; that God had a work for me to do, and that my name should be had for good and evil among all nations, kindreds and tongues, or that it should be both good and evil spoken of among all people."

This experience occurred September 21, 1823. See Cowdery's Letters, Messenger and Advocate, Kirtland, Ohio, 1834; or Pearl of Great Price, p. 49, 1851. Though only in his fifteenth year, with but little apparent promise of prominence, this has been most graphically fulfilled as a first prediction.

When Joseph Smith asked God in fervent prayer which of the existing churches he should join, he was answered, "do not join any of them, for their creeds are all wrong and an abomination in my sight." Does the following confirm it?

"Rev. J. D. Williamson said before the Presbytery at Cleveland, Ohio: 'To suppose that those Westminster divines reached the high water mark of biblical statement of truth is to my mind preposterous. I have read and reread chapter third on God's eternal decree, and my moral sense has been no less shocked than when I first read the confession. I find also that the idea of God which this chapter presents is utterly abhorrent. It is as it now stands a chilling document, instead of being warm with the love of God.' "—Cleveland Plain Dealer, Oct. 8, 1889.

"Rev. T. A. Goodwin, of the M. E. church, said at Indianapolis, Ind., in February, 1890: 'For more than seventeen years the church has been tinkering at her creeds until they are a theological hodge podge, in many cases widely departing from the faith once delivered to the saints. From the time of the apostles' creed to this day, creed building and repairing has been a chief occupation, until creeds are as numerous as sands upon the sea shore, and they all claim to be in harmony with the apostles' creed and the Bible as well. But what of Methodism and some other isms? For nearly three hundred years it has been uncomfortably quartered in a house of theological patchwork. The whole needs to be torn down and reconstructed from cellar to garret, so as to make a symmetrical and congruous structure, consistent with itself by being consistent throughout with the Bible.' " This exposes the imperfections of that creed, and of the societies represented at that particular time.

"The St. Louis 'Globe Democrat' of March 3d, 1890, contains the following from Talmage on 'Why a new creed is needed:' 'I was sorry to have the question disturbed at all. The creed did not hinder us from offering the pardon and the comfort of the gospel to all men, and the Westminster Confession has not interfered with me one minute. But now that the electric lights have been turned on, the imperfections of that creed— and everything that man fashions is imperfect—let us put the old creed respectfully aside and get a brand new one. I move for a creed for all our denominations made out of Scripture quotations pure and simple. That would take the earth for God. That would be impregnable against infidelity and Apollyonic assault. That would be beyond hunman criticism. The denomination, whatever its name be, that can rise up to that will be the church of the millennium, will swallow up all other denominations and be the one that will be the bride when the Bridegroom cometh.' "

These were the churches Mr. Smith had been attending and four of the family belonged to the Presbyterian. Much more could be added, but this fully confirms his second prediction.

In Book of Mormon, 2d Nephi 12: 6, as to what the Book of Mormon would be called, occurs this: "A bible, a bible, we have got a bible, and there cannot be any more bible." Though the believers in the book protested from the first that it was not a bible, it has been so called and is yet, Mormon Bible, Golden Bible, etc. We have then a third prediction fulfilled. Those in Mr. Foster's testimony in the preceeding pages relative to Rev. George C. Cookman and Stephen A. Douglass are here referred to as a fourth and fifth prediction and fulfillment.

A REVELATION AND PROPHECY BY THE PROPHET, SEER AND REVELATOR, JOSEPH SMITH, GIVEN DECEMBER 25TH, 1832.

"Verily, thus saith the Lord, concerning the wars that will shortly come to pass, beginning at the rebellion of South Carolina, which will eventually terminate in the death and misery of many souls. The days will come that war will be poured out upon all nations, beginning at that place: for behold, the Southern States shall be divided against the Northern

States, and the Southern States will call on other na
tions, even the nation of Great Britain, as it is called,
and they shall also call upon other nations, in order to
defend themselves against other nations; and thus war
shall be poured out upon all nations.

"And it shall come to pass, after many days, slaves
shall rise up against their masters,·who shall be mar
shalled and disciplined for war.

"And it shall come to pass also, that the remnants
who are left of the land will marshall themselves, and
shall become exceeding angry, and shall vex the Gen
tiles with a sore vexation; and thus, with the sword,
and by bloodshed, the inhabitants of the earth shall
mourn; and with famine, and plague, and earthquakes,
and the thunder of heaven, and the fierce and vivid
lightning also, shall the inhabitants of the earth be
made to feel the wrath, and indignation, and chasten
ing hand of an Almighty God, until the consumption
decreed hath made a full end of all nations; that the
cry of the Saints, and of the blood of the Saints, shall
cease to come up into the ears of the Lord of Sabaoth,
from the earth, to be avenged of their enemies.

"Wherefore, stand ye in holy places, and be not
moved, until the day of the Lord come; for behold it
cometh quickly, saith the Lord. Amen."—"Pearl of
Great Price," published at Liverpool, England, in 1851.

No prophetic utterance was ever more strikingly
fulfilled. This, therefore, is a sixth.

Iowa State Register, for January 26th, 1894, con
tained this:

"MORMONS, 'LATTER DAY SAINTS,' ETC.

"VERONA, Michigan.--Please answer in Sunday
Register:

"1.   Was Joseph Smith, the Mormon leader, really a prophet?

"2.   Was he at any time convicted of a crime?

"3.   Is there any difference between the sects calling themselves 'Latter Day Saints' in Utah and those who go under the same name and have their headquarters at Lamoni, Iowa?

"4.   Have the Latter Day Saints of Lamoni a special permit or any extraordinary authority from the United States government, in other words, any special privileges which other churches do not enjoy?   WEST.

"ANS.—1.   He claimed that gift, and made some predictions, which were startlingly fulfilled years afterward.

"2.   He was arrested between fifty and seventy-five times, once under the charge of 'murder, treason, burglary, arson, and larceny,' but was never, to the best of my knowledge, convicted of any of these crimes. He was in jail at Carthage, Illinois, at the time of his assassination.

"3.   The main difference between the 'Latter Day Saints' of Utah and those of Iowa is that the latter never practiced polygamy.   The Iowa branch is under the leadership of a son of 'Joseph the Prophet,' and is known as 'The Reorganized Church of Jesus Christ of Latter Day Saints.'"

The court records would show it if Mr. Smith had been convicted of crime, and it would have been published all over the world.   His murderers knew the just operation of law would again exonerate him, and so they dyed their hands in his innocent blood.

Of the Danite Band Abomination Joseph Smith wrote October 1838:

"When a knowledge of Avard's rascality came to the Presidency of the Church, he was cut off from the Church, and every means used to destroy his influence, at which he was highly incensed, and went about whispering his evil insinuations, but finding every effort unavailing, he again turned conspirator, and sought to make friends with the mob.

"And here let it be distinctly understood, that these companies of tens and fifties got up by Avard, were altogether separate and distinct from those companies of tens and fifties organized by the brethren for self defense, in case of an attack from the mob, and more particularly that in this time of alarm no family or person might be neglected; therefore, one company would be engaged in drawing wood, another in cutting it, another in gathering corn, another in grinding, another in butchering, another in distributing meat, etc., so that all should be employed in-turn, and no one lack the necessaries of life. Therefore, let no one hereafter, by mistake or design, confound this organization of the Church for good and righteous purposes, with the organization of the Danites, of the apostate Avard, which died almost before it had an existence."

Joseph, on page 525, says further, that Avard, who was taken into the camp of the mob, Friday, October 2d, 1838, "told them that Daniteism was an order of the Church, and by his lying tried to make the Church a scape goat for his sins."

When in Liberty jail, Missouri, December 16th, 1838, Joseph wrote to the Church, and said of Dr. Avard, "We have learned also since we have been in prison that many false and pernicious things, which were calculated to lead the Saints astray and do great injury, have been taught by Dr. Avard, who has represented them as coming from the Presidency; and we have reason to fear that many other designing and corrupt characters, like unto himself, have taught many things which the Presidency never knew of until after they were made prisoners, which, if they had known, they would have spurned them and their authors as as they would a serpent.

"Thus we find that there have been frauds, secret abominations, and evil works of darkness going on, leading the minds of the weak and unwary into confusion and distraction, and all of which have been endeavored to be palmed upon the Presidency, who were ignorant of these things which were practiced upon the Church in our name."—Times and Seasons Vol. 1, Millenial Star, Vol. 16, p. 459.

"Joseph Smith always denied that he had in any way authorized the formation of the Danite band; and in fact, in public he repeatedly repudiated them and their deeds of violence. * * The outrages committed by these Danites, and others like them, caused the expulsion of the Saints from Missouri."—Ann Eliza, Wife No. 19, p. 48.

CHAPTER II.

COL. PITCHER AND GEN. DONIPHAN SPEAK OF TIMES AND SCENES IN MISSOURI. —EXPULSION DOCUMENT OF 1833 AND 1838.

MORMON HISTORY.

"Of the many pioneer citizens of Jackson county, Missouri, who were present and took part in the Mormon difficulties of the memorable year of 1833, but few now live. It is, however, fortunate for the historian that a few yet remain to relate the story of the events of those troublous times, nearly half a century ago, as they occurred, without prejudice. Among the very few of the pioneers still living is Col. Thomas Pitcher, of Independence, who has been a citizen of Jackson county for almost fifty-five years, and who, during the troubles of 1833, was a colonel of the state militia, and took a prominent part in all of the events of the early history of the county. Knowing these facts, a Journal representative at Independence was sent to Col. Pitcher to interview him upon the Mormon history of Jackson county. After learning the object of the visit, the colonel lighted his pipe and related the following facts: I came to Jackson county, in the month of November, 1826, and located four miles southwest of Independence. The Mormon immigration to the county commenced in the fall of 1830, and continued until the autumn of 1832. During the first two years of their residence in the county, they and the citizens got along together very peaceably, and no one had any thought of a difficulty until the spring of 1833. In the latter part of 1831 the Mormons established a newspaper in Independence, called the 'Morning and Evening Star,' which was edited by one W. W. Phelps. This paper published the so called revelations of Joseph Smith and other leading elders of the church, and other doctrines of their religion. The Mormons, as a rule, were an ignorant and a fanatical people, though there were some very intelligent men among them. The troubles of 1833, which led to their expulsion from the county, were originated by these fanatics making boasts that they intended to possess the entire county, saying that God had promised it to them and they were going to have it. This of course caused ill feeling toward them, which continued to grow more and more bitter, until the final uprising took place. One Saturday, about the middle of July, 1833, a citizens' meeting was held at the Court House in Independence, to decide what was to be done with the Mormons who were pouring into the county, and to devise some means to put a stop to their seditious boasts as to what they proposed to do, etc. This meeting determined to destroy the Mormon printing office, located a short distance south of where Chrisman & Sawyer's bank building now stands, which determination was carried into effect that afternoon.

" 'Did the citizens give the Mormons any notice of what they intended to do?'

" 'No, I don't think they gave them any notice whatever, but when they had determined upon destroying the printing office, they immediately proceeded to do so.'

" 'Did the Mormons make any resistance?'

" 'No, they did not. Some of them tried to argue the case, but it was of no avail. The printing office was a two story brick building, and I don't think its destruction occupied over an hour.'

" 'How many citizens were engaged in the affair?'

" 'I suppose there must have been over a hundred, altogether.'

" 'Was there any personal violence or other indignities offered the Mormons at that time?'

" 'Nothing of any particular consequence. Several were knocked down, but as a general thing the Mormons had sufficient discretion to keep out of the way.' * *

" 'Were the Mormons allowed to dispose of their lands and other property before they left the county?'

" 'No, they did not have time, but afterwards a great many came back and disposed of their lands without molestation.'

" 'Did they own much property in the county?'

" 'Yes, they owned a large amount of land all over the county, and a great deal of property in the town of Independence.' * *

" 'Do you think, colonel, that the slavery question had anything to do with the difficulties with the Mormons?'

" 'No, I don't think that matter had anything to do with it. The Mormons, it is true, were northern and eastern people, and "free soilers," but they did not interfere with the negroes and we did not care whether they owned slaves or not.' * *

" 'Did the Mormons practice or advocate polygamy while in Jackson county?'

" 'No, they did not. Polygamy, at that time, had not been heard of.'—Kansas City Journal." Herald, June 15, 1881.

"There is probably no man in Western Missouri who is better acquainted with the various causes of the difficulties between the citizens of Jackson and Caldwell counties and the Mormons during the years of 1833 and 1838, than Gen. Alexander W. Doniphan, then a resident of Clay county, but now of Richmond, Ray county, Missouri, and there is, perhaps, no one who took such an active part in the events of those years who can now look back and relate the history of these troubles as dispassionately as he can. In view of these facts a representative of the Journal called upon Gen. Doniphan at his rooms at the Hudgins' House at Richmond, for the purpose of interviewing him upon the subject. The general, after learning the object of the visit, seemed very willing to communicate all he knew in regard to the history of the Mormon troubles, and after a few introductory remarks, related the following:

" 'I came to Missouri in 1830, and located in Lexington, where I lived until April, 1833, when I removed to Liberty, Clay county. The Mormons came to Jackson county in 1830, and I met Oliver Cowdery, John Whitmer and Christian Whitmer, three of the Elders, in Independence, during the spring of 1831. Peter Whitmer was a tailor and I employed him to make me a suit of clothes.'

" 'What kind of people were the Mormons?'

" 'They were northern people, who, on account of their declining to own slaves and their denunciation of the system of slavery, were termed "free soilers." The majority of them were intelligent, industrious and law abiding citizens, but there were some ignorant, simple minded fanatics among them, whom the people said would steal.' * * 'Governor Boggs used the expression "that the Mormons leave the state or be exterminated," whereas this order was entirely illegal. I paid no attention to it. In my report to Gov. Boggs I stated to him that I had disregarded that part of his order, as the age of extermination was over, and if I attempted to remove them to some other state, it would cause additional trouble. The Mormons commenced immediately after this to move to Nauvoo, Illinois, and I know nothing further about them. While the Mormons resided in Clay county, they were a peaceable, sober, industrious and law-abiding people, and during their stay with us not one was ever accused of a crime of any kind.'

"Gen. Doniphan is now in his seventy-third year, but is still hale and hearty. He is a man of fine appearance and intellect, and is well known and highly respected all over the State. He has resided in Richmond during the past several years. His statements as given above may be relied upon as strictly the truth in every particular. There are a few old citizens still living near Independence who were in this county during the troubles of 1833, whose statements will be given in the near future.—Kansas City Journal." Herald, July 1, 1881.

Not a crime—not even a personal misdemeanor—of any kind could the mob find to charge the Saints with.

An account from the Western Monitor, of Fayette, Missouri, the 2d of August, 1833. In this will be

seen the alleged grounds and all the reasons the mob
could trump up in justification of their barbarous doing:

"MORMONISM!

"At a meeting of the citizens of Jackson county,
Missouri, called for the purpose of adopting measures
to rid themselves of the sect of fanatics called Mormons, held at Independence on the 20th day of July,
1833; which meeting was composed of gentlemen from
every part of the county, there being present between
four and five hundred persons.

"The meeting was organized by calling Colonel
Richard Simpson to the chair, and appointing James
H. Flournoy and Col. Samuel D. Lucas, secretaries.
It was resolved that a committee of seven be appointed
to report an address to the public, in relation to the
object of this meeting, and the chair named the following gentleman to wit: Russel Hicks, Esq., Robert
Johnson, Henry Chiles, Esq., Colonel James Ham-
bright, Thomas Hudspeth, Joel F. Chiles, and •James
M. Hunter.   The meeting then adjourned, and convened again, when Robert Johnson, the chairman of
said committee, submitted for the consideration of the
meeting, the following address, etc.:

"This meeting, professing to act not from the
excitement of the moment, but under a deep and abiding conviction that the occasion is one that calls for
cool deliberation, as well as energetic action, deem it
proper to lay before the public an expose of our peculiar situation in regard to this singular sect of pretended
Christians, and a solemn declaration of our unalterable
determination to amend it.

"The evil is one that no one could have foreseen,

and is therefore unprovided for by the laws, and the delays incident to legislation would put the mischief beyond remedy.

"But little more than two years ago some two or three of this people made their appearance in the Upper Missouri, and they now number some twelve hundred souls in this county; and each successive autumn and spring pours forth its swarm among us, with a gradual falling of the character of those who compose them, until it seems that those communities from which they come were flooding us with the very dregs of their composition. Elevated as they mostly are but little above the condition of our blacks either in regard to property or education, they have become a subject of much anxiety on that part, serious and well grounded complaints having been already made of their corrupting influence on our slaves.

"We are daily told, and not by the ignorant alone, but by all classes of them, that we, (the Gentiles), of this county are to be cut off, and our lands appropriated by them for inheritances. Whether this is to be accomplished by the hand of the destroying angel, the judgments of God, or the arm of power, they are not fully agreed among themselves.

"Some recent remarks in the Evening and Morning Star, their organ in this place, by their tendency to moderate such hopes and repress such desires, show plainly that many of this deluded and infatuated people have been taught to believe that our lands were to be won from us by the sword. From this same Star we learn that for want of more honest or commendable employment, many of their society are now preaching through the states of New York, Ohio, and Illinois, and that their numbers are increased beyond every rational calculation, all of whom are required as soon as convenient, to come up to Zion, which name they have thought proper to confer on our little village. Most of those who have already come are characterized by the profoundest ignorance, the grossest superstition, and the most abject poverty.

"Indeed, it is a subject of regret by the Star itself, that they have come not only to lay an inheritance, which means some fifteen acres of wild land for each family, but destitute of the means of procuring bread and meat. When we reflect on the extensive field in which the sect is operating, and that there exists in every country a leaven of superstition that embraces with avidity notions the most extravagant and unheard of, and that whatever can be gleaned by them from the purlieus of vice, and the abodes of ignorance, it is to be cast like a waif into our social circle, it requires no gift of prophecy to tell that the day is not far distant when the civil government of the country will be in their hands, when the sheriff, the justices, and the county judges will be Mormons, or persons wishing to court their favor from motives of interest or ambition.

"What would be the fate of our lives and property in the hands of jurors and witnesses who do not blush to declare, and would not upon occasion hesitate to swear that they have wrought miracles, and have been the subjects of miraculous and supernatural cures; have converse with God and his angels, and possess and exercise the gifts of divination and of unknown tongues, and fired with the prospect of obtaining inheritances without money and without price, may be better imagined than described. * *

"One of the means resorted to by them, in order to drive us to emigrate, is an indirect invitation up, like the rest, to the land of Zion. True, they say this was not intended to invite, but to prevent their emigration; but this weak attempt to quiet our apprehension is but a poor compliment to our understandings. The article alluded to contained an extract from our laws, and all necessary directions and cautions to be observed by colored brethren, to enable them upon their arrival here to claim and exercise the rights of citizenship. Contemporaneous with the appearance of this article was the expectation among the brethren here, that a considerable number of this degraded cast were only awaiting this information before they should set out on their journey. With the corrupting influence of these on our slaves, and the stench both physical and moral that their introduction would set afloat in our social atmosphere, and the vexation that would attend the civil rule of these fanatics, it would require neither a visit from the destroying angel nor the judgments of an offended God to render our situation here insupportable. True, it may be said, and truly no doubt, that the fate that has marked the rise and fall of Joanna Southcote and Ann Lee will also attend the progress of Joe Smith, but this is no opiate to our fears, for when the fabric falls the rubbish will remain.

"Of their pretended revelations from heaven— their personal intercourse with God and his angels—the maladies they pretend to heal by the laying on of hands —and the contemptible gibberish with which they habitually profane the Sabbath, and which they dignify with the appellation of unknown tongues, we have nothing to say, vengeance belongs to God alone. But as to the other matters set forth in this paper, we feel called on by every consideration of self-preservation, good society, public morals, and the fair prospects, that if not blasted in the germ, await this young and beautiful county, at once to declare, and we do hereby most solemnly declare:

"That no Mormon shall in future move and settle in this county.

"That those now here, who shall give a definite pledge of their intention within a reasonable time to remove out of the county, shall be allowed to remain unmolested until they have sufficient time to sell their property and close their business without any material sacrifice.

"That the editor of the Star be required forthwith to close his office and discontinue the business of printing in this county; and as to all other stores and shops belonging to the sect, their owners must in every case strictly comply with the terms of the second article of this declaration, and upon failure, prompt and efficient measures will be taken to close the same.

"That the Mormon leaders here are required to use their influence in preventing any further emigration of their distant brethren to this county, and to counsel and advise their brethren here to comply with the above requisition.

"That those who fail to comply with these requisitions be referred to those of their brethren who have the gifts of divination, and of unknown tongues, to inform them of the lot that awaits them.

"Which address being read and considered, was unanimously adopted. And thereupon it was resolved that a committee of twelve be appointed forthwith to

wait on the Mormon leaders, and see that the foregoing
requisitions are strictly complied with by them, and
upon their refusal, that said committee do, as the organ
of this county, inform them that it is our unwavering
purpose and fixed determination, after the fullest considerations of all the consequences and responsibilities
under which we act, to use such means as shall insure
their full and complete adoption, and that said committee, so far as may be within their power, report to this
present meeting.   And the following gentlemen were
named as said committee:

"Robert Johnson, James Campbell, Colonel Moses
Wilson, Joel F. Chiles, Hon. Richard Fristoe, Abner
F. Staples, Gan. Johnson, Lewis Franklin, Russel
Hicks, Esq., Colonel S. D. Lucas, Thomas Wilson, and
James M. Hunter, to whom was added Colonel R.
Simpson, chairman.

"And after an adjournment of two hours, the
meeting again convened, and the committee of twelve
reported that they had called on Mr. Phelps, the editor
of the Star, Edward Partridge, the bishop of the sect,
and Mr. Gilbert, the keeper of the Lord's storehouse,
and some others, and that they declined giving any
direct answer to the requisitions made of them, and
wished an unreasonable time for consultation, not only
with their brethren here, but in Ohio.

"Whereupon it was unanimously resolved by the
meeting, that the Star printing office should be razed to
the ground, the type and press secured.   Which resolution was, with the utmost order, and the least noise and
disturbance possible, forthwith carried into execution,
as also some other steps of a similar tendency, but no
blood was spilled nor any blows inflicted.   The meet-

ing then adjourned till the 23d inst., to meet again to know further concerning the determination of the Mormons.

"Resolved that a copy of these proceedings be posted up at the post office in this place for the information of all concerned; and that the secretaries of this meeting send copies of the same to the principal editors in the eastern and middle states for publication, that the Mormon brethren may know at a distance that the gates of Zion are closed against them—that their interests will be best promoted by remaining among those who know and appreciate their merits.

RICHARD SIMPSON, Chairman

S. D. LUCAS, |
J. H. FLOURNOY, | Secretaries.

Times and Seasons, vol. 6, pp 832, 833, 834.

In the official address of Major General Clark to the forces driving the Saints out of Missouri, November, 1838, he said: "It now devolves upon you to fulfill the treaty that you have entered into, the leading items of which I now lay before you. The first of these you have already complied with, which is that you deliver up your leading men to be tried according to law. Second, that you deliver up your arms—this has been attended to. The third is that you sign over your properties to defray the expenses of this war—this you have also done. Another thing yet remains for you to comply with—that is, that you leave the state forthwith; and whatever your feelings concerning this affair, whatever your innocence it is nothing to me."

CHAPTER III.

INTERVIEW AT PAINESVILLE, OHIO, AND
LETTERS OF SAMUEL MURDOCK.—
INTERVIEW OF CITIZENS OF
PALMYRA, NEW YORK.

FACTS FROM PAINESVILLE, OHIO.

"Pres. J. Smith, Plano, Illinois:

"Dear Sir:—One week ago today I arrived in this city, to look after the interests of the Reorganized Church in its action in the state courts, to recover the possession of the Kirtland Temple property, in Lake county. * *

"So far, among the former acquaintances of Joseph Smith, Jr., I have failed to find one who will say that he was not a good citizen and an honest man. 'Joe Smith,' say they, 'was an honorable man and a gentleman in every particular, let the histories say what they may.' Now, if these things are true, history greatly belies the man and in the eternal fitness of things, time must correct the false and fickle stories and vindicate his memory. My information is derived from such men as Messrs. Quinn, Storm, Burrows and Axtell, who are foremost citizens of the county. These parties say that among some of the fanatical and ignorant there is existing great prejudice and hatred against the early Mormons, and I have found in Kirtland two persons who are terribly bitter, but neither of these had any acquaintance with the parties and base their knowledge on the 'stories told'. One of these is the present pastor of the Methodist Church in Kirtland, and who is now under the charge of being not only a fanatic, but crazy, and his congregation ask his removal; the other, a Mr. Harvey, of Kirtland, a member of the Baptist Church, but ignorant, can neither read nor write, and abuses his own wife for differing from him in religion, and teaches his children to abuse their mother.

"As a sample of my testimony I give you my conversation with I. P. Axtell, Esq., a large farmer and director in the First National Bank of Painesville for many years; a man of energy and experience, and as early as 1844, a member of the Whig convention at Baltimore, which nominated Henry Clay for President. The conversation was as follows:

"Q.—When did you come to this county, Mr. Axtell?

"A.—My father moved here with his family in the year 1830. I was but a boy then.

"Q.—What was your father's business?

"A.—He was a Baptist minister, and kept a hotel then.

"Q.—Did you know Joseph Smith?

"A.—Yes, sir. I have seen him many a time; he was often at my father's house; and I with many young people, often went to Kirtland to see him and his people. I knew his father also, who at the time I knew him had charge of the Kirtland Temple. He took me with others through the Temple at one time; he appeared to be a fine old man.

"Q.—When did your father become acquainted with Mr. Smith?

"A.—In about six weeks after he came to the county he first met him; he went out of his way one day six miles to see Joseph Smith and Sidney Rigdon. He said he found them in Kirtland township, they had been there but a short time and occupied a small log house. He found them to be quite intelligent men, and he said pleasant talkers, and quite free to converse upon their religious views, which at that time was known as the 'new sect.' My father always said Joseph Smith was a conscientious and upright man.

"Q.—Did you know any other persons of the new society?

"A.—O, yes, a great many. I knew Mr. Pratt very well. He was a smart and a square man all around. Those men were neither knaves nor rogues; that is my opinion of them. I suppose some of them may have been. It was just as in all other bodies of the kind, there will be some bad ones, but I don't know of any that were. There were a good many stories circulated about them that I knew to be false. At one time an ox was found in Kirtland township, killed and skinned; and there was a great to do about the Mormons having killed it. My brother was sheriff at the time, and with others went up to investigate the matter, and he says that there was not the least evidence which showed that the Mormons had any hand in killing the ox. Persons around, however, who hated their religion would tell that they did.

"Q.—How was it that people did not like them? Were they not good citizens?

"A.—Yes, they were as good citizens as those of any society. It was the fanatics in religion that tried to drive those men out. There were a great many conservative men in our county at that time who held these fanatics back, and if it had not been for this they would have gone in and killed them all. But our intelligent and honorable citizens prevented this.

"Q.—What about the Kirtland Bank swindle? Mr. Axtell, you are a banker, and know how that was, do you not?

"A.—Yes, I know about that bank; they started in Kirtland. These parties went into the banking business as a great many others in the state of Ohio and other states. They got considerable money out at first, and their enemies began to circulate all manner of s ories against them and as we had a great many banks then that issued what was known as 'wild-cat" money, the people began to get alarmed at so many stories, and would take the other banks' issue instead of the Kirtland; and so much of it was forced in at once that the bank was not able to take it up. Had the people let these people alone there is no reason that I know of why the Kirtland bank should not have existed to this time, and on as stable a basis as other banks.

"Q.—Then you think it was the fault of the enemies of the bank that it failed?

"A.—Yes, I do; and it was not the only one that failed either by a good many, and with which Smith had nothing to do.

"Q.—What then do you consider the prime causes of the expulsion of the Mormons from Kirtland?

"A.—The ignorance and fanaticism of their accusers did it; they thought public sentiment would tolerate it and they did it. The same as Roger Williams was driven out and the witches burned in Massachusetts. My position is that no fanatic, either in religion or politics, should be permitted to hold an office of trust in this country.

"The above is a fair average sample of the testimony of those I have met and talked with as to the character of the early Mormons in this county, among those who lived here and knew these people. A gentleman of Willoughby, this county, suggested to me, that another reason was, their persecutors wanted their property, and said he, 'They got from them thousands of dollars worth too' After canvassing the sentiment here of these men, I feel a good deal like Col. R. G. Ingersoll when he offered the gold for the evidence of Tom. Paine's dying declarations; and I now affirm that if any of the great newspapers of the day, like the Chicago Times, Tribune or Inter-Ocean wish to test the truth of the statements and publish the facts by a correspondent through their columns; I will undertake the task of accompanying their correspondent and if the general integrity, uprightness, honesty and patriotism, of these men are not maintained by the evidence, I will forfeit to the one the one hundred dollars in gold. A letter will reach me at any time directed, Glenwood, Iowa.

"Hastily, I am very respectfully yours,
"E. L. KELLEY.
"PAINESVILLE, Ohio, Feb. 19th, 1880."

SAMUEL MURDOCK PROTESTS.

"ELKADER, Iowa, April 13th, 1893.
"Editor Dubuque Daily Times:

"DEAR SIR:—In your article on the Mormon Church contained in your daily issue of April 12, you say: 'It was founded by an ignorant, dissipated member of a vicious family which had a well-earned reputation of being thieves and drunkards, etc.' Knowing your reputation for kindness, fairness, and sympathy, I do not believe that you would willfully or knowingly inflict a pang or a pain in the bosom of any one of our fellow creatures unless it was done without a knowledge on your part of the true facts in any case.

"I have no more sympathy or feeling for either branch of the Mormon Church than you have, but I have a strong sympathetic feeling, and friendship for some of the Smith family who are still living, and to whom your language above quoted, does great injustice, and I also know that when you hear from me a few facts, your kindness will prompt you to repair in some manner the wrong you have inflicted upon them.

"Kirtland is situated in the county in which I was raised from youth to manhood, and at the time Smith and his Mormons settled there I was nearly a man grown, and some of them were my immediate neighbors, with whose children I was often schoolmates, and I often met their prophet, Joseph Smith, although I was not personally acquainted with him. I was, however, intimately acquainted with Mr. Cowdery, one of his scribes, and to whom I was indebted for his special kindness to me, as well as for the many lessons of instruction I received from him as my preceptor in the schoolroom, and a Mormon as he was, I shall ever cherish his memory. A more amiable, generous, kind hearted man, I have not met since. I lived among the daily talk and excitement of the 'New Faith' or 'Latter Day Saints,' as they were sometimes called at that time. From the time they settled in my county until they left it, I must say that during all that time I never heard Joseph Smith called a thief, a drunkard or a vicious

man, even by his worst enemies, and my recollection of
him to this late day is that he was a tall, graceful, good-
looking man, continually wearing a smile on his face for
everyone, and that he was a kind-hearted, generous
friend and companion, and that it was his winning manners by which he succeeded more than anythingelse.

"Dupe, impostor, crazy fanatic, were the common
words applied to him by the Gentiles of these days, but
never thief, drunkard, or vicious.

"But all this is not where your language referred
to, cuts the deepest, and inflicts the most pain, for this
same Joseph Smith has a brother, the Rev. William B.
Smith, who is one of the old pioneers of Clayton county,
and who is still living among us, and a man whom I
have known for nearly forty years, and for nearly half
of that time, he has lived within a stone's throw of my
dwelling, and I do know that the citizens of Elkader,
and those of the county generally, will sustain me when
I say that there is not a single stain upon his character.
A kind, honest, just, and upright man is his life long
reputation here.

"He has preached to us, lectured to us, pronounced funeral services over our dead, sat upon our
juries, mingled in our conventions, acted as chaplain
on our national holidays, and may be seen mingling
with his fellows at every reunion of both the old settlers
and the G. A. R., and, although he is a strong defender
of his brothers, and a devoted Mormon of the anti-
polygamy sect, yet, unless he is drawn out, no one
would ever know from any of his public or private talk
that he was a Mormon.   When the first gun was fired
on Fort Sumpter he took the stump to arouse the people to the impending danger, and then shouldered his

rifle, bid adieu to his family, enlisted in the Union
army, and when the war was over came home with an
honorable discharge. He has raised up in this county
a bright and honorable family, all of whom are doing
well, and not one of whom has ever caused him to
blush, and it is here again where the language of your
article cuts like a knife. Deluded as they were, there
was among the early Mormons the best and noblest of
mankind, and where they missed it, was by admitting
among them without knowing it, rascals, horse thieves,
and murderers, and then defending them without investigation on the belief that the charge against them was
Gentile persecution.

"SAMUEL MURDOCK.

"The above communication was inspired by an
editorial appearing in the Times the date stated. There
were no intentions of saying anything to the detriment
of those of the faith of today, and what was said of the
founder of the sect was in line with the leading encyclopedias, all of which give detailed account of the work
of Joseph Smith during the days of organizing the Mormon Church.—Editor Times."

CITIZENS OF PALMYRA, NEW YORK, INTERVIEWED.

Elders W. H. and E. L. Kelley, having visited and
interviewed the old settlers in and around Palmyra,
New York, reported the following to the Saints' Herald,
regarding what they learned about Joseph Smith and
his family associations:

"Here is where they lived, and where, the stories
say, lived those who knew of their bad character, etc.
We were among some of their old neighbors, all unbelievers in the faith they taught, and we remembered

some of the names of the parties published by their enemies as knowing facts against them, and determined to "beard the lion in his den," and hear the worst, let it hurt whom it would.   So we set about it in good earnest, to interview, if possible, all of those referred to by the enemies of these men, as having a knowledge of them, and with one writing during each interview, we obtained the following as the result:

"Having the names of Messrs. Bryant, Booth, and Reed, obtained from a published communication in the 'Cadillac News,' of Michigan, about a year ago, by Rev. A. Marsh, of that place, who had received it from a brother Rev., one C. C. Thorn, of Manchester, New York, who claimed to have interviewed the above named gentlemen, and obtained from them wonderful revelations about the Smith family, Cowdery, etc., making Mr. Bryant to say that Smith was 'a lazy, drinking fellow, loose in his habits every way;' and Mr. Booth to say that their reputation was 'bad,' and that Oliver Cowdery was 'a law pettifogger,' and 'cat's-paw of the Smiths, to do their dirty work,' etc.; and Mr. Reed to say, 'they were too low for him to associate with,' with a citation of the black sheep story, etc.; all of whom were 'astonished beyond measure' at the progress of this 'imposture, which they thought would not amount to anything.'   All of which was sent to Rev. A. Marsh, of Cadillac, in order to counteract the influence which had been created in favor of the faith in that place, by the efforts of M. H. Bond and myself.

"Believing then that the whole story was a trumped up thing, I was determined to call on these gentlemen, and ascertain whether this pious Rev. told the truth about what they said or not.

"At about 10 a. m. we called at the house of Mr. Bryant, and knocked at the door, which was answerd by a lady who gave her name as Mary Bryant. She gave us seats in the room where her husband, William Bryant, was sitting. He is now eighty-five years of age, tall, and lean in flesh, and, during our interview, sat in a stooping posture, with open mouth. His wife informed us that for the last few years his mind had been somewhat impaired. She has a good memory, is seventy-five years of age, intelligent, and seemingly a great talker. We announced that the purpose of our visit was to ascertain some facts from the old settlers, with reference to the people known as Mormons, who used to live there, as it is understood to have been the home of the Smith family and others at the time the Book of Mormon is alleged to have been discovered.

"To this Mr. Bryant in a slow voice replied, 'Yes, that big hill you saw coming along, is where they say Joe Smith got the plates; you must have seen it coming along. Well, you can't find out much from me; I don't know much about them myself; I have seen Joe Smith once or twice; they lived about five miles from where I did; was not personally acquainted with any of them —never went to any of their meetings, and never heard one preach.'

"What do you know about the character of the family? How were they for honesty? Were they industrious or lazy? We want to know their character among their old neighbors.

" 'Well, I don't know about that. I never saw them work; the people thought young Joe was a great liar.'

"What made them think that?

" 'They thought he lied when he said he found that gold bible.'

"Before this what was thought of him, as to his telling the truth?

" 'I never heard anything before this.'

"What else did he lie about? And how did he get the name of being such a great liar?

" 'The people said he lied about finding the plates; I don't know whether he lied about anything else; they were all a kind of a low, shiftless set.'

"What do you mean by that?

" 'The people said they were awful poor, and poor managers. Joe was an illiterate fellow. If you come from Palmyra, you could have got Tucker's work there and it would have told you all about them. I have read a great deal about them.'

"Yes, we have seen Tucker's work, but there are too many big stories in that. Thinking people don't believe them; they ridicule them, and demand the facts; we wish to get some facts which we can stand by

" 'I don't know anything myself; I wish I did. Have you been to see Mr. Reed? He lives up north of Manchester; he knows.'

"Mrs. Bryant.—'My husband don't know anything about them; they did not live in the same neighborhood that we did, and he was not acquainted with them; he don't know anything.'

"Well, were they drunkards?

"Mr. Bryant.—'Everybody drank whiskey in them times.'

"Did you ever see Joe Smith drunk or drinking?

" 'No, I can't say that I did; I only saw him once or twice, when he came to the woolen mill where I worked.'

"Did you not see Joe drink sometime?

" 'N-o-e.'

"Mrs. Bryant.—'He ought not to say anything, for he knows nothing about them; then it has been a long time ago.'

"Have you stated now all you know about them?

"Mr. Bryant.—'Yes; I never knew much about them anyway.'

"Did you know any of their associates—Cowdery, Harris or others?

" 'No, I never knew any of them.'

"Mrs. Bryant.—'I knew Cowdery; Lyman Cowdery, I believe, was his name. They lived next door to us; they were low shacks,—he was a lawyer,—he was always on the wrong side of every case, they said.'

"Did he ever teach school?

" 'No, not this one.'

"Did you know any other one?

" 'No, I only knew this one and his family; I know they borrowed my churn once, and when it came home, I had to scour it all over before I used it. My father owned the largest house there was in the country at that time.'

"How were they about being honest, and telling the truth?

" 'I don't remember anything about that, now.'

"Were they religious people—pious?

" 'No they did not belong to any church; I know they didn't, for there were only two churches there, the Baptist and Methodist,—sometimes the Universalists preached there—they did not belong to either of those churches.'

"Mr. Bryant.—'He (Cowdery), was strong against

the Masons; he helped to write Morgan's book, they said.'

"What do you know, now, about the Smiths, or others; you have lived here about seventy-five years, have you not, Mrs. Bryant?.

" 'Yes, I have lived here all my life, but I never knew.anything about the Smith's myself; you will find it all in Tucker's work.   I have read that.   Have you been to see Mr. Booth?   He lives right up·here, on the road running south; he knows all about them, they say.'

"Very good; we will call and see him.   Thank you for your kindness in allowing us to trouble you.

" 'Oh, it is no trouble; I wish we knew more to tell you.'

"We then called upon Mr. David Booth, an intelligent gentleman, hale and hearty, and upwards of seventy years of age—and make known our business.

"Mr. Booth promptly stated that he knew nothing of the Smiths, or their character; did not live in their neighborhood, and never saw either of them; did not know anything about them, or their book.

"Did you know the Cowderys?

" 'I knew one—the lawyer.'

"What kind of a character was he?

" 'A low pettifogger.'

"What do you mean by that?

" 'Why, he was not a regular lawyer, but took small cases and practiced before the justices of the peace.   We call them pettifoggers here.'

"What was his given name?

" 'Lyman; he never taught school; guess he was no church member; he was a Mason; that was all there was to him.   They called him "loose Cowdery," ' '

"What did they mean by that?

" 'Why, he would take small cases; would be on the wrong side, and pettifog before justices, was the reason, I suppose.'

"Are you certain his name was Lyman? Wasn't it Oliver?

" 'It has been a long time ago. I think may be his name was Oliver.'

"Did he drink?

" 'Everybody drank then. I never saw Cowdery drink.'

"Mr. Bryant, here in the village, told us that he was a strong Anti Mason, and helped to write Morgan's work.

" 'Oh, that is all nonsense; they don't know anything about it. Mr. Bryant hasn't been here more than thirty-five years; his wife was raised here—is his second wife. Cowdery was a strong Mason, so they all said; that is all the religion he had.'

"Do you know Rev. Thorn, a Presbyterian minister at Manchester?

" 'Yes, I know him.'

"What kind of a fellow is he?

" 'He is a pretty sharp fellow, and will look after his bread and butter, you may depend on that.'

"Did he ever interview you on this subject?

" 'No, sir; he never did.'

"Did he not call to see what you knew about the Smiths and Cowderys about a year ago?

" 'No, he never did, to my recollection.'

"Did you know he had a statement of yours published in Michigan, in regard to this, last year?

" 'No, sir; I never heard of it before.'

"Did you ever give him one to publish?

" 'I never did—did not know he wanted one.'

"He will look out for himself, will he?

" 'He will that; that is him.'

"You have lived here all your life. Tell us of some one who can tell us all about the people we wish to learn about—some of the old settlers.

" 'Squire Pierce and Mr. Reed live a few miles north from here, in the neighborhood where the Smiths lived; they know all about them, they say. The Smiths never lived in this neighborhood.'

"Do you know Thomas H. Taylor, of Manchester?

" 'Yes.'

"What kind of a fellow is he?

" 'He is a pretty smart fellow; can do most anything he undertakes; he is a lawyer, and lectures sometimes.'

"Mr. Booth, we were told, is a Free Methodist. His address is Shortville, Ontario Co., New York.

"Following the directions of Mr. Booth, we repassed the town of Manchester, and at one o'clock, p. m., arrived at the house of Ezra Pierce, a very pleasant and hospitable New York farmer, quite well informed in the political history of the country, especially on the Democratic side. Approaching the subject of the deired interview to him, he quickly answered by saying:

" 'Well, gentlemen, I must first ask you a question, because I went on to give my statement to some parties once, and as it did not suit them, they began to abuse and insult me; said that I lied about it. Let me ask: Are you Mormons?'

E. L.—I am a lawyer, myself; this other gentleman can speak for himself. We don't propose to be anything, especially during this interview; we are here to try to find out some facts, and we don't care who they hit; it is facts that we are after, and you may be sure there will be no abuse, no matter which side they are on.

" 'All right; that's fair, go ahead.'

"Were you acquainted with the Smith family?

" 'Oh, yes, I pulled sticks with Joe for a gallon of brandy once at a log rolling; he was about my age. I was born in 1806. I lived about three miles from the Smiths. Was not very well acquainted with them, but knew them when I saw them. I knew young Joe, who claimed to have found the plates, and old Joe, his father.'

"Did young Joe drink?

" 'Everybody drank them times.'

"Did you ever see young Joe drink.

" 'No, I never did; it was customary in those early days for everybody to drink, more or less. They would have it at huskings, and in the harvest field, and places of gathering; the Smiths did not drink more than others.'

"What about Joe's learning?

" 'I know that he was ignorant; and he knew no more about hieroglyphics than that stove,' pointing to the stove in the room.

"Well, go on and state what kind of a family they were—all about them.

" 'They were poor, and got along by working by the day; the old man had a farm up there, and a log house upon it. The old man Smith and Hyrum were coopers; I never went to the same school that the boys did—they dug for money sometimes; young Joe, he had a stone that he could look through and see where the money was; there were a good many others who dug with them, and Joe used to play all kinds of tricks upon them.'

"Who said they dug for money?

" 'Oh, I have heard it lots of times. If my brother was living, he could tell you all about it.'

"Others dug besides the Smiths, did they?

" 'Yes; there were others who dug; but I always heard that the Smiths dug the most; one of the Chase's, a young lady had a stone, which she claimed she could look through and see money buried.'

"Did any body dig for her?

" 'Yes, I guess they did. They said so.'

"Then young Joe had some opposition in the see-ing money business?

" 'That is what everybody said.'

"Who was this Miss Chase? Where does she live?

" 'She is dead now; she was a sister to Abel Chase, who lives upon the Palmyra Road. Have you seen him? He will know all about this. He has been in the cave with the Smiths where the sheep bones were found—people used to think they were making counter-feit money.'

"Did you ever see any of it?

" 'No.'

"Did any of the neighbors?

" 'No; I never heard any say they did.'

"Did any one ever catch them trying to pass coun-terfeit money?

" 'No; oh! I don't say they made any; it was only talked around.'

"Who talked it; their friends or enemies, and when was it talked?

" 'Well, they were not their friends of course; I never heard it while they lived here; after they went to Kirtland, Ohio, people were talking it.'

"Young lady, a daughter of Mr. Pierce:

" 'The sheets, the sheets, pa; what was it about the sheets? Ma said old Mr. Smith come here with the sheets—and she told him to leave. How was it?' (looking to other members of the house).

"The sheets; what kind of sheets? (I began to think of ghosts and hobgoblins).

" 'The sheets, or the leaves, he was carrying around in an old sack, or something.'

"Our feelings were relieved somewhat when we learned on further inquiry, that Mr. Smith had called upon them when the Book of Mormon was first published, with a few unbound volumes for sale, and was ordered out of the house by 'ma;' nothing like ghosts being connected with the event.

"Squire, did you really think they were in the counterfeit money business?

" 'No; I never thought they did that.'

"Tell us about the cave you spoke of.

" 'The cave is over there in the hill now—a large cave.'

"In what hill? The hill they call 'Mormon Hill?'

" 'No; it is about a mile from that, but what are you so particular about it for?'

"We want to go and see it—we want to see the thing itself. Now you have been there, give us the description, while we write it down, so that we can find it.

" 'No; I never saw it; besides it is all caved in now, so you could not see anything. There is no cave there now, it is all fallen in.'

"The young lady.—'Well, why are you so particular for, anyway; what good will it do?'

"We wish to know just how much truth there is to these stories; and get some facts that we can stand on.

"Y. L.—'But what good will it do?'

"Just this; there has been a great many stories told about these people, and the finding of the plates; some believe there is truth in the stories, and some believe they are lies. We are investigating the matter to satisfy ourselves what there is in it.

"Y. L.—'Now, you had better turn your backs upon it, and let it go; that is the way to do, there is no truth in it.'

"That is just the thing at issue. Some say there is truth in it, some say there isn't. It is right to investigate and prove all things; and we wish to find what there is in this.

"Y. L.—'But what good will it do to find out the truth about the Book of Mormon?'

"If it is what it claims to be, we wish to know it; if false, we wish evidence to prove that.

"Y. L.—'What; you spending your time trying to find out about that? If I only knew where your wives are, I would write to them and let them know just what you are doing.'

"All right; do so. (Here we gave our names and addresses).

"Did you ever read that book?

"Y. L.—'No; I never saw one.'

"Well, I have; and there is something strikingly strange about it. It is certain that no one, or multitude of men, ever possessed sufficient inventive genius to produce it, or one similar to it, and have it so perfect in its doctrinal teachings, history and general make up, as to baffle the skill of learned critics to detect the error and deception. This book bids defiance to the whole learned world to prove it false; did you ever think of that?

"Y. L.—'No; but what good will it do, if it is true?'

"If really true; Joseph Smith obtained the plates, and men are telling falsehoods about him; and there has been a divine communication from heaven in our own day, which is contrary to the whole of the traditionary religious belief of the age. It unites with the testimony given in the Bible concerning Jesus being the Christ; and that he is indeed, the Redeemer of the world; hence, another witness testifying in favor of His mission and work. Quite a necessary thing when we take into consideration the unbelief and skepticism there is in the world at the present time, and it is on the increase. Then it is very gratifying and instructive to know about the ancient inhabitants of this country, their origin, habits of life, form of government, laws and religion.

"Y. L.—'But does this book teach the same as the Bible—our Bible?'

"The teachings of the two books are the same, so far as religious duties and life are concerned. Besides it is urged that many prophecies of the Bible refer to the coming forth of this book, and we confess that we are not enabled to explain satisfactorily the passages referred to, in any other light.

"Y. L.— 'Why what are some of them? I never heard of that before.'

"The twenty-ninth chapter of Isaiah is one directly in point, where the prophet speaks with reference to a sealed book coming forth, the words of which were to be delivered to a learned man, but he could not be able to read them; and the book itself was to be delivered to an unlearned man, and he would be enabled to read it. Also the stick of Joseph in the hand of Ephraim, recorded in the thirty-seventh chapter of Ezekiel. It is interpreted by the learned that the stick of Judah, there mentioned, is the Bible; and the Latter Day Saints hold the stick of Joseph referred to, is the Book of Mormon. Then in the tenth of John, where Jesus says: 'Other sheep I have which are not of this fold,' etc., relates to Israelitish people who had to come to this continent, and were unknown to the Jews, but known to Jesus. It is held, too, that the fourteenth chapter of the book of Revelations refers to this event, where John saw an angel flying through the midst of heaven having the everlasting gospel to preach to all people, just previous to the hour of God's judgment; and many other passages. Did you never read them?

"Y. L.—'No; write some of them down, and I will examine them.' (Here we wrote down some references).

"Y. L.—'Don't this book teach polygamy?'

"'Oh, no; it is much more outspoken and emphatic against that sin than the Bible. (Quoting a passage from the Book of Jacob). The people in Utah, known as Mormons, treat it as you would a last year's almanac. They say it was good in its time, but they have outgrown it.

"Y. L.—'Are there any other people who believe in that book?'

"Yes; the Latter Day Saints who may be found in almost every State and Territory in the Union, and

other parts of the world. An intelligent class of people, who have taken pains to examine all sides relating
to this subject, and have become convinced that there
is truth in it. They do not believe in going to Utah;
neither are they more like them in faith and doctrine
than are the Methodists, Baptists, Presbyterians, etc.
They have a publishing house at Plano, Illinois, about
fifty-six miles from Chicago, and are an orderly class
of people. It was very easy for people in the days of
Jesus to say that He was an imposter—was possessed of
the devil—born of fornication—a glutton and a wine
bibber; an enemy of mankind generally, but He was
true, and the Christ just the same. Sensible people
examined into the facts, then, relating to Him and His
doctrine; and the foolish were moved by gossip, stories
and popular rumor, until they raised their hands and
rejected the best friend of the human race. It is just
as easy for people to cry in this age 'Old Joe Smith—
Gold Bible—Money digger, Imposter,' etc. But what
are the facts in the case? That is what we wish to
know. I am a Latter Day Saint minister myself, not
of choice, but from conviction, by force of evidence
adduced on that side of the question; I expect to continue to be one until convinced that it is not right, and
it will take something more than stories to do it.

"The Squire.—'Well, if he believes that Joe Smith
was a prophet, that's enough; you can't do anything
with him. I never knew one to change yet.'

"Now Squire, what do you know about it?

" 'I don't know anything about it.'

"Now, I am ready to affirm that the Book of Mormon is a work of divine authenticity, and that Joseph
Smith was a prophet of God; and I say that I can

prove it from the Bible and other evidences, and am willing to undertake to do it right here, or in Palmyra, or Manchester, where it is admitted the thing first started.

"Y. L.—'Why, I don't believe you would be safe to do that here.'

"You don't? Have you such a class of people here, that they will break the laws of the country, and refuse liberty of speech and conscience? Don't dare to speak my sentiments in a country in which I have followed the flag, and bore arms for its defense, in order to continue a perpetual union? A country in which every ounce of powder and pound of lead is pledged to maintain human rights and religious equality and freedom?

" 'Oh, I guess they would let you, too; I will take that back. It is right to let all have the privilege of speaking their minds.'

"Of course, Squire, I should not expect you to believe in this, for it is difficult for any one to believe a matter without evidence; and you say you never heard one of them preach; never attended their meetings; never read one of their books, and have read a great many things written against them. Now would any of us have ever believed in Jesus if we had never read anything that he and the apostles said; never read any of their books; but just took the stories their enemies circulated about them—read the books put out by the pretended pious Jews against them? And don't you know that it is from that standpoint that the Jews reject Jesus and the teachings of the apostles, unto this day? They say they have hundreds of witnesses to one that Jesus was a law-breaker, and a deceiver; and the apostles false witnesses.

" 'Yes, that is true.'

"Y. L.—'Can you speak in tongues and prophesy?'

"Suppose I can't, what has that to do with the principle? Jesus says, 'These signs shall follow them that believe.' It is in the Bible. I am not responsible for it.

" 'But can you speak in tongues? That is my question.'

"I have heard a great many of the Saints speak in tongues and interpret. Have heard them speak in prophecy, and have seen the sick healed many times.

" 'But can you prophesy and speak in tongues?'

"Well, what would you think, if I was to tell you that I can?

" 'Why, I should say you was crazy.'

"That is just what I thought.

" 'We have institutions in which ministers are educated now, and we don't need such things.'

"Yes; I know there are a good many who seem to think they know more than Paul and Peter did about Christ and his doctrine; have gone on to invent creeds and systems; but did you never think that this is the greatest evil of the age—the very thing that keeps men in fetters, ignorance and superstition. Here is a Roman Catholic institution, that educates its priests to teach Catholicism; and after they go through the training, they know nothing else; hence, start out in their little groove to make Catholics. They do not know anything else, nor will they listen to others, in order that they may become informed. It is the abominable system of training is the difficulty. Take the Methodist ministers, or Baptist, or Episcopalian, or Quakers, or Disciples, or Adventists, or others; and each has to pass through their respective institutions of training, and when through, they start out, not to preach what is in the Bible, for many of them are forbidden to talk doctrine, but to proselyte to their peculiar creeds; fortify and build them up.   One to teach sprinkling for baptism; another pouring, or immersion; another no baptism at all, or only that of the Spirit; one that you must keep Sunday, and others, Saturday; another that you will be saved by works; another by faith and grace, without works; one sprinkles infants, and others don't; all owing to what school he was educated in.   If any courageous spirit endeavors to break away from the creed, they will whip him into the traces or throw him out.   There is no genuine Christian unity and love between them, but each rejoices at the others downfall, for the sake of the advantage; not because it is according to the Bible, but according to the Creed.

" 'Well, I guess there is a good deal of truth in that.'

"In this age of the conflict of ideas and investigation, people are getting tired of myths, and are digging deep and searching for facts, in religion as well as everything else.   If religion is a truth, the facts should show it; if false, the world ought to know that.   We believe in discussion—'proving all things, and holding fast that which is good.'   Hearing everybody; investigating everything possible.   But we must go.

"Mr. Pierce having referred us to Mr. Reed, Orlando Saunders, and Abel Chase, we took leave of him and his intelligent family, and called next at the residence of Mr. Orin Reed.

"He was at his home, doing some work about the barn.   He is a gentleman of about seventy years of age, hard of hearing, and of pleasant and intelligent countenance. Breaking the object of our call to him, he readily informed us that he knew nothing whatever in regard to the character of Joseph Smith, or his family.

"Mr. Reed, were you not acquainted with the Smith family, or some of those early connected with them?

" 'No, I was not. I lived in the town of Farmington when the Smiths lived here. I knew nothing about any of them; was not personally acquainted with them, and never heard any of them preach, nor never attended any of their meetings. I have seen Hyrum Smith. He bought a piece of land near here, and lived on it sometime after the others left; but I don't know anything against him.'

"We were given your name by a number of persons, who claimed that you did know all about them, Mr. Reed?

" 'Is that so? Well, they are mistaken; I don't know anything about it. I think Mr. Orlando Saunders, living up on the road to Palmyra, will know more about that people than any one around here. He was better acquainted with them, or lived right by them, and had a better opportunity of knowing them.'

"Yes, we have his name already, but have not seen him yet. Do you know Mr. Thorn, the Presbyterian minister at Manchester, over here.

" 'Yes, I know him slightly.'

"Did you not make a statement to him in regard to the character of these men; that they were low persons, and not good associates, or something of the kind?

" 'I never did.'

"Did he call on you to find out what you knew about it?

" 'No, sir, he never did; at least he never let me know anything about it, if he did.'

"Did you ever see a statement he sent to Michigan last year, and had published, purporting to be what you and others knew about the Smiths and Cowderys?

" 'No, I never did; did not know that one was ever published before.'

"You think we can find out about these persons from Mr. Saunders, then, Mr. Reed?

" 'Yes; he is more likely to know than any one round here.'

"Leaving Mr. Reed, we at once drove to the house of Mr. Orlando Saunders, and found that gentleman, with his wife and two sons, at supper. Mr. Saunders is a man seventy-eight years old, in April, 1881; a fair type of the intelligent New York farmer, seemingly well-to-do in this world's goods, and quite active for a man of his years; and withal, has an honest and thoughtful face.

"Entering upon conversation with reference to our business, Mr. Saunders at once said:

" 'Well, you have come to a poor place to find out anything. I don't know anything against these men, myself.' (Evidently judging that we wanted to get something against them, only.)

"Were you acquainted with them, Mr Saunders?

" 'Yes, sir; I knew all of the Smith family, well; there were six boys; Alvin, Hyrum, Joseph, Harrison, William, and Carlos, and there were two girls; the old man was a cooper; they have all worked for me many a day; they were very good people; Young Joe, (as we called him then), has worked for me, and he was a good worker; they all were. I did not consider them good managers about business, but they were poor people; the old man had a large family.'

"In what respect did they differ from other people, if at all?

" 'I never noticed that they were different from other neighbors; they were the best family in the neighborhood in case of sickness; one was at my house nearly all the time when my father died; I always thought them honest; they were owing me some money when they left here, that is, the old man and Hyrum did, and Martin Harris. One of them came back in about a year and paid me.'

"How were they as to habits of drinking and getting drunk?

" 'Everybody drank a little in those days, and the Smiths with the rest; they never got drunk to my knowledge.'

"What kind of a man was Martin Harris?

" 'He was an honorable man. Martin Harris was one of the first men of the town.'

"How well did you know young Joseph Smith?

" 'Oh! just as well as one could very well; he has worked for me many a time, and been about my place a great deal. He stopped with me many a time, when through here, after they went west to Kirtland; he was always a gentleman when about my place.'

"What did you know about his finding that book, or the plates in the hill over here?

" 'He always claimed that he saw the angel and received the book, but I don't know anything about it. Have seen it, but never read it as I know of; didn't care anything about it.'

"Well, you seem to differ a little from a good many of the stories told about these people.

" 'I have told you just what I know about them, and you will have to go somewhere else for a different story.'

"Mr. Saunders, giving us the directions to the house of Abel Chase, we next called upon him and as-certained the following:

"Mr. Chase.— 'I am sixty-seven years old. Knew the Smiths; the old man was a cooper. I was young and don't remember only general character. They were poorly educated, ignorant and superstitious; were kind of shiftless, but would do a good day's work. They used to call Joe, "Lobby Joe." He got a singu-lar looking stone, which was dug up out of my father's well; it belonged to my brother Willard, and he could never get it. His mother, old Mrs. Smith, got the stone from mother.'

"How do you know Joe ever had it?

" 'Oh, I don't know that; but my brother could never get it back.'

"Your sister had a stone she could look through and see things, so they have told us; did you ever see that, Mr. Chase?

" 'Yes, I have seen it, but that was not the one that old Mrs. Smith got.'

"Well, could you see things through that?

" 'I could not; it was a dark looking stone; it was a peculiar stone.'

"Do you really think your sister could see things by looking through that stone, Mr. Chase?

" 'Well, she claimed to; and I must say there was something strange about it.'

"Where is your sister now?

" 'She is not living now: my brother Willard is dead, also. He would know more than I do about those things.'

"How did the stone look, you say Mrs. Smith got?

" 'I don't know; I never saw that.

"How do you know she got it?

" 'They said she did; I was young, and don't remember myself.'

"Did you ever see the Smiths dig for money; or did you ever see the cave where they say they met at?

" 'No. I never saw them dig, myself; I never saw the cave.'

"Well; you were a young man then, how did it come you lived so near, and never saw them do these things?

" 'I was young, and never went where they were. Don't know anything about it but what I have heard. If you will see Mr. Guilbert, at Palmyra, he can tell you more about it than any person else; he knows it all and has been getting everything he could for years to publish against them; he was in with Tucker in getting out Tucker's work.'

"All right, Mr. Chase, we will see him this evening if possible. Good day, sir, Much obliged for the trouble.

" 'Oh! it is no trouble; I only wish I could tell you more.'

"Early in the evening we called upon Mr. John H. Gilbert, at his residence, and made known our desire for an interview, etc. He seemed quite free to give us all the information he had upon the subject, and said he had been for the past forty-five or fifty years doing all he could to find out what he could about the Smiths and Book of Mormon. He is a man seventy-nine years of age, and quite active even in this time of life.

"What did you know about the Smiths, Mr. Gilbert?

" 'I knew nothing myself; have seen Joseph Smith a few times, but not acquainted with him. Saw Hyrum quite often. I am the party that set the type from the original manuscript for the Book of Mormon. They translated it in a cave. I would know that manuscript today if I should see it. The most of it was in Oliver Cowdery's handwriting. Some in Joseph's wife's; a small part though. Hyrum Smith always brought the manuscript to the office; he would have it under his coat, and all buttoned up as carefully as though it was so much gold. He said at the time it was translated from plates by the power of God, and they were very particular about it We had a great deal of trouble with it. It was not punctuated at all. They did not know anything about punctuation, and we had to do that ourselves.'

"Well; did you change any part of it when you were setting the type?

" 'No, sir; we never changed it at all.'

"Why did you not change it and correct it?

" 'Because they would not allow us to; they were very particular about that. We never changed it in the least. Oh, well; there might have been one or two words that I changed the spelling of; I believe I did change the spelling of one, and perhaps two, but no more.'

'·Did you set all of the type, or did some one help you?

" 'I did the whole of it myself, and helped to read the proof too; there was no one who worked at that but myself. Did you ever see one of the first copies? I have one here that was never bound. Mr. Grandin, the printer, gave it to me. If you ever saw a Book of Mormon you will see that they changed it afterwards.'

"They did! Well, let us see your copy; that is a good point. How is it changed now?

" 'I will show you,' (bringing out his copy). 'Here on the title page it says,' (reading) ' "Joseph Smith, Jr, author and proprietor." Afterwards, in getting out other editions they left that out, and only claimed that Joseph Smith translated it.'

"Well, did they claim anything else than that he was the translator when they brought the manuscript to you?

" 'Oh, no; they claimed that he was translating it by means of some instruments he got at the same time he did the plates, and that the Lord helped him.'

"Was he educated, do you know?

" 'Oh, not at all then; but I understand that afterwards he made great advancement, and was quite a scholar and orator.'

"How do you account for the production of the Book of Mormon, Mr. Gilbert, then, if Joseph Smith was so illiterate?

" 'Well, that is the difficult question. It must have been from the Spaulding romance—you have heard of that, I suppose. The parties here then never could have been the authors of it, certainly. I have been for the last forty-five or fifty years trying to get the key to that thing; but we have never been able to make the connecting yet. For some years past I have been corresponding with a person in Salt Lake, by the name of Cobb, who is getting out a work against the Mormons; but we have never been able to find what we wanted.'

"If you could only connect Sidney Rigdon with Smith some way, you could get up a theory.

" 'Yes; that is just where the trouble lies; the manuscript was put in our hands in August, 1829, and all printed by March, 1830, and we can not find that Rigdon was ever about here, or in this state, until sometime in the Fall of 1830. But I think I have got a way out of the difficulty now. A fellow that used to be here, by the name of Saunders, Lorenzo Saunders, was back here some time ago, and I was asking him about it. At first he said he did not remember of ever seeing Rigdon until after 1830 sometime; but after studying it over a while, he said it seemed to him that one time he was over to Smith's, and that there was a stranger there he never saw before, and that they said it was Rigdon I told him about Cobb, of Utah, and asked him if he would send Cobb his affidavt, that he saw Rigdon before the book was published, if he (Cobb), would write to him; he finally said he would, and I wrote to Cobb about it, and gave Saunders' address, and after a long time, I got a letter from him, saying he had written three letters to Saunders, and could get no answer. I then sat down and wrote Saunders a letter myself, reminding him of his promise, and wrote to Cobb also about it; and after a long time Cobb wrote me again, that Saunders had written to him; but I have never learned how satisfactory it was, or whether he made the affidavit or not.'

"Is that Saunders a brother of the Saunders living down here, Orlando Saunders?

" 'Yes, sir; they are brothers.'

"Is he older or younger?

" 'Younger; about fifteen years younger.'

"Then he must have been quite young before the Book of Mormon was published?

" 'Yes, he was young.'

"This Saunders down here don't talk like a great many people; he seems to think the Smiths were very good people; we have been there today.

" 'Oh, I don't think the Smiths were as bad as people let on for. Now Tucker, in his work, told too many big things; nobody could believe his stories.'

"Did the Smiths ever dig for money?

" 'Yes; I can tell you where you can find persons who know all about that; can take you to the very place.'

"Can you? All right, give us their names.

" 'The Jackaway boys—two old bachelors, and their sister, an old maid, live together, right up the street going north, near the north part of the town; they can tell you all about it, and show you the very places where they dug.'

"What will you take for your copy of the Book of Mormon; or will you sell it?

" 'Yes, I will sell it.'

"How much for it?

" 'I will take Five Hundred Dollars for it, and no less: I have known them to sell for more than that.'

"Well, I am not buying at those figures, thank you.

"What kind of a man was Martin Harris?

" 'He was a very honest farmer, but very superstitious.'

"What was he before his name was connected
with the Book of Mormon?

" 'Not anything, I believe; he was a kind of a
skeptic.'

"What do you mean by his being superstitious?
Was he religious?

" 'Well, I don't know about that; but he pretended to see things.'

"What do you think of the Book of Mormon, as a
book; you are well posted in it?

" 'Oh, there is nothing taught in the book but
what is good; there is no denying that; it is the claim
of being from God that I strike at.'

"Well, is it any more wonderful than that God
gave the Bible?

" 'No, not a bit; and there is a good deal more
evidence to show that that is divine than there is for
some of the books in the Bible.   Why, it is all nonsense
to think that Moses wrote some of the books attributed
to him, in the Bible.'

"Then you don't believe the 'fish story,' either,
Mr. Gilbert?

" 'No; nor that Jonah swallowed the whale.'

"How about Sampson catching the three hundred
foxes, and the firebrands?

" 'Yes, that is a good one; you fellows will do.'

"Much obliged, Mr. Gilbert.

" 'You are quite welcome.   I wish I could give
you more than I have.'

"Acting upon Mr. Gilbert's advice, we at once
called upon the Jackways, and found the older of the

boys and the sister, ready to talk of what they knew. They had Tucker's work on the small table by; which they offered to sell us for three dollars, and then we could read for ourselves; but being quite familiar with its weaknesses, we declined to purchase at the price.

"The conversation upon the main topic was as follows:

"What is your age?

" 'I will be sixty-six years old on my next birthday,' said Mr. Jackway. (The lady did not answer).

"How far did you live from town at the time the Smiths, and those of their comrades, were in this country?

" 'One-half mile south of Palmyra.'

"Were you acquainted with Joseph Smith and his early followers?

" 'Yes, I knew them; seen them a many a time—old Joe and young Joe.'

"How far did you live from them?

" 'It was about a mile.'

"You know about their digging for money, so Mr. Gilbert said; he sent us to you?

" 'Oh, yes, I can show you the places now; there are three places over there where they dug.'

"Well, we want to see them. Did you help them dig?

" 'No, I never helped them.'

"Well, you saw them digging?

" 'No, I never saw them digging.'

"How do you know they dug the holes you refer to?

" 'I don't know they dug them; but the holes are there.'

"Did anybody else dig for money at that time there?

" 'I believe there were some others that dug; but I did not see them.'

"Do you know any of them?

" 'I only know one now; he lives up at Can-andaigua.'

"(Mr. Jackway gave us the name, but for some cause we fail to find it in our notes).

"What do you know about the Smiths' character?

" 'I don't know much about that.'

"Would they steal, get drunk, &c?

" 'Don't know anything about their stealing. Joe and his father got drunk once.'

"Where was that?

" 'It was in the hay field; Joe and his father wrestled, and Joe threw the old man down and he cried.'

"What did he cry for?

" 'Because Joe was the best man I guess.'

"What did they drink to make them drunk?

" 'They drank cider.'

"Got drunk so they could not walk, on cider, did they?

" 'No; they could walk, but they cut up and acted funny?

"Did you ever see them drink, or drunk, any other time?

"No; not as I remember.'

"What kind of a woman was the old lady Smith?

" 'I don't know; I never was at the house. She was kind in sickness.'

"Quite a number here in town, today, have told us it was two and a half to three miles from Palmyra to where the Smiths lived; how is that?

" 'Yes it was about three miles.'

"(How Jackway lived within half a mile of town and only a mile from them he did not explain).

"Where was Joe when he was translating his book?

" 'At home; it was translated in the farmhouse.'

"Mr. Gilbert, across here, said it was done in a cave; now you don't agree? What does Tucker say? (reading Tucker).

" 'They all differ. Now, Tucker has a statement from Willard Chase in his book, and Chase said Tucker never called on him at all to find out what he knew.'

"Lady.—'Yes; I have heard Willard Chase say Tucker never even asked him for what he knew, and Chase lived next door to him, too. Chase is dead now.'

"Well, did you ever see Hulbert or Howe, that published works?

" 'Yes; Hulbert came around first, I believe, soon after the thing started, and they had gone to Kirtland, Ohio, trying to find things against them; and there have been a good many around trying to connect Sidney Rigdon with them.'

"What kind of men were Martin Harris and Oliver Cowdery?

" 'Harris was an industrious, honest man; lived north here, two miles. The Cowderys were as good as the general run of people. Have you seen Dr. Stafford? He lives at Rochester. His father, William Stafford, is the one that furnished the "black sheep" Tucker tells about there.'

"He is? Well, do you know about that?

" 'No; only what Tucker says there.'

"Taking leave of the Jackways, in due time we called upon Dr. John Stafford, at Rochester, New York. He is now a retired physician, being too aged and infirm to practice. Answering a question as to the character of Joseph Smith, he said:

" 'He was a real clever, jovial boy. What Tucker said about them was false, absolutely. My father, William Stafford, was never connected with them in any way. The Smiths, with others, were digging for money before Joe got the plates. My father had a stone, which some thought they could look through, and old Mrs. Smith came there after it one day, but never got it. Saw them digging one time for money; (this was three or four years before the Book of Mormon was found), the Smiths and others. The old man and Hyrum were there, I think, but Joseph was not there. The neighbors used to claim Sally Chase could look at a stone she had, and see money. Willard Chase used to dig when she found where the money was. Don't know as anybody ever found any money.'

"What was the character of Smith, as to his drinking?

" 'It was common then for everybody to drink, and to have drink in the field; one time Joe, while working for some one, after he was married, drank too much boiled cider. He came in with his shirt torn; his wife felt bad about it, and when they went home, she put her shawl on him.'

"Had he been fighting and drunk?

" 'No; he had been scuffling with some of the boys. Never saw him fight; have known him to scuffle; would do a fair day's work if hired out to a man; but were poor managers.'

"What about that black sheep your father let them have?

" 'I have heard that story, but don't think my father was there at the time they say Smith got the sheep. I don't know anything about it.'

"You were living at home at the time, and it seems you ought to know if they got a sheep or stole one from your father?

" 'They never stole one, I am sure; they may have got one sometime.'

"Well, Doctor, you know pretty well whether that story is true or not, that Tucker tells. What do you think of it?

" 'I don't think it is true. I would have heard more about it, that is true. I lived a mile from Smiths; am seventy-six years old. They were peaceable among themselves. The old woman had a great deal of faith that their children were going to do something great. Joe was quite illiterate. After they began to have school at their house, he improved greatly.'

"Did they have school in their own house?

" 'Yes, sir; they had school in their house, and studied the Bible.'

"Who was their teacher?

" 'They did not have any teacher; they taught themselves.'

"Did you know Oliver Cowdery?

" 'Yes; he taught school on the Canandaigua road, where the stone school house now stands; just three and a half miles south of Palmyra. Cowdery was a man of good character.'

"What do you know about Martin Harris?

" 'He was an honorable farmer; he was not very

religious before the Book of Mormon was published. Don't know whether he was skeptical or visionary. Old Joe claimed he understood geology, and could tell all kinds of minerals; and one time, down at Manchester, in the grocery, the boys all got pretty full, and thought they would have some fun, and they fixed up a dose for him.' (We omit the ingredients of the dose, because improper for publication).

"If Smith was as illiterate as you say, Doctor, how do you account for the Book of Mormon?

" 'Well, I can't; except that Sidney Rigdon was connected with them.'

"What makes you think he was connected with them?

" 'Because I can't account for the Book of Mormon any other way.'

"Was Rigdon ever around there before the Book of Mormon was published.

" 'No; not as we could ever find out. Sidney Rigdon was never there, that Hulburt, or Howe, or Tucker could find out.'

"Well, you have been looking out for the facts a long time, have you not, Doctor?

" 'Yes; I have been thinking and hearing about it for the last fifty years, and lived right among all their old neighbors there most of the time.'

"And no one has ever been able to trace the acquaintance of Rigdon and Smith, until after the Book of Mormon was published, and Rigdon proselyted by Pratt, in Ohio?

" 'Not that I know of.'

"Did you know the Pratts,—Parley or Orson Pratt?

" 'No; have heard of them.'

"Did you know David Whitmer?

" 'No; he lived in Seneca county, New York.'

"Have you told now all you know about the Smiths and the Book of Mormon?

" 'All that I can recollect.'

"Here we bade the Doctor, whom we found to be quite a gentleman,—affable, and ready to converse,— good day.

"During the time of making the interviews in Manchester, we accidentally met the Thomas H. Taylor, referred to by Mr. Booth in the interview with him. He is a Scotchman by birth, of advanced age, but very robust and active. Somewhat of the knock-down and drag-out style; is a public speaker and lecturer, and practices law to some extent. He claims to be one of the original parties with John Brown at Harper's Ferry —all through the fight there—and previous to the war of the rebellion, was engaged in piloting the darkey to Canada and freedom. He was a soldier throughout the war, and saw hard service. In religion he follows Col. Robert G. Ingersol. To our inquiries if he was acquainted with the Smiths, and the early settlers throughout that part, sometimes called Mormons, he said:

" 'Yes; I knew them very well; they were very nice men too; the only trouble was they were ahead of the people; and the people, as in every such case, turned out to abuse them, because they had the manhood to stand for their own convictions. I have seen such work all through life, and when I was working with John Brown for the freedom of my fellow man, I often got in tight places, and if it had not been for Gerritt Smith, Wendell Phillips and some others, who gave me their influence and money,

I don't know how I would ever got through.'

"What did the Smiths do that the people abused them so?

" 'They did not do anything. Why! these rascals at one time took Joseph Smith and ducked him in the pond that you see over there, just because he preached what he believed, and for nothing else. And if Jesus Christ had been there, they would have done the same to him. Now, I don't believe like he did; but every man has a right to his religious opinions, and to advocate his views, too; if people don't like it, let them come out and meet him on the stand, and shew his error. Smith was always ready to exchange views with the best men they had.'

"Why didn't they like Smith?

" 'To tell the truth, there was something about him they could not understand; someway he knew more than they did, and it made them mad.'

"But a good many tell terrible stories about them being low people, rogues, and liars, and such things. How is that?

" 'Oh! they are a set of d—d liars. I have had a home here, and been here, except when on business, all my life—ever since I came to this country, and I know these fellows; they make these lies on Smith, because they love a lie better than the truth. I can take you to a great many old settlers here who will substantiate what I say, and if you want to go, just come around to my place across the street there, and I'll go with you.'

"Well, that is very kind, Mr. Taylor, and fair; if we have time we will call around and give you a chance; but we are first going to see these fellows who, so rumor says, know so much against them.

" ·All right; but you will find they don't know anything against those men when you put them down to it; they could never sustain anything against Smith.'

"Do you think Smith ever got any plates out of the hill he claimed to?

" 'Yes; I rather think he did.   Why not he find something as well as anybody else.   Right over here, in Illinois and Ohio, in mounds there, they have discovered copper plates since, with hieroglyphics all over them; and quite a number of the old settlers around here testified that Smith showed the plates to them— they were good, honest men, and what is the sense in saying they lied?   Now, I never saw the Book of Mormon—don't know anything about it, nor care; and don't know as it was ever translated from the plates. You have heard about the Spaulding Romance; and some claim that it is nothing but the books of the Bible that were rejected by the compilers of the Bible; but all this don't prove that Smith never got any plates.'

"Do you know Rev. Thorn, here in Manchester?

" 'The Presbyterian preacher?'

"Yes, that is the one.

" 'I know him.'

"What kind of a fellow is he?

" 'Well, originally he was nothing.   He got some money, and went off to college a while, and came back a Presbyterian preacher.   He knows just what he got there, and feels stuck up, and is now preaching for his bread and butter; and if they should take away his salary, he wouldn't last twenty-four hours.'

"We are much obliged, Mr. Taylor, for your kindness.

" 'You are welcome, and if you will drive back, I will go with you and show you persons who can tell you all about those people.'

"We thus left Mr. Taylor, but for want of time, could not then return and accept his kind offer to show us around; hope to be able to do so some time in the future.

"These facts and interviews are presented to the readers of the Herald impartially—just as they occurred —the good and bad, side by side; and allowing for a possible mistake, or error, arising from a misapprehension, or mistake in taking notes, it can be relied upon as the opinion and gossip had about the Smith family and others, among their old neighbors.   It will be remembered that all the parties interviewed are unbelievers in, and some bitter enemies to, the faith of the Saints; and it is not unreasonable to suppose that they all told the worst they knew.   So we submit it to the readers without comment, with the expectation of sending each one of the parties interviewed a copy when published.

"WM. H. KELLEY.

"COLDWATER, Michigan, March, 1881."

CHAPTER IV.

THE SPAULDING MANUSCRIPT STORY IN BRIEF.

The supporters of the "story" give the date of its writing as 1809-12.   The decease of Spaulding in 1816.   Mrs. Spaulding the custody of the manuscript till 1834, when at the instance of W. H. Sabine, Henry Lake, Aaron Wright and others it was delivered to one D. P. Hurlbut, who turned it over to E. D. Howe, who stated in his book, published soon after, that "it did not read like we expected and we did not use it."   It was then lost between forty and fifty years.

In 1880 Elder T. W. Smith wrote something for the Pittsburg, Pennsylvania, Leader; that paper declining to publish the article, the matter was disposed of, setting forth solid facts in the following terse and pithy manner:

"In reply to many criticisms, Mr. Smith, the Mormon preacher of Pittsburg, sends us a small letter of about forty pages, which he requests us to print as 'an act of justice' to him. * * We have to be just to our readers as well as to Mr. Smith, and can not therefore surrender the space where they have a right to look for news, to the missionary efforts of any sect whatever. It should be sufficient justice to Elder Smith to say right now and here, as we frankly do, that the evidence by which it is sought to prove that 'Joe' Smith or Sidney Rigdon stole the manuscript copy of Rev. Solomon Spaulding's romance, and made the Book of Mormon out of it, is FATALLY DEFECTIVE. The thing can not be proved. The Mormons SUCCESSFULLY RIDDLE the testimony of those who assert it, and very fairly demand that Spaulding's romance be produced and the comparison made or the slander be dropped. The fact that this romance, though alleged to have remained in Gentile hands, never has been produced, and can not be now, is prima facie evidence that it is not the original of the Book of Mormon."—Pittsburg Leader, February 20, 1880.

The following year Mr. Smith wrote E. D. Howe who replied as follows:

"PAINESVILLE, Ohio, July 26th, 1881.

"SIR:—Your note of 21st is before me,—and I will answer your queries seriatim.

"1st.—The manuscript you refer to was not marked on the outside or inside 'Manuscript Found.' It was a common-place story of some Indian wars along the borders of our Great Lakes, between the Chicagoes and Eries, as I now recollect—not in Bible style—but purely modern.

"2d.—It was not the original 'Manuscript Found,' and I do not believe Hurlbut ever had it.

"3d.—I never saw or heard read the 'Manuscript Found,' but have seen five or six persons who had, and from their testimony, concluded it was very much like the Mormon Bible.

"4th.—Never succeeded in finding out anything more than was detailed in my book of exposure published about fifty years ago.

"5th. — The manuscript that came into my possession I suspect was destroyed by fire forty years ago.

"I think there has been much mist thrown around the whole subject of the origin of the Mormon Bible and the 'Manuscript Found,' by the several statements that have been made by those who have been endeavoring to solve the problem after sleeping quietly for half a century. Every effort was made to unravel the mystery at the time, when nearly all the parties were on earth, and the result published at the time, and I think it all folly to try to dig out anything more.

"Yours, etc.,

"E. D. HOWE."

Howe being unable to use the manuscript to defeat the Book of Mormon, suppressed it and concluded that "much mist" has been thrown around the "whole subject," and that "every effort had been made to unravel the mystery at the time."

The "mist has cleared away!" Extracts from Prof. J. H. Fairchild and L. L. Rice on the matter:

" 'There seems no reason to doubt that this is the long-lost story. Mr. Rice, myself, and others, compared it with the Book of Mormon, and could detect no resemblance between the two, in general or in detail. There seems to be no name or incident common to the two. The solemn style of the Book of Mormon, in imitation of the English Scriptures, does not appear in the manuscript. The only resemblance is in the fact that both profess to set forth the history of lost tribes. Some other explanation of the origin of the Book of Mormon must be found, if any explanation is required.' Signed, James H. Fairchild."—Bibliotheca Sacra, p. 173.

"HONOLULU, Sandwich Islands,
"March 28th, 1885.

"MR. JOSEPH SMITH:—The Spaulding Manuscript in my possession came into my hands in this wise. In 1839–40 my partner and myself bought of E. D. Howe, the Painesville Telegraph, published at Painesvile, Ohio. The transfer of the printing department, types, press, etc., was accompanied with a large collection of books, manuscripts, etc., this manuscript of Spaulding among the rest. So, you see, it has been in my possession over forty years. But I never examined it, or knew the character of it, until some six or eight months since. The wrapper was marked, 'Manuscript Story— Conneaut Creek.' The wonder is, that in some of my movements, I did not destroy it with a large amount of rubbish that had accumulated from time to time.

"It happened that President Fairchild was here on a visit at the time I discovered the contents of it, and it was examined by him and others with much curiosity. Since President Fairchild published the fact of its existence in my possession, I have had application for it from half a dozen sources, each applicant seeming to think that he or she was entitled to it. Mr. Howe says he was getting up a book to expose Mormonism as a fraud at an early day, when the Mormons had their headquarters at Kirtland, he obtained it from some source, and it was inadvertently transferred with the other effects of his printing office. A. B. Deming, of Painesville, who is also getting up some kind of a book, I believe on Mormonism, wants me to send it to him. Mrs. Dickinson, of Boston, claiming to be a relative of Spaulding, and who is getting up a book to show that he was the real author of the Book of Mormon, wants it. She thinks, at least, it should be sent to Spaulding's daughter, a Mrs. Somebody—but she does not inform me where she lives. Deming says that Howe borrowed it when he was getting up his book, and did not return it, as he should have done, etc.

"This manuscript does not purport to be 'a story of the Indians formerly occupying this continent,' but is a history of the wars between the Indians of Ohio and Kentucky, and their progress in civilization, etc. It is certain that this manuscript is not the origin of the Mormon Bible, whatever some other manuscript may have been. The only similarity between them, is, in the manner in which each purports to have been found— one in a cave on Conneaut Creek—the other in a hill in Ontario county, New York. There is no identity of names, of persons or places; and there is no similarity of style between them. As I told Mr. Deming, I should as soon think the Book of Revelations was written by the author of Don Quixotte, as that the writer of this Manuscript was the author of the Book of Mormon. * *

"Deming and Howe inform me that its existence is exciting great interest in that region. I am under a tacit, but not a positive pledge to President Fairchild, to deposit it eventually in the Library of Oberlin College. I shall be free from that pledge when I see an opportunity to put it to better use.

"Yours, etc.,
"L. L. RICE.

"P. S.—Upon reflection, since writing the foregoing, I am of the opinion that no one who reads this Manuscript will give credit to the story that Solomon Spaulding was in any wise the author of the Book of Mormon. It is unlikely that any one who wrote so elaborate a work as the Mormon Bible, would spend his time in getting up so shallow a story as this, which at best is but a feeble imitation of the other. Finally I am more than half convinced that this is his only writing of the sort, and that any pretence that Spaulding was in any sense the author of the other, is a sheer fabrication. It was easy for anybody who may have seen this, or heard anything of its contents, to get up the story that they were identical.   L. L. R."

Now the following extract:

"HONOLULU, Sandwich Islands, May 14th, 1885.
"MR. JOSEPH SMITH.

"DEAR SIR:—I am greatly obliged to you for the information concerning Mormonism in your letters of April 30th and May 2d. As I am in no sense a Mormonite, of course it is a matter of curiosity, mainly, that I am interested in the history of Mormonism.

"Two things are true concerning this manuscript in my possession: First, it is a genuine writing of Solomon Spaulding; and second, it is not the original of the Book of Mormon.   Very respectfully yours,

"L. L. RICE."

In a postscript Mr. Rice says he found the following endorsement on the manuscript:

"The writings of Solomon Spaulding, proved by Aaron Wright, Oliver Smith, John N. Miller and others. The testimonies of the above named gentlemen are now in my possession.   (Signed)   D. P. HURLBUT."

Extract from Mr. Rice's letter:

"HONOLULU, H. I., June 12, 1885.
"PRESIDENT J. H. FAIRCHILD:—Herewith I send you the Solomon Spaulding Manuscript, to be deposited

in the Library of Oberlin College, for reference by any one who may be desirous of seeing or examining it. * *

"Truly yours, etc.,

"L. L. RICE."

"OBERLIN COLLEGE, OBERLIN, O.,

"July 23, 1885.

"I have this day delivered to Mr. E. L. Kelley a copy of the Manuscript of Solomon Spaulding, sent from Honolulu by Mr. L. L. Rice, to the Library of Oberlin College, for safe keeping, and now in my care. The copy was prepared at Mr. Kelley's request, under my supervision, and is, as I believe, an exact transcript of the original manuscript, including erasures, misspellings, etc.   JAS. H. FAIRCHILD,

"Prest. of Oberlin College."

The correspondence in full on the matter, from these gentlemen, is contained in the "Manuscript Found," published from the copy President Fairchild prepared. Can be bought at Herald Office, Lamoni, Iowa, at 25 cents.

This entire batch of Spaulding story nonsense and alleged evidences in support of it was exposed by Benjamin Winchester in a pamphlet in 1840, at Philadelphia, Pennsylvania; by John E. Page in a pamphlet in 1843, at Pittsburg, Pennsylvania, and by various others at divers times and places, especially in the Braden–Kelley debate on sale at Herald Office, Lamoni, Iowa; also White–Box debate on sale at Ensign Office, Independence, Missouri Also treated in brief in J. R. Lambert's late work issued at Herald Office, entitled "Objections to the Book of Mormon and Doctrine and Covenants Examined and Refuted."

CHAPTER V.

TESTIMONY AND AFFIDAVITS.

TESTIMONY OF KATHERINE SALISBURY.

"STATE OF ILLINOIS, ⎫ ss.
   "Kendall County. ⎰

"I, Katherine Salisbury, being duly sworn, depose and say, that I am a resident of the State of Illinois, and have been for forty years last past; that I will be sixty-eight years of age, July 28th, 1881.

"That I am a daughter of Joseph Smith, senior, and a sister to Joseph Smith, Jr., the translator of the Book of Mormon. That at the time the said book was published, I was seventeen years of age; that at the time of the publication of said book, my brother, Joseph Smith, Jr., lived in the family of my father, in the town of Manchester, Ontario county, New York, and that he had, all of his life to this time made his home with the family.

"That at the time, and for years prior thereto, I lived in and was a member of such family, and personally knowing to the things transacted in said family, and those who visited at my father's house, and the friends of the family, and the friends and acquaintances of my brother, Joseph Smith, Jr., who visited at or came to my father's house.

"That prior to the latter part of the year A. D. 1830, there was no person who visited with, or was an acquaintance of, or called upon the said family, or any member thereof to my knowledge, by the name of Sidney Rigdon; nor was such person known to the family, or any member thereof, to my knowledge, until the last part of the year A. D. 1830, or the first part of the year 1831, and some time after the organization of the Church of Jesus Christ, by Joseph Smith, Jr., and several months after the publication of the Book of Mormon.

"That I remember the time when Sidney Rigdon came to my father's place, and that it was after the removal of my father from Waterloo, N. Y., to Kirtland, Ohio. That this was in the year 1831, and some months after the publication of the Book of Mormon, and fully one year after the Church was organized, as before stated herein.

"That I make this statement, not on account of fear, favor, or hope of reward of any kind, but simply that the truth may be known with reference to said matter, and that the foregoing statements made by me are true, as I verily believe.

"KATHERINE SALISBURY.

"Sworn to before me, and subscribed in my presence, by the said Katherine Salisbury, this 15th day of April, A. D. 1881.

"J. H. JENKS, Notary Public."

"PRINCEVILLE, Ill.; March 14th, 1872.

"BRO. JOSEPH:—I learn of late that some of the opposers of the Church of Jesus Christ of Latter Day Saints are resorting to an old story, that the Book of Mormon was manufactured from a romance of one

Solomon Spaulding, and was accomplished by one Sidney Rigdon. * *

"In the spring of 1833 or 1834, at the house of Samuel Baker, near New Portage, Medina county, Ohio, we, whose signatures are affixed, did hear Elder Sidney Rigdon, in the presence of a large congregation, say he had been informed that some in the neighborhood had accused him of being the instigator of the Book of Mormon. Standing in the door-way, there being many standing in the door-yard, he, holding up the Book of Mormon, said, 'I testify in the presence of this congregation, and before God and all the Holy Angels up yonder, (pointing towards heaven), before whom I expect to give account at the judgment day, that I never saw a sentence of the Book of Mormon, I never penned a sentence of the Book of Mormon, I never knew that there was such a book in existence as the Book of Mormon, until it was presented to me by Parley P. Pratt, in the form that it now is.'

"PHINEAS BRONSON,
"HIEL BRONSON,
"MARY D. BRONSON.

"Brother Hiel thinks it was in 1834, but sister Mary, his wife, and I, think it was in 1833, so we have put it in 1833 or 1834.

"PHINEAS BRONSON."

Herald, June 6, 1891.

"Statement of William B. Smith, the surviving brother of Joseph and Hyrum Smith, who in the closing years of a long life is waiting the summons of the pale reaper to call him to his answer and his rest:

" '* * No such man as Elder Rigdon ever visited my father's house, to my certain knowledge, prior to the publication of the Book of Mormon. And the first knowledge I ever had of Elder Rigdon was not until it was publicly announced that he had become a convert to the faith and doctrine of Mormonism, through the instrumentality of P. P. Pratt and Oliver Cowdery, who had presented him with the Book of Mormon while on a mission from the state of New York to the town of Kirtland, state of Ohio, where Elder Rigdon at the time held a prominent position as a Disciple minister in the Christian Church. * * No stranger from a distance could have visited your father, holding private or public conference with him, without the family knowing it; and to my certain knowledge no strangers visited about my father's house during that period of time in which the work of translating the found record was going on.

" 'Witness my testimony and seal,

" 'W. B. SMITH.' "

Herald, June 6, 1891.

The following is from the Braden–Kelley debate, at Lamoni, Iowa, 1891, as reported by the Independent Patriot:

KELLEY.—"I will offer an affidavit of Jno. W. Rigdon, son of Sidney Rigdon, a lawyer of Cuba, New York. This affidavit was given a short time ago. Subscribed and sworn to before me this 17 of April, 1891. W. F. Bement, Notary Public. Seal. I read this to show you where his witnesses are with reference to this matter.

"[All testimony condensed.]

"About 1832, while my father was preaching at Mentor, O., Martin Harris and Oliver Cowdery called upon him and presented to him the Book of Mormon, and told him it was found by Joseph Smith engraved

on gold plates, and that Smith translated the engravings, and the book was a true translation. That they
had seen the plates, that Harris had written the translation given by Joseph Smith. They asked him to read
it and give them his opinion of it. He gave them permission to preach in his church, and went to hear them.
At the close he told the congregation that they had
listened to some strange doctrine, but it was their duty
to investigate. Cowdery and Harris left next morning,
but returned in about six weeks. They asked my father
if he had read the book, and he said he had. They
asked what he thought of it. He asked if Joseph
Smith was a man of intelligence. Cowdery said Smith
had about as much knowledge as he had. Father replied if that was the 'case Smith was not the author of
the book.

"Some time after this father met Joseph Smith
for the first time in the state of New York. After being
in Smith's company for some time, he joined the Mormon Church, removed to Kirtland, and began preaching Mormonism. He afterward went to Missouri,
thence to Nauvoo, Ill. After Smith's death, my father
claimed it was his right to lead the church, but B.
Young was chosen. In 1847, father removed to Friendship, New York, where he remained until his death,
July 14, 1876, aged 84. He retired to private life after
removing to Friendship. Would occasionally lecture.
Large crowds always came out when it was announced
that he would speak. By his calm and dignified de-
meanor he gained the respect of all.

"In answer to the statements of Clark Braden in
'Saints' Herald,' under 'Christianity vs. Mormonism,'
I have only to quote Horatio Seymour who pronounced

Rigdon a very eloquent man; Martin Grover, one of New York's greatest jurists, who said Sidney Rigdon's knowledge of the history of the world, and the political history of our country, was perfectly surprising to him, and that he was a very learned and eloquent man. Prof. Hatch frequently said Rigdon was the best historian he ever saw and one of the most eloquent men he ever listened to. Also Rev. Braden's statements about Rigdon's extravagant yarns, highfalutin rant, his visions, the power while speaking, and falling in trances in the pulpit, have no truth in them whatever.

"Sidney Rigdon was a devout Christian from his youth to his grave. He preached and talked the Bible on all occasions when necessary, to his children and all. He died having a firm belief in the Christian religion. I never knew one who was a stronger believer in the Christian religion than he. I therefore pronounce such assertions as positively untrue.

"I am probably better acquainted with S. Rigdon than any living person. Had better opportunities through business and family relations to know his character, history, and religious belief than any one else. Religion was his favorite theme.

"On returning from Salt Lake City in 1865, where I had interviews with the leading dignitaries of the Mormon Church at that place on the subject of Mormonism and the Book of Mormon, I asked my father to tell me the facts as to the production of this book. My father stated that all he knew of the origin of the book was what Harris, Cowdery and J. Smith told him. That Smith during the fifteen years he was intimate with him, never stated anything else than that he found it engraven on gold plates which he found in a hill in New

York. He said after investigation he was confident that the story about Spaulding writing the Book of Mormon was untrue. He said the story about his writing the book was false. That he never saw the book until it was presented to him by Oliver Cowdery at Mentor, O. Knowing my father as I do, I am confident he told me the truth.

"My father never saw Solomon Spaulding in his life, nor did he steal any of his MSS. as stated by Rev. Braden.

"My mother survived my father about ten years. After father's death, in conversation with her about the Book of Mormon, she always told me that my father obtained it from Cowdery and Harris at Mentor, O., and that the stories about father having written it were untrue. Father and mother told me this same story in my youth and manhood, and they told it in their old age, and they never told any other. I am not a member of any religious denomination, and do not pretend to say how that book came into existence. But I am as certain as that I exist, that S. Rigdon never wrote any part of the Book of Mormon, and that he never saw it until Harris and Cowdery presented it to him at Mentor, O."

This affidavit shows up all these tales from Howe's work. This man testifies to nothing but what he knows. And the way he writes and the intelligence he was shown in getting up his own affidavit that his father might be placed correctly before the world, show that he is a gentleman in the highest sense.

Extract from Elder E. L. Kelley's article to Herald, bearing date November 7, 1894:

"Whatever may have been the opinion of the

enemies of Elder Rigdon touching his bold denunciation of the story implicating him in plotting or aiding
in anywise in the production of the Book of Mormon,
it must be admitted that all subsequently discovered
facts corroborate the statements of the witness, Rigdon,
and are at variance with the questionable yarns hawked
about the world by the enemies of this man, who hoped
to accomplish by these tales his overthrow, together
with the new faith which he had espoused.

"The times and places definitely settled by this
corroborative evidence, as to the whereabouts, occupation, and business of Elder Rigdon during the years
mentioned, are as follows:

"1. November 2, 1826. Solemnized a marriage
contract between John G. Smith and Julia Giles, in
Geauga county, Ohio.

"2. December 13, 1826. Returns and record of
marriage.

"3. January, 1827. Held public meetings in
Mantua, Ohio. ('Hayden's History of the Disciples of
the Western Reserve,' page 237.)

"4. February, 1827. Preached funeral discourse
of Hannah Tanner, Chester, Ohio.

"5. March, April, 1827. Held protracted meetings in Mentor, Ohio, baptizing Nancy M. Sanford,
William Dunsen and wife and others.

"6. June 5, 1827. Solemnized Marriage between
Theron Freeman and Elizabeth Waterman, Geauga
county, Ohio.

"7. June 15, 1827. Baptized Thomas Clapp and
others, Mentor, Ohio.

"8. July 3, 1827. Solemnized marriage between
James Gray and Mary Kerr, Mentor, Ohio.

"9. July 19, 1827. Solemnized marriage between Alden Snow and Ruth Parker, Kirtland, Ohio.

"10. August 23, 1827. Meeting with the ministerial Association, New Lisbon, Ohio. (Hist. Dis., pp. 55–57.

"11. October 9, 1827. Solemnized marriage of Stephen Sherman and Wealthy Matthews, Mentor, Ohio.

"12. October 20, 1827. Ministerial Council at Warren, Ohio. (His. Dis. p. 137.)

"13. November, 1827. Preaching at New Lisbon, Ohio. (His. Dis., pp. 72–75.)

"14. December 6, 1827. Solemnized marriage of Oliver Wait and Eliza Gunn, at Concord, Geauga county, Ohio.

"15. December 13, 1827. Solemnized marriage of Roswell D. Cottrell and Matilda Olds, Concord, Ohio.

"16. January 8, 1828. Return of marriage made at Chardon, Ohio.

"17. February 14, 1828. Solemnized marriage between Otis Herrington, Lyma Corning, Mentor, Ohio.

"18. March, 1828. Instructing class in theology in Mentor, Ohio, Zebulon Rudolph being a member; also held great religious meetings in Mentor and Warren, Ohio. (His. Dis., p. 198.)

"19. March 31, 1828. Returns made to Chardon, Ohio.

"20. April, 1828. Holds great religious revival at Kirtland, Ohio. (His. Dis., p. 194.)

"21. May, 1828. Meets Campbell at Shalersville, Ohio, and holds protracted meetings. (His. Dis., p. 155.)

"22. June, 1828. Baptized Henry H. Clapp, Mentor, Ohio.

"23. August, 1828. Attended great yearly association at Warren, Ohio.

"24. September, 1828. Solemnized marriage between Luther Dille and Clarissa Kent.

"25. September 18, 1828. Solemnized marriage between Nachore Corning and Phœbe E. Wilson, Mentor, Ohio.

"26. October 13, 1828. Returns made to Chardon, Ohio.

"27. January 1, 1829. Solemnized marriage between Albert Churchill and Anna Fosdick, Concord, Ohio.

"28. February 1, 1829. Solemnized marriage between Erastus Root and Rebecca Tuttle.

"29. February 12, 1829. Returns made to Chardon, Ohio.

"30. March, 1829. Protracted meeting, Mentor, Ohio.

"31. April 12, 1829. Protracted meeting, Kirtland, Ohio.

"32. July 1, 1829. Organized church at Perry, Ohio. (His. Dis., p. 346.)

"33. August 13, 1829. Solemnized marriage between John Strong and Ann Eliza Moore, Kirtland, Ohio.

"34. September 14, 1829. Solemnized marriage between Darwin Atwater and Harriet Clapp, Mentor, Ohio.

"35. September, 1829. Meeting at Mentor, Ohio; baptized J. J. Moss, disciple minister of note.

"36. October 1, 1829. Solemnized marriage between Joel Roberts and Relief Bates, Perry, Ohio.

"37. October, 1829. At Perry, Ohio. (His. Dis., pp. 207–409.)

"38. November, 1829. Wait Hill, Ohio; baptized Alvin Wait. (His. Dis., pp. 204–207.)

"39. December 31, 1829. Solemnized marriage between David Cloudler and Polly Johnson, Chagrin, Ohio.

"40. January 12, 1830. Returns to Cleveland, Ohio.

"41. March 1830. Mentor, Ohio.

"42. June 1–30, 1830. Mentor, Ohio. (Millennial Harbinger, p. 389.)

"43. July, 1830. Protracted meeting at Pleasant Valley, Ohio; baptized forty-five.

"44. August, 1830. With Alexander Campbell at Austintown, Ohio. (His. Dis., p. 209.)

"45. November 4, 1830. Solemnized marriage between Lewis B. Wood and Laura Cleveland, Kirtland, Ohio.

"46. December, 1830. Was converted to the faith of and united with the Church of Jesus Christ of Latter Day Saints, under the preaching of P. P. Pratt and Oliver Cowdery.

"The following certificates of the proper officers, touching the record—evidence of the marriages, will show the correctness of transcript as to these dates:

"The State of Ohio, } SS. Probate Court.
"Geauga county.

"I, H. K. Smith, Judge of the Probate Court in and for said county, hereby certify that the above and foregoing certificate, numbering from one to sixteen were truly taken and copied from the record of marriages in this county, preserved in this office, where the same, by law, are required to be kept. In testimony whereof, I have hereunto set my hand and affixed the seal of said court, at Chardon, this 27th day of April, A. D., 1891.

"(SEAL)   (Signed)   H. K. SMITH, Probate Judge.

"IN THE PROBATE COURT.

"State of Ohio,   ⎱ S. S.
"Cuyahoga County. ⎰

"I, Henry C. White, judge of said court, do hereby certify that the foregoing is a true and correct transcript taken from the marriage records in this office, where the same is by law required to be kept.

"(Signed)   HENRY C. WHITE, Probate Judge.
"(SEAL)   By H. A. SCHWAB, Dp. Clk."

EMMA SMITH'S TESTIMONY.

Interview with Emma Smith shortly before her death, April 30, 1879:

"QUESTION.—Who performed the marriage ceremony for Joseph Smith and Emma Hale? When? Where?

"ANSWER.—I was married at South Bainbridge, New York; at the house of Squire Tarbell, by him, when I was in my 22d or 23d year.

"We here suggested that Mother Smith's History gave the date of the marriage as January 18th, 1827. To this she replied:

"I think the date correct. My certificate of marriage was lost many years ago, in some of the marches we were forced to make.

"In answer to a suggestion by us that she might mistake about who married father and herself, and that it was rumored that it was Sidney Rigdon, or a Presbyterian clergyman, she stated:

"It was not Sidney Rigdon, for I did not see him for years after that. It was not a Presbyterian clergy-

man.   I was visiting at Mr. Stowell's, who lived in
Bainbridge, and saw your father there.   I had no intention of marrying when I left home, but, during my
visit at Mr. Stowell's, your father visited me there.
My folks were bitterly opposed to him, and, being im-
portuned by your father, aided by Mr. Stowell who
urged me to marry him, and preferring to marry him
to any other man I knew, I consented.   We went to
Squire Tarbell's and were married.   Afterwards, when
father found that I was married, he sent for us.   The
account in Mother Smith's History is substantially correct as to date and place.   Your father bought your
uncle Jesse's [Hale] place, off father's farm, and we
lived there till the Book of Mormon was translated, and
I think, published.   I was not in Palmyra long.

"Q. How many children did you lose, mother,
before I was born?

"A. There were three.   I buried one in Pennsylvania, and a pair of twins in Ohio.

"Q. Who were the twins that died?

"A. They were not named.

"Q. Who were the twins whom you took to raise?

"A. I lost twins.   Mrs. Murdock had twins and
died.   Bro. Murdock came to me and asked me to take
them, and I took the babes   Joseph died at eleven
months.   They were both sick when your father was
mobbed.   The mob who tarred and feathered him, left
the door open when they went out with him, the child
relapsed and died.   Julia lived, though weaker than the
boy.

"Q. When did you first know Sidney Rigdon?
Where?

"A. I was residing at father Whitmer's, when I

first saw Sidney Rigdon. I think he came there.

"Q. Was this before or after the publication of the Book of Mormon?

"A. The Book of Mormon had been translated and published some time before. Parley P. Pratt had united with the Church before I knew Sidney Rigdon, or heard of him. At the time the Book of Mormon was translated there was no church organized, and Rigdon did not become acquainted with Joseph and me till after the Church was established in 1830. How long after that I do not know, but it was some time.

"Q. Who were scribes for father, when translating the Book of Mormon?

"A. Myself, Oliver Cowdery, Martın Harris, and my brother, Reuben Hale.

"Q. Was Alva Hale one?

"A. I think not. He may have written some, but if he did, I do not remember it.

"Q. What about the revelation on polygamy? Did Joseph Smith have anything like it? What of spiritual wifery?

"A. There was no revelation on either polygamy, or spiritual wives. There were some rumors of something of the sort, of which I asked my husband. He assured me that all there was of it was, that, in a chat about plural wives, he had said, 'Well, such a system might possibly be, if everybody was agreed to it, and would behave as they should, but they would not, and, besides, it was contrary to the will of heaven.'

"No such thing as polygamy, or spiritual wifery, was taught, publicly or privately, before my husband's death, that I have now, or ever had any knowledge of.

"Q. Did he not have other wives than yourself?

"A. He had no other wife but me, nor did he to my knowledge ever have.

"Q. Did he not hold marital relation with women other than yourself?

"A. He did not have improper relations with any woman that ever came to my knowledge.

"Q. Was there nothing about spiritual wives that you recollect?

"A. At one time my husband came to me and asked me if I had heard certain rumors about spiritual marriages or anything of the kind; and assured me that if I had, that they were without foundation; that there was no such doctrine, and never should be with his knowledge or consent. I know that he had no other wife or wives than myself, in any sense, either spiritual or otherwise.

"Q. What of the truth of Mormonism?

"A. I know Mormonism to be the truth; and believe the Church to have been established by divine direction. I have complete faith in it. In writing for your father, I frequently wrote day after day, often sitting at the table close by him, he sitting with his face buried in his hat, with the stone in it, and dictating hour after hour with nothing between us.

"Q. Had he not a book or manuscript from which he read, or dictated to you?

"A. He had neither manuscript nor book to read from.

"Q. Could he not have had, and you not know it?

"A. If he had had anything of the kind he could not have concealed it from me.

"Q. Are you sure that he had the plates at the time you were writing for him?

"A. The plates often lay on the table without any attempt at concealment, wrapped in a small linen table cloth, which I had given him to fold them in. I once felt of the plates, as they thus lay on the table, tracing their outline and shape. They seemed to be pliable like thick paper, and would rustle with a metallic sound when the edges were moved by the thumb, as one does sometimes thumb the edges of a book.

"Q. Where did father and Oliver Cowdery write?

"A. Oliver Cowdery and your father wrote in the room where I was at work.

"Q. Could not father have dictated the Book of Mormon to you, Oliver Cowdery and the others who wrote for him, after having first written it, or having first read it out of some book?

"A. Joseph Smith [and for the first time she used his name direct, having usually used the words, 'your father,' or 'my husband] could neither write nor dictate a coherent and well-worded letter, let alone dictating a book like the Book of Mormon. And, though I was an active participant in the scenes that transpired, and was present during the translation of the plates, and had cognizance of things as they transpired, it is marvelous to me, 'a marvel and a wonder,' as much so as to any one else.

"Q. I should suppose that you would have uncovered the plates and examined them?

"A. I did not attempt to handle the plates, other than I have told you, nor uncover them to look at them. I was satisfied that it was the work of God, and therefore did not feel it to be necessary to do so.

"Major Bidamon here suggested: Did Mr. Smith forbid your examining the plates?

"A. I do not think he did. I knew that he had them, and was not specially curious about them. I moved them from place to place on the table, as it was necessary in doing my work.

"Q. Mother, what is your belief about the authenticity or origin of the Book of Mormon?

"A. My belief is that the Book of Mormon is of divine authenticity—I have not the slightest doubt of it. I am satisfied that no man could have dictated the writing of the manuscripts unless he was inspired; for, when acting as his scribe, your father would dictate to me hour after hour, and when returning after meals, or after interruptions, he would at once begin where he had left off, without either seeing the manuscript or having any portion of it read to him. This was a usual thing for him to do. It would have been improbable that a learned man could do this, and for one so ignorant and unlearned as he was, it was simply impossible.

"Q. What was the condition of feeling between you and father?

"A. It was good.

"Q. Were you in the habit of quarreling?

"A. No. There was no necessity for any quarreling. He knew that I wished for nothing but what was right, and, as he wished for nothing else, we did not disagree. He usually gave some heed to what I had to say. It was quite a grievous thing to many that I had any influence with him.

"Q. What do you think of David Whitmer?

"A. David Whitmer I believe to be an honest and truthful man. I think what he states may be relied on.

"Q. It has been stated sometimes that you apostatized at father's death, and joined the Methodist Church. What do you say to this?

"A. I have been called apostate, but I have never apostatized, nor forsaken the faith I at first accepted, but was called so because I would not accept their new fangled notion.

"Q. By whom were you baptized? Do you remember?

"A. I think by Oliver Cowdery, at Bainbridge.

"Q. You say that you were married at South Bainbridge, and have used the word Bainbridge. Were they one and the same town?

"A. No. There was Bainbridge and South Bainbridge; some distance apart; how far I don't know. I was in South Bainbridge.

"These questions and the answers she had given to them, were read to my mother by me, the day before my leaving Nauvoo for home, and were affirmed by her. Major Bidamon stated that he had frequently conversed with her on the subject of the translation of the Book of Mormon, and her present answers were substantially what she had always stated in regard to it.

"JOSEPH SMITH."

CHAPTER VI.

EXTRACTS FROM GOV. FORD, BANCROFT AND MRS. E. M. AUSTIN.

EXTRACTS FROM GOV. THOMAS FORD'S HISTORY OF ILLINOIS, 1854.

"In the year 1840, the people called Mormons came to this state and settled in Hancock county, and as their residence amongst us led to a mobocratic spirit; which resulted in their expulsion, it is proper here to notice other incidents of this sort in our previous history. In 1816 and 17, in the towns of the territory, the country was overrun with horsethieves and counterfeiters. They were so numerous and so well combined together in many counties, as to set the laws at defiance. Many of the sheriffs and justices of the peace were of their number, and even some of the judges of the county courts, and they had numerous friends to aid them and sympathize with them, even amongst those who were least suspected. When any of them were arrested, they escaped from the slight jails of those times, or procured some of their gang to be on the jury, and they never lacked witnesses to prove themselves innocent. (MS lacking page will be found preceeding the next in order 233.) This gang built a fort in Pope county, and set the government at open defiance. In the year 1831, the honest portion of the people in that region assembled under arms, in great numbers, and attacked the fort with small arms and one piece of artillery."—p. 233.

"In 1837 a series of mobs took place in Alton, which resulted in the destruction of an abolition press, and in the death of one of the rioters and of one of the abolitionists." Then follows ten pages relating the killing of this abolitionist, Rev. Elijah P. Lovejoy, a Presbyterian preacher. (p. 234). "Previous to the year 1840, other mobs were rife in the northern part of the state."—p. 245. "Then again, the northern part of the state was not destitute of its organized bands of rogues, engaged in murders, robberies, horse-stealing and in making and passing counterfeit money. These rogues were scattered all over the north, but the most of them were located in the counties of Ogle, Winnebago, Lee and De Kalb. In the county of Ogle, they were so numerous, strong and well organized, that they could not be convicted for their crimes."—p. 246. Hancock, where the Mormons lived, is not of the number.

Of Nauvoo regulations: "The common council passed many ordinances for the punishment of crime. The punishments were generally different from, and vastly more severe than the punishments provided by the laws of the state."—p. 266.

"A vast number of reports were circulated all over the country, to the prejudice of the Mormons."—p. 269.

"The people affected to believe that with this power in the hands of an unscrupulous leader, there was no safety for the lives or property of any who should oppose him. They affected, likewise, to believe that Smith inculcated the legality of perjury, or any other crime in defiance, or to advance the interest of

true believers. * * It was likewise asserted." * *
p. 327.   The readers attention is called to the phrases in
the above, "affected to believe," "affected likewise to
believe," "it was likewise asserted."

"This one principle and practice of theirs arrayed
against them in deadly hostility all aspirants for office
who were not sure of their support, all who have been
unsuccessful in elections, and all who were too proud
to court their influence, with all their friends and con-
nections.   These also were the active men in blowing
up the fury of the people, in hopes that a popular
movement might be set on foot, which would result in
the expulsion or extermination of the Mormon voters.
For this purpose public meetings had been called,
inflammatory speeches had been made, exaggerated reports had been extensively circulated, committees had
been appointed who rode day and night to spread the
reports, and solicit the aid of neighboring counties.
And at a public meeting at Warsaw, resolutions were
passed to expel or exterminate the Mormon population."
p. 330.

EXTRACTS FROM BANCROFT'S NEW HISTORY OF
UTAH, ISSUED 1890.

Bancroft gives twenty-six pages of titles of authorities, in the way of books and documents cited in the
preparation of his work, thirty-four or more on each
page.

On page seven of preface, says of works written
against Mormonism: "Most of these are written in a
sensational style, and for the purpose of deriving profit
by pandering to a vitiated public taste, and are wholly
unreliable as to facts."

"Thus is organized the Church of Jesus Christ of

Latter Day Saints, in accordance with special revelations and commandments and after the manner set forth in the New Testament."—p. 66.

"The same night Joseph was arrested by a constable on a charge of disorderly conduct, and for preaching the Book of Mormon. * * Again he was acquitted, and again escaped from the crowd outside the courthouse, whose purpose it was to tar and feather him, and ride him on a rail. These persecutions were instigated, it was said, chiefly by Presbyterians. While Joseph rested at his home at Harmony, further stories were circulated, damaging to his character, this time by the Methodists."—p. 68.

"On the night of the 25th of March, 1832, Smith and Rigdon were seized by a mob, composed partly of the Campbellites, Methodists. and Baptists of Hiram, twelve or fifteen being apostate Mormons."—p. 90.

"The spirit of mobocracy was aroused throughout the entire country."—p. 91.

"Thus it appears that the Missouri state militia, called out in the first instance to assist the Mormon militia in quelling a Missouri mob, finally joins the mob, against the Mormon militia. In none of their acts had the Saints placed themselves in an attitude of unlawful opposition to the state authorities; on the other hand, they were doing all in their power to defend themselves and support law and order, save in the matter of retaliation." * *

"General Atchison was at Richmond in Ray county, when the governor's exterminating order was issued. 'I will have nothing to do with so infamous a proceeding,' he said, and immediately resigned."—p. 130.

" 'In the name of humanity, I protest against any such cold blooded murder,' says General Doniphan."—p. 131.

"But when the testimony on both sides is carefully weighed it must be admitted that the Mormons in Missouri and Illinois, were, as a class, a more moral, honest, temperate, hard-working, self-denying, and thirfty people, than the Gentiles by whom they were surrounded."—p. 164.

"Of all that has been laid at their door, I find little proved against them."—p. 165.

"Early in June, 1844, was issued the first number of the Nauvoo Expositor, the publishers being apostate Mormons and Gentiles. The primary object of the publication was to stir up strife in the church, and aid its enemies in their work of attempted extermination."—p. 170.

Gov. Ford is quoted in respect to the Mormons of Nauvoo: "Upon the conclusion of my address I proposed to take a vote on the question whether they would strictly observe the laws, even in opposition to their prophet and leaders. The vote was unanimous in favor of this proposition."—p. 176.

"The govenor took his departure on the morning of the 27th of June. * * The prison was guarded by eight men, detailed from the Carthage Greys, their company being in camp on the public square, a quarter of a mile distant, while another company under Williams, also the sworn enemies of the Mormons, was encamped eight miles away, there awaiting the development of events."—p. 178.

"In view of this state of affairs, which was more like old time feudalism than latter-day republicism,

Gov. Ford made an inspection of the city, and declared that fewer thefts were committed in Nauvoo, in proportion to the population, than in any other town in the state."—p. 208.

"This is why the people of Missouri and Illinois drove them out—not because of their religion or immorality, for their religion was nothing to the Gentiles, and their morals were as good, or better, than those of their neighbors."—p. 368.

"The only way the Mormons can live in peace with Gentile neighbors, is for them to follow the example of their brethren, the Josephites—leave politics and government out of their ethics." * * p. 369.

"The New Testament is all against plurality of wives, and though it nowhere, in so many words, condemns the system, the books of Mormon and Doctrine and Covenants do."—p. 572.

"The most successful of the recusant sects was the one established by Joseph Smith, the prophet's son, who, with his brothers Alexander H. and David Hyrum, remained at Nauvoo after the exodus. * * He at first refused, but in 1860, the number of members being then considerably increased by the breaking up of other parties, he accepted the call as prophet and began to preach the faith of his father, as he affirmed, in its original purity, repudiating the claims of Brigham and the doctrine of polygamy."—p. 644.

"At first singly, then by dozens, and afterwards by scores, converts were gathered into this fold, and in the spring of 1864, the Josephites in Zion mustered more than three hundred, the number of proselytes elsewhere being, at this date, between two and three thousand. Persecution followed, as they claimed, and early

in the summer about one half of the Josephites in Salt
Lake City started eastward, so great being the excitement that General Connor ordered a strong escort to
accompany them as far as Green River. To those who
remained protection was also afforded by the authorities."—p. 645.

EXTRACTS FROM "MORMONISM" BY MRS. E. M. AUSTIN,
A RECENT ANTI-MORMON WRITER FROM
PERSONAL OBSERVATION.

"There were now (1831) hundreds who were called
people of good sense and judgment, men who were
valued in good society, yet they were firm believers in
Mormonism."—Mormonism, p. 62.

Of those in Kirtland in the early days of the church,
she says: "The members now numbered about one
hundred persons, the greater part of whom were the
brightest and best of the community, merchants, lawyers and doctors. All were united in the belief that
God had set his hand again—the second time—to recover the house of Israel."—Mormonism, pp. 58, 59.

Copied from Herald.

CHAPTER VII.

COURT DECISIONS.

KIRTLAND TEMPLE SUIT.—FINDINGS OF THE
COURT IN LAKE COUNTY, OHIO.

The following are the findings of the Court in
which the late suit of the Reorganized Church for the
quieting the title to the Kirtland Temple, was tried:

"In Court of Common Pleas, Lake County, Ohio,
February 23d, 1880. Present: Hon. L. S. Sherman,
Judge; F. Paine, Jr., Clerk; and C. F. Morley, Sheriff.

"Journal Entry, February Term, 1880.

"The Reorganized Church of Jesus Christ of Latter Day Saints: Plaintiff. Against

"Lucian Williams, Joseph Smith, Sarah F. Videon,
Mark H. Forscutt, the Church in Utah, of which John
Taylor is President and commonly known as the Mor-
mon church, and John Taylor, President of said Utah
Church: Defendants.

"Now at this term of the Court came the Plaintiff
by its attorneys, E. L. Kelley, and Burrows and Bos-
worth, and the Defendants came not, but made default;
and thereupon, with the assent of the Court, and on
motion and by the consent of the Plaintiff a trial by
jury is waived and this cause is submitted to the Court
for trial, and the cause came on for trial to the Court
upon the pleadings and evidence, and was argued by

counsel; on consideration whereof, the Court do find as matters of fact: * *

"That the said Plaintiff, the Reorganized Church of Jesus Christ of Latter Day Saints, is a Religious Society, founded and organized upon the same doctrines and tenets, and having the same church organization, as the original Church of Jesus Christ of Latter Day Saints, organized in 1830, by Joseph Smith, and was organized pursuant to the constitution, laws and usages of said original Church, and has branches located in Illinois, Ohio, and other States.

"That the church in Utah, the Defendant, of which John Taylor is President, has materially and largely departed from the faith, doctrines, laws, ordinances and usages of said original Church of Jesus Christ of Latter Day Saints, and has incorporated into its system of faith the doctrines of Celestial Marriage and a plurality of wives, and the doctrine of Adam-God worship, contrary to the laws and constitution of said original Church.

"And the Court do further find that the Plaintiff, the Reorganized Church of Jesus Christ of Latter Day Saints, is the True and Lawful continuation of, and Successor to the said original Church of Jesus Christ of Latter Day Saints, organized in 1830, and is entitled in law to all its rights and property.

"And the Court do further find that said defendants, Joseph Smith, Sarah F. Videon and Mark H. Forscutt, are in possession of said property under a pretended title, derived from a pretended sale thereof, made by order of the Probate Court of Lake County, on the petition of Henry Holcomb, as the administrator of said Joseph Smith, as the individual property of said

Smith; and the Court finds that said Smith had no title
to said property, except as the Trustee of said Church,
and that no title thereto passed to the purchasers at said
sale, and that said parties in possession have no legal
title to said property.

"And the Court further finds that the legal title to
said property is vested in the heirs of said Joseph
Smith, in trust for the legal successor of said original
Church, and that the Plaintiffs are not in possession
thereof."

APPEALED CASE IN CANADA COURT.

"Chief Justice Armour, and other Judges concurr-
ing, said: 'I have read the evidence over, and find
nothing contrary to the doctrine of Christ in the teaching of the Reorganized Church of Jesus Christ of Latter
Day Saints.'   'The great trouble is the Latter Day
Saints' doctrine is Christian in the highest sense, and
the rest of the religious world is opposed to them because they (the Saints) cling so closely to the Bible.'
'It seems as though it is jealousy, not justice, that
moves the action in this case.'   'These people teach
that one man should have one wife only, and they stand
by that.'   'The doctrine of this church is surely according to the Bible.'   'God has a body.'   'Yes, they teach
that God has body, parts and passions.   I think that
doctrine very elementary.   Don't you believe that God
has a body?   Does not the Bible say that God made
man in his own image?   Now, I am a man; I have a
body.   This point appears to be in their favor.'   'I
am surprised to see this trial, it seems as if some of the
Christians are wanting to go back to the dark ages;
they would have us try heresy here.'   'This is not pros-
ecution but persecution.'

"THE DECISION.

"Rev. V. Dickhout.—J. C. Cartwright, Q. C., and Dymond for the Crown. W. M. German (Welland) for the defendant. Case stated by the Police Magistrate for the Town of Niagara Falls, before whom the defendant was charged for that he did on the 19th May, 1893, at that town, unlawfully and without lawful authority, solemnize a marriage between Abraham H. Taylor and Alice E. Vance. The question raised by the case was whether the defendant as a priest of 'The Reorganized Church of Jesus Christ of Latter Day Saints' was entitled as a minister of 'a church or denomination' within the meaning of R. S. O , ch. 131, sec. 1, to solemnize a marriage. Counsel for the Crown contended, as Christianity was part of the law of the Province, the words of the statute must be read as meaning 'Christian church or denomination,' and that the body in question was not a Christian body. At the conclusion of the argument the judgment of the court was delivered by Armour C. J., as follows: We think it quite clear that this conviction can not be maintained. The defendant was clearly a duly ordained minister of this religious body, and there is no doubt that it is a religious denomination within the words of the statute. Assuming that Christianity is the law of the land in a sense, there is nothing contrary to Christianity in the tenets of this body. It is true they have something supplemental to the Bible, but that is the case with every church or denomination. The Church of England has its creeds and the Presbyterian Church its confession. That does not make the church an anti-Christian one. The statute does not say 'Christian,' but 'religious.' If it said 'Christian' it would exclude Jews. The funda-

mental law of the country makes no distinction between
churches or denominations.   Every person is at liberty
to worship his Maker in the way he pleases.   We have,
or ought to have, in this country, perfect freedom of
speech and perfect freedom of worship.   Conviction
quashed."—Toronto Globe, Mail, Nov. 29th, 1893.

UNITED STATES CIRCUIT COURT.—TEMPLE LOT CASE.—DECISION BY JUDGE PHILLIPS.

"Beyond all cavil, if human testimony is to place
any matter forever at rest, this church was one in doctrine, government, and purpose from 1830 to June,
1844, when Joseph Smith, its founder, was killed.   It
had the same federal head, governing bodies, and faith.
During this period there was no schism, no secession,
no 'parting of the ways,' in any matter fundamental,
or affecting its oneness.

"The only authorized and recognized books of doctrine and laws for the government of the church from
1830 to 1846 were the Bible, the Book of Mormon, and
the Book of Doctrine and Covenants.   The Book of
Doctrine and Covenants, which consisted principally of
claimed divine revelations to Joseph Smith, was the
edition published at Kirtland, Ohio, in 1835, and at
Nauvoo in 1845.

"No possible question could be made that had this
church, with its central governing power resident at
Nauvoo, asserted right of control over this property
up to 1845, it would have been recognized by the
ecclesiastical body and by Courts of Chancery, as the
beneficiary of the trust recognized by Edward Partridge
from 1832 and declared by him in his trust deed of
1839.

"Joseph Smith was killed at Carthage, Illinois, in June, 1844. He was the President and the inspiring spirit of the church. His violent death struck with dismay the hearts of his followers; and out of the confusion incident thereto was born disorder, schism, and ambition for leadership. Disintegration set in and the church split into factions, which under the lead of different heads, scattered to different parts of the country. Among the 'Quorum of Twelve'—representing the Apostles—was one Brigham Young, a man of intellectual power, shrewd and aggressive, if not audacious. Naturally enough such a man gathered around him the greater numbers, and it was an easy matter for him to seize the fallen reigns of the Presidency. He led the greater portion of Mormons out to what was known as 'Winter Quarters,' near Omaha, and thence to Salt Lake Valley in Utah, then a dependency of Old Mexico. From this settlement has sprung the powerful ecclesiastical body known as the Salt Lake or Utah Church. While the Respondents are wary of claiming alliance with this Salt Lake Church, it is evidently 'the power behind the throne' in the defense of this suit; and claim is made by Respondents' Counsel that it in fact absorbed the Mormon Church, and is the real successor to the ancient church.

"There can be no question of the fact that Brigham Young's assumed presidency was a bold and bald usurpation. The Book of Doctrine and Covenants (printed in 1846) page 411, containing a revelation to Joseph Smith, January 19, 1841, gave unto them 'my servant Joseph, to be a presiding elder over all my church, to be a translator, a revelator, a seer and a prophet. I give unto him for counselors my servant Sidney Rig-

don, and my servant William Law, that these may con-
stitute a quorum and first presidency, to receive the
oracles for the whole church. I give unto you, my
servant Brigham Young, to be a president over the
twelve traveling council.' So that Brigham Young
was but president over the 'Twelve,' a traveling council. The book clearly taught that the succession should
descend lineally and go to the firstborn. Joseph Smith
so taught, and, before his taking off, publicly pro-
claimed his Son Joseph, the present head of Complainant Church, his successor, and he was so annointed.

"The book also contains the following, when referring to Joseph Smith:

" 'But verily, verily, I say unto you, that none else
shall be appointed unto this gift except it be through
him, for if it be taken from him he shall not have power,
except to appoint another in his stead; and this shall
be a law unto you, that ye receive not the teachings of
any that shall come before you as revelations, or commandments; and this I give unto you, that you may
not be deceived, that you may know they are not of
me. For verily I say unto you; that he that is ordained of me, shall come in at the gate and be ordained
as I have told you before, to teach those revelations
which you have received, and shall receive through him
whom I have appointed.'

"Brigham Young's assumption of this office (under
the claim of something like a transfiguration) was itself
a departure from the law of the church.

"The Book of Mormon itself inveighed against the
sin of polygamy. True it is that Brigham Young taught
that these denunciations of the book were leveled at the
Indians—the Lamanites. But I confess to an utter

inability to interpret human language if this be correct.
In chapter 1, Book of Jacob, in speaking of the people
of Nephi, the favored people, they were arraigned for
growing hard of heart and indulging themselves somewhat in wicked practices, such as like unto David of
old, desiring 'many wives and concubines,' as also did
Solomon, David's son; and in chapter two, same book,
after alluding to the filthiness evidently of the Indian
tribes, it says:

" 'Behold, the Lamanites, your brethren, whom ye
hate, because of their filthiness and the cursings which
hath come upon their skins, are more righteous than
you; for they have not forgotten the commandment of
the Lord, which was given unto our fathers, that they
should have, save it were one wife, and concubines they
should have none.....And now this commandment
they observe to keep, wherefore, because of this obser-
vance in keeping this commandment, the Lord God
will not destroy them, but will be merciful unto them,
and one day they shall become a blessed people.'

"How it can be that the Lamanites please God in
sticking to one wife, and the Nephites displease him by
imitating David and Solomon in multiplying wives, and
yet polygamy is to be a crown of righteousness in the
teachings of the Angel Mormon, challenges my power
of comprehension.   It requires transfiguration to do so.

"Conformably to the Book of Mormon, the Book of
Doctrine and Covenants expressly declares "that we
believe that one man should have but one wife, and one
woman but one husband.'   And this declaration of
the church on this subject reappeared in the Book of
Doctrine and Covenants, edition of 1846 and 1856.
Its first appearance as a dogma of the church [the dog-

ma of polygamy] was in the Utah Church in 1852.

"Claim is made by the Utah Church that this doctrine is predicated of a revelation made to Joseph
Smith in July, 1843. No such revelation was ever
made public during the life of Joseph Smith, and under
the law of the church it could not become an article of
faith and belief until submitted to and adopted by the
church. This was never done.

"No more complete and caustic refutation of this
claim made by Brigham Young can be found than in
exhibit 'W' in this case, in a book entitled 'The
Spiritual Wife System Proven False,' issued by Granville Hedrick, the head of the Respondent Church, in
1856. He ridiculed the pretension of Brigham Young
that he had this revelation, unproclaimed, locked up in
his private chest for nine years. He says:

" 'Now how strangely inconsistent, that the revelation should be given nine or ten years before its time,
and have to lie eight or nine years under his patent
lock before it would be time to proclaim it. Here,
then, we have a specimen of an abortive revelation,
come before its time, and had to be put in the sacred
desk, under a patent lock, for eight or nine years, and
shown occasionally—just often enough to get the thing
used to it so that when it got old enough it could go
abroad. So much for this curious revelation, come in
an abortion—got burned up—then locked up—and now
has gone forth to damn everybody that don't believe it.
Why! It is a perfect phœnix.'

"When the present President of the Salt Lake
Church, Wilford Woodruff, was on the witness stand, he
testified that on the 15th of November, 1844, there was
no marriage ceremony in the church except that pub-

lished in the [Book of Doctrine and Covenants] edition of 1835. He was then asked why the church, of which he is President, in the publication of the Book of Doctrine and Covenants in the Salt Lake edition of 1876, eliminated the section on marriage as found in the 1835 edition and in all editions thereof published up to 1876, and inserted in lieu thereof the claimed revelation on polygamy of July, 1843. 'Answer. I do not know why it was done, It was done by the authority of whoever presided over the church, I suppose. Brigham Young was the President then.'

"The Utah Church further departed from the principles and doctrines of the Original Church by changing in their teaching the first statement in the Article of Faith, which was, 'We believe in God, the Eternal Father, and in his Son, Jesus Christ, and in the Holy Ghost,' and in lieu thereof taught the doctrine of 'Adam God worship,' which, as announced in Journal of Discourses by Brigham Young, is as follows:

" 'When our father Adam came into the Garden of Eden, he came into it with a celestial body, and brought Eve, one of his wives, with him. He helped to make and organize this world. He is Michael the Archangel, the Ancient of Days, about whom holy men have written and spoken—He is our Father and our God, and the only God with whom we have to do.'

"It has introduced societies of a secret order, and established secret oaths and covenants, contrary to the book of teachings of the old church. It has changed the duties of the President, and of the Twelve, and established the doctrine to 'Obey Counsel,' and has changed the order of the 'Seventy, or Evangelists.'

"The next important and interesting question is,

Does the Complainant Church represent the beneficiaries of this property?

"In controversies of this character, respecting the rightful ownership of church property, the civil judicatories have nothing to do with the question as to which faction expounds the sounder theology, or moral philosophy, and which best accords with reason and common sense.   A good Chancellor may be an indifferent theologian; and when he should lay aside the ermine for the surplice he might prove more bigot than justiciary.   As said in Smith vs. Pedigo, 33 N. E. Rep. 777, 'Religious doctrines and practices are listened to by the Courts solely as facts upon which civil rights and the right to property are made to depend, regardless of the ultimate truth or soundness of such doctrines, practices, and beliefs.'

"In case of disorganization and factional divisions of an ecclesiastical body, the settled rule of the civil courts is that 'the title to church property * * is in that part of it which is acting in harmony with its own law, and the ecclesiastical laws and usages, customs and principles, which were accepted among them before the dispute began, and the standards for determining which party is right.'   The right of ownership abides with that faction, great or small, which is 'in favor of the government of the church in operation, with which it was connected at the time the trust was declared.' McRoberts vs. Moudy, 19 Mo. App. 26; Roshi's Ap. 69 Pa. St. 462; Baker et al. vs. Thales, 9 Pick. 488; Whitlick vs. Whitelick, 83 Ind. 130.

"The Courts will adjudge the property 'to the members, however few in numbers they may be,' who adhere to the form of church government, or acknowledge the church connection, for which the property was acquired.' (Judge Strong's lecture on Relation of Civil Law to Church Property, pages 49–59.)

"Justice Caton in Ferraria et al., vs. Vanconcellos et al., 31 Ill. 54, 55, aptly states the rule to be, 'That, where a church is erected for the use of a particular denomination or religious persuasion, a majority of the members cannot abandon the tenets and doctrines of the denomination and retain the right to the use of the property; but such secessionists forfeit all right to the property, even if but a single member adheres to the original faith and doctrine of the church. This rule is founded in reason and justice.... Those who adhere to the original tenets and doctrines, for the promulgation of which a church has been erected, are the sole beneficiaries designed by the donors; and those who depart from and abandon those tenets and doctrines cease to be beneficiaries, and forfeit all claim to the title and use of such property.'

"No matter, therefore, if the church at Nauvoo became a prey to schisms, after the death of Joseph Smith, and presented as many frightful heads as did the dragon which the Apostle John saw in his vision on the Isle of Patmos, if there was one righteous left in Sodom, the promise of the covenant and of the law of the land is to him. It is neither good law nor Bible history to say that because the Saints became scattered and without an organism, the faithful lost the benefit of the church property. Forsooth the children of Israel were carried captive to Babylon,—'the mother of harlots and abominations of the earth,'—they did not cease to be children of the covenant, nor lose their interest in Jerusalem.

"A considerable number of the officers and members of the church at Nauvoo did not ally themselves with any of the factions, and wherever they were they held onto the faith, refused to follow Brigham Young to Utah, and ever repudiated the doctrine of polygamy, which was the great rock of offense on which the church split after the death of Joseph Smith.

"In 1852 the scattered fragments of the church, the remnants of those who held to the fortunes of the present Joseph Smith, son of the so-called 'Martyr,' gathered together sufficiently for a nucleus of organization. They took the name of 'The Reorganized Church of Jesus Christ of Latter Day Saints,' and avowed their allegiance to the teachings of the ancient church; and their epitome of faith adopted, while containing differences in phraseology, in its essentials is but a reproduction of that of the church as it existed from 1830 to 1844. Today they are twenty-five thousand strong.

"It is charged by the Respondents, as an echo of the Utah Church, that Joseph Smith, 'the Martyr,' secretly taught and practiced polygamy; and the Utah contingent furnishes the evidence, and two of the women, to prove this fact. It perhaps would be uncharitable to say of these women that they have borne false testimony as to their connection with Joseph Smith; but, in view of all the evidence and circumstances surrounding the alleged intercourse, it is difficult to escape the conclusion that at most they were but sports in 'nest hiding.' In view of the contention of the Salt Lake party, that polygamy obtained at Nauvoo as early as 1841, it must be a little embarrassing to President Woodruff of that organization when he is confronted, as he was in the evidence in this case, with a published card in the church organ at Nauvoo in October, 1843, certifying that he knew of no other rule or system of marriage than the one published in the Book of Doctrine and Covenants, and that the 'secret wife system,' charged against the church, was a creature of invention by one Dr. Bennett, and that they knew of no such society. That certificate was signed by the leading members of the church, including John Taylor the former President of the Utah Church. And a similar certificate was published by the Ladies Relief Society of the same place, signed by Emma Smith, the wife of Joseph Smith, and Phoebe Woodruff, wife of the present President Woodruff. No such marriage ever occurred under the rules of the church, and no offspring came from the imputed illicit intercourse, although Joseph Smith was in the full vigor of young manhood, and his wife, Emma, was giving birth to healthy children in regular order, and was enciente at the time of Joseph's death.

"But if it were conceded that Joseph Smith and Hyrum, his brother, did secretly practice concubinage, is the church to be charged with those liaisons, and the doctrine of polygamy to be predicated thereon of the church? If so, I suspect the doctrine of polygamy might be imputed to many of the Gentile churches. Certainly it was never promulgated, taught, nor recognized, as a doctrine of the church prior to the assumption of Brigham Young.

"It is next charged against Complainant Church that it has added to the Articles of Faith other revelations of the Divine will, alleged to have been made to Joseph Smith, the present head of Complainant Church.

If so, how can this be held to be heretical, or a departure, when in the Epitome of Faith of the ancient
church, is this article, 'We believe all that God has revealed, all that he does now reveal, and we believe that
he will yet reveal many great and important things pertaining to the kingdom of God.' And in the Book of
Doctrine and Covenants, paragraph 2, section 14, it is
taught that such revelations might come through him
whom the prophet might ordain.

"In the very nature of the doctrine of the church,
that God in the fullness of time makes known his will
to the church by revelation, additional revelations were
to be expected. No specification is made by learned
Counsel as to wherein the alleged new revelations declare any doctrine at variance with that taught in ante-
cedent revelations.

"It is next charged that the Complainants have a
new Bible. The basis for this is that Joseph Smith,
the founder of the Church, was as early as 1830 engaged in a translation of the Bible, which he is alleged
to have completed about 1833 or 1834. This work
seems to have been recognized also in a revelation in
section 13, paragraph 15, and in section 58. The evidence shows that this manuscript was kept by his wife
and delivered to the present Joseph Smith, her son,
and was published by a committee of the church. It is
not claimed by Joseph Smith that this translation is a
substitute for the King James' translation, nor has it
been made to appear that it inculcates any new religious
tenet different from that of the ancient church. In
this day of multifarious and free translations of the
Bible it should hardly be imputed a heresy in this
church to take some liberties with the virgin Greek and

Hebrew. It is also charged that the Complainant Church has only eleven representing the Quorum of the Twelve. I believe the New Testament records it as a historical fact that 'Peter stood up with the eleven,' after the apostasy of Judas Iscariot. There is nothing in the Code of the present church to prevent the filling out of the 'Twelve.'

"There are some other minor objections to the present organization; the answer to which is so obvious that it scarcely need be made.

"Who are the Respondents and in what do they believe? Looking at their answer in this case, and their evidence, the idea occurs that in theory they are Ecclesiastical Nondescripts, and in practice 'Squatter Sovereigns.' They repudiate polygamy while looking to Salt Lake City for succor. They deny in their answer that this property was ever bought for the church, or impressed with a trust therefor, and yet, when their head men were on the witness stand they swore they are a part and parcel of the original church, founded and inspired by Joseph Smith, 'the Martyr,' and that today they hold the property in question in trust for that church.

"They are commonly called 'Hedrickites' because their head is Granville Hedrick, who himself was a member of Complainant organization as minister, and participated actively in its General Conference as late as 1857, receiving 'the right hand of fellowship,' and moving the conference to works of evangelization in his region of the country. It is inferable from the testimony in this case that they reject measurably the standard Book of Doctrine and Covenants, and according to the testimony of Respondent Hill they 'repudiate the doctrine taught by the church in general after 1833, 1834 and 1835.' And also the law relating to 'tithes and offerings,' and the doctrine of baptism for the dead, which was taught by the Mother Church. They also seem to reject the law relating to the Presidency, and of 'the Twelve Traveling High Council,' and also 'the Quorum of Seventy Evangelists.'

"They are but a small band, and their seizure of the Temple Lot, and attempt thus to divert the trust, invoke the interposition of a Court of Equity to establish the trust and prevent its perversion.

"LACHES.

"It is urged by Respondents that the claim of Complainant is stale, and that a Court of Equity will not afford relief where party complaining has been guilty of laches. There are several answers to this objection. In the first place, this is an express trust in favor of Complainant, arising on the Partridge deed of 1839. The statute of limitation does not run against an express trust. There was no repudiation of the trust by the trustees. Laches is a question determined by the circumstances of the particular case.

"The delay in bringing this action is not inexcusable. The beneficiaries of the trust were driven from the State in 1838–9 by military force, and were not permitted to return to the State. A public hostile feeling and sentiment were excited against them, which would have blazed up from the slumbering fires at any time thereafter prior to the Civil War, had they returned here and attempted to occupy this property. No one better knew this than the Respondents when they laid hands to this property. The Complainants were not here 'to stand by' while parties were giving and receiving deeds to this property. No improvements were made on, and no visible possession taken of the Temple Lot, until 1882, within ten years of the institution of this suit, and when the trust deed had been on record twelve years. Up to this hostile action of Respondents the Complainant had a right to assume that the trust character of this property was intact, and that the lot was open for their entry at any time when the auspicious hour came to build on it.

"In the language of Chief Justice Fuller in Simmons Creek Coal Company vs. Doran, 142 U. S. 444, 'There was no delay, therefore, in the assertion of its rights after they were invaded.' See also Burke vs. Bachus (Minn.), 53 N. W. Rep. 458.

"A Court of Equity has jurisdiction in this case. It belongs to it to remove clouds from title, 'the relief being granted on the principle of quia timet.' It is peculiarly its province in a case like this to vindicate the trust, to determine the real beneficiaries of the trust estate, and to prevent its diversion.

"Decree will go in favor of Complainant, establishing the trust in its favor against Respondents, removing the cloud from the title, enjoining Respondents from asserting title to the property, and awarding the possession to the Complainant."

Decision in full text can be had at Herald office, Lamoni, Iowa, or Ensign office, Independence, Missouri, at fifteen cents per copy.

[THE END.]

INDEX.

PART I.

PART III.

NOTES.

The dagger (†) used and explained in the preface appleis to copyrighted works.

The quotation credited to "Star of the West," on page 45, was in print on that page before the reference to it by the author in Herald and Ensign appeared. The statement of Boudinot on page 93 and Dr. West on 94 should have been on page 45.

Of copper plates found by Mr. Morehead, page 91 he said in letter, to the author, of February 11th, 1895, "I found lots of copper plates in the Hopewell Mounds of Ross County, Ohio, but none of them were inscribed." The eagle, he gave cut of in his Archæologist, May, 1884, published at Waterloo, Indiana.

The plates found by Mr. Peet, described on page 91, he gave cut of in his magazine soon after he discovered them.   R. E.